THE CLASH WITH DISTANT CULTURES

Richard J. Payne

THE CLASH WITH DISTANT CULTURES

Values, Interests, and Force in American Foreign Policy

STATE UNIVERSITY OF NEW YORK PRESS

Production by Ruth Fisher
Marketing by Fran Keneston

Published by
State University of New York Press, Albany

© 1995 State University of New York

For information, address the State University of New York Press,
State University Plaza, Albany, NY 12246

Library of Congress Cataloging-in-Publication Data

Payne, Richard J., 1949 -
    The clash with distant cultures: values, interests, and force in
American foreign policy/Richard J. Payne.
        p.   cm.
    Includes bibliographical references (p.   ) and index.
    ISBN 0-7914-2647-5 (CH: acid-free). — ISBN 0-7914-2648-3 (PB:
acid-free)
    1. United States — Foreign relations — 1989 2. United States —
Military policy. 3. Politics and culture — United States —
History — 20th century. I. Title.
    E881.P28 1995   94-47454
    327.73 — dc20   CIP

10 9 8 7 6 5 4 3 2 1

To Roger Fisher
Mentor and Friend

CONTENTS

Acknowledgments   xi

Introduction   xiii

Chapter 1: Foreign Policy Begins at Home:
           Cultural Influences on
           U.S. Behavior Abroad   1
           Culture and Foreign Policy   4
           Public Opinion and Foreign Policy   14
           Ideology, Myth, and American Foreign Policy   18
           American Exceptionalism and Foreign Policy   22
           A Religious Nation: Church and State Inseparable   26
           Race, Culture, and American Foreign Policy   31

Chapter 2: Cultural Roots of Force in
           American Foreign Policy   35
           The Link Between Internal and External Violence   38
           America's Historical Experiences and Its Use of Force   47
           America's Historical Experiences and the Rule of Law   54
           A Culture of Violence   56
           Television and the Culture of Violence   59
           Sports, Violence, and Foreign Policy   61

The Government: Reinforcing the Culture
of Violence   63
Flight from Responsibility   66
Americans' Quest for Absolute Security   67
Foreign Policymaking by Analogy   68

**Chapter 3: Cultural Barriers to International
Negotiations   71**
The Negotiation Process   75
American Perceptions of Diplomacy
and American Exceptionalism   82
Isolationism, Interdependence, and Negotiations   87
Impatience as a Barrier to Negotiation   90

**Chapter 4: Operation Desert Storm:
No Negotiations, No Compromise   93**
American Perceptions of Arabs   96
Perception of the Threat   98
Demonizing the Enemy: Hussein as Hitler   101
Foreign Policy by Analogy: World War II
and Vietnam   104
Barriers to a Negotiated Settlement   106
America's Impatience and Sanctions   112
Bush's March to War   115
War and Religion   118
The Enemy Must Be Destroyed   121
Avoiding Responsibility   126
A New World Order: America as a
Redeemer Nation   128

**Chapter 5: The Palestinian-Israeli Conflict:
Negotiating Peace Patiently   131**
American Perceptions of and Cultural Links
with Israel   134
American Perceptions of Palestinians   139
Ignoring UN Resolutions and the Rule of Law 141
Israel's Violations of Human Rights in the
Occupied Territories   147
Israeli Settlements in the Occupied Territories 153
Negotiating with Friends   155
War Brings Peace   162

**Chapter 6: Bosnia: Cultural Distance
and U.S. Military Inaction   165**
The Collision of Distant Cultures   166
Perception of the Threat   171

Ethnic Cleansing: Downplaying
the World War II Analogy   176
Ignoring the Rule of Law   179
Reluctance to Use Force: Stressing the Vietnam
Analogy   182
Arming the Bosnian Muslims   189
Ineffective Negotiations: Rewarding Agression?   193

Chapter 7: Resolving Conflicts Peacefully   **199**

Notes   **215**

Bibliography   **253**

Index   **267**

ACKNOWLEDGMENTS

An analysis of cultural influences on foreign policy requires one to take an interdisciplinary approach. Consequently, this book is essentially a collaborative project. Several colleagues read parts of the manuscript, raised questions, and offered suggestions. I am particularly indebted to Denis Thornton, Ann Cohen, Jamal Nassar, Ron Pope, Carlos Parodi, Elizabeth Davis, Fred Roberts, and Robert Hunt of the Department of Political Science at Illinois State University, Jean Bethke Elshtain of the Department of Political Science at the University of Chicago, David D. Newsom of the Woodrow Wilson Department of Government and Foreign Affairs at the University of Virginia, Saadia Touval of Harvard's Center for International Affairs and the U.S. Institute of Peace, Robert Jervis of the Institute of War and Peace at Columbia University, Seymour Martin Lipset of the Institute of Public Policy at George Mason University, and Steve Yetiv of the Center for Middle Eastern Studies at Harvard University. Sociologists who were extremely helpful are: Richard Stivers, F. James Davis, Barbara Heyl, Maura Toro-Morn, Shailer Thomas, Wib Leonard, and Anne Wortham of Illinois State University. Jane Guyer, professor of anthropology at Johns Hopkins University and Boston University, Linda Giles of the Anthropology Department at Illinois State University, Jeanne Howard and Mary Cunningham of the Social Work Department, Laura Berk and Karen Pfost of the Psychology Department, Paul Holsinger, Joe Grabill, John Freed, Gerlof Homan, Sheila Hufeld, Louis Perez, David Cheesebrough, and David MacDonald of the History Department at Illinois State University, and Katherine McCarthy of the University of Pittsburgh provided many helpful suggestions.

I would like to thank Jeff Taylor, George Bode, Amy Atchison, David Harmon, Shannon Matteson, Laura Long, Tasha Welch, Vaseema Nooruddin, Ben Chapman, Sinead Rice, Vassilios Damiras, Kathy Sawyer, and Bonita Taylor for helping me with the research. I am extremely grateful to Garold Cole, Carol Ruyle, Joan Winters, Pat Werdell, and Sharon Wetzel at Illinois State University for their invaluable assistance in locating library materials, to Paul Schollaert, Dean of the College of Arts and Sciences, and Gregory Aloia, Dean of the Graduate School at Illinois State University for supporting my research efforts, to Shannon Matteson, Laura Long, Ben Chapman, and Linda Fuller for their word processing skills, and to Michele Steinbacher-Kemp for preparing the index.

Many friends read parts of the manuscript, provided useful criticism, and helped to make the book accessible to a general audience. I am especially indebted to Debbie Schroeder, Michele Steinbacher-Kemp, Jane Lee, Jackie Salome, Paula Monroe, Lucille Holcomb, Cyndi Hamlin, William Diggins, Gloria-Jean Davis, Donna Richter, and Sue Barbour. Above all, I would like to thank my son Jason, the most important critic, for his insights and support.

INTRODUCTION

The end of the Cold War and the demise of the Soviet Union help make cultural conflicts among and within nations more obvious as well as more prevalent than was the case during the intense, ideological East-West struggle. Cultural differences, mobilized by leaders for political, economic, and social purposes, have literally determined life and death in places such as Bosnia, Rwanda, and Somalia. The pervasive and increasing influence of cultural considerations in international politics is underscored by growing racial and religious problems throughout much of Europe, especially in France, Germany, and Britain; the proliferation of ethnic conflicts in the former Soviet Union, the former Yugoslavia, and elsewhere; and increased attacks by some Islamic groups on Jewish and Western targets. Samuel P. Huntington observes that the fundamental source of conflict in this new world will not be primarily ideological or primarily economic. The great divisions among humankind and the dominating source of conflict will be cultural. The principal conflicts of global politics will occur between nations and groups of different civilizations."[1]

Are the dominant American cultural values more conducive to military confrontation with nations that are culturally distant than to nonviolent strategies and negotiations to settle disputes with them? In the radically altered strategic international system, American cultural values are likely to play a more prominent role both in foreign affairs in general and in conflict resolution in particular.

If domestic politics plays a significant role in a democratic society's foreign policy, then that society's dominant values ultimately affect, to varying degrees, how it conducts its relations with other countries.[2] Elected representatives, the president in particular, reflect and are motivated by the values of elective majorities of voters in their constituencies. These values play a crucial role in shaping most policymakers' perceptions of and, consequently, approaches to international conflicts. While foreign policymaking is viewed by most political scientists and scholars specializing in international relations and foreign affairs as primarily a rational, unemotional, and sophisticated process, analysis of U.S. policies toward the Persian Gulf, the Palestinian-Israeli, and the Bosnian conflicts suggests that the underlying cultural values of most ordinary Americans play a major role in determining the choice of foreign policy instruments for dealing with problems.

Realism, the dominant approach to the study of international relations since World War II, downplays the significance of internal factors and ideational considerations in the formulation and implementation of a country's foreign policies. This traditional approach is seriously challenged by post-Cold War developments, which buttress the view that culture is one of the most decisive but often overlooked determinants of international behavior. Although culture is not always the dominant or most important factor in some conflicts, it has the potential to influence decisions. In several cases, the values, beliefs, and activities of ordinary Americans have helped to convince policymakers to negotiate. Examples discussed in Chapter Seven include Central America and South Africa.

With a rich national mythology that stresses independence, expansion, and the consolidation of a vast area through war with distant others (Native Americans), the United States, as discussed in Chapter Two, has generally viewed force in positive terms. Responding militarily to Iraq's alleged involvement in a plot to assassinate former President Bush during his 1993 visit to Kuwait, President Clinton emphasized that "from the first days of our Revolution, America's security has depended on the clarity of this message: Don't tread on us."[3] Violence is regarded by many Americans as efficacious in settling disputes in which American interests are directly threatened, whereas negotiations, especially with countries and groups perceived as dangerous and culturally distant, are often seen as an indication of weakness, naiveté, and indecisiveness.

The belief that force is the ultimate problem-solver is undergirded by our limited experience with military defeats and the consequences of war for many Americans. No wars have been fought on the U.S. mainland in living memory, a fact which tends to make force a more attractive instrument of U.S. foreign policy—especially when a quick victory is certain and the costs are perceived to be relatively low. On the other hand, there is also a strong component of the culture that favors nonviolence and the peaceful resolution of disputes. These conflicting tendencies contribute to the ambivalence many Americans feel toward war, even when they think it is necessary.

This study analyzes Washington's choice of instruments for dealing with international conflicts within the broader context of American values, historical experiences, and major characteristics of contemporary U.S. culture. As Chapter One shows, culture is complex, contains contradictory elements, and is generally understood in a pluralist sense, as differentiation within a collectivity. This book examines the linkage between the United States' tendency to use force in foreign policy and what is increasingly viewed as a culture of violence in America. Content analysis of speeches and statements by various presidents, State Department officials, and members of Congress regarding the Persian Gulf, the Middle East from 1967 to 1993, and the Bosnian conflict demonstrates that leaders constantly and deliberately appeal to cultural values to mobilize public support for military activities against culturally distant states, as well as for negotiations with friendly countries. The Bosnian war shows how culture drives conflicts and how it can complicate international negotiations.

While external factors and political leadership help to determine foreign policy behavior, any significant use of force must generally gain widespread public consent. Charles Ostrom and Brian Job conclude that: "the absolute and relative levels of popular support turn out to be the most important influence on the political use of major force."[4] Because most American leaders appear to be hypersensitive to popular approval in public opinion polls, the society's cultural values often have a direct or indirect influence on many of the country's international activities. Most Americans expect their leaders to appear forceful and strong. James Meernik, for example, finds that the President's reputation as a credible protector of U.S. interests rests in large part on his willingness to take forceful action when such interests are threatened. To do less would be to risk creating an impression of weakness.[5]

A central thesis of this book is: (1) the stronger the cultural similarities and interdependence between the United States and another country, the less likely Americans are to perceive themselves in conflict with it and to use force against it to settle disputes; (2) conversely, the greater the cultural distance between the United States and another society, the more likely Americans are to perceive it to be in conflict with the United States and to threaten or resort to violence to resolve conflicts with it that endanger America's perceived interests; and (3) when significant American interests are not at stake in a country that is culturally distant, the United States is less inclined either to rely on military might or to vigorously pursue negotiations to resolve major conflicts in that society. The case study of the Palestinian-Israeli dispute demonstrates the first part of this thesis, the Gulf War the second, and the Bosnian conflict the third.

Presidents' personalities help to determine which aspects of U.S. culture are emphasized, and, consequently, influence the choice of foreign policy instruments. Leaders such as Jimmy Carter who transcend racial and ethnic boundaries at home are generally empathetic toward countries that are culturally distant from America, and are relatively predisposed to resolve conflicts with them through negotiations. Carter's successes include the Horn of Africa, Zimbabwe, Panama, Nicaragua, North Korea, and Haiti. Carter's ability to empathize with both the Israelis and the Arabs was a major factor in the success of the Camp David negotiations. Carter represents that component of the culture that downplays the use of force. Ronald Reagan and George Bush, on the other hand, reacted militarily to perceived Third World challenges to American interests, to demonstrate the country's resolve and to punish evil transgressors. Clinton, reflecting in part his generation's ambivalence toward war, has adopted policies which, while ambiguous, lean toward negotiations to settle problems. Despite their divergent approaches, Carter, Reagan, Bush, and Clinton have appealed to different aspects of the nation's complex and inconsistent culture to obtain support for their methods of conflict resolution. But most policymakers are influenced by the dominant culture, which often favors using violence to protect U.S. interests.

Dramatic, unprecedented, and largely unpredicted changes in world politics in the post-Cold War period challenge American foreign policymakers to develop a clearer definition of national interests and to rethink how the United States has historically attempted to resolve conflicts. Given the growing influence of culture in post-Cold War conflicts, American policymakers might improve the effectiveness of U.S. policies by becoming more self-aware regarding the cultural biases implicit in many of their actions and statements. Cultural traits of violence are likely to serve the United States poorly in dealing with the ambiguities of a multipolar world. To protect and advance its interests, America will have to emphasize the non-violent component of its culture and develop a more careful blend of toughness and softness, of military force and diplomacy.

Chapter One

Foreign Policy Begins at Home: Cultural Influences on U.S. Behavior Abroad

A nation's response to international conflicts is influenced by the interaction of many internal and external factors, some of them more dominant than others in different crises. These include the country's historical experiences, its self-perception, its perception of other countries, its perception of the threat, the quality of its leadership, its economic and military capabilities, bureaucratic politics, the interests and values of the policy-relevant elites, the dynamics of the policy-making process, the personalities of prominent decision makers, regional and international responses to the problem, and the views of major allies.

At a more fundamental, but often overlooked, level, a nation's choice of one course of action over another and its selection of instruments to implement it are often determined by complex, and largely subconscious, aspects of culture. Michael Vlahos, director of the center for the Study of Foreign Affairs at the U.S. Department of State, contends that "the way people

1

think and behave at very sophisticated levels is driven by culture."[1] Similarly, Eugene W. Rostow, a former Under-Secretary of State for Political Affairs and Director of the U.S. Arms Control and Disarmament Agency, observes that "the web of traditions, beliefs, and habits which constitute a culture defines the goals it aspires to reach through political action, and sets limits on its capacity to achieve change."[2] This is particularly true of U.S. foreign policy, primarily because various historical myths and perceptions provide an essential part of the bedrock upon which a national sense of belonging, patriotism, purpose, and rationality rests. American presidents constantly refer to these myths to gain support for their policies, including the use of force.

To a much greater extent than most other countries, the United States is not just a geographic entity; it is an ideology or set of beliefs. The dominant culture, which embodies that creed, profoundly affects the content of foreign policy, and directly and significantly shapes responses to international problems. Public discourse, policy debates, all the abstract analytical models, and various methods of solving problems are ultimately anchored in the "American Way." The relative newness of the United States as a nation, its isolation from European quarrels, its endemic provincialism, its unmatched racial and ethnic diversity, and the fact that the country was founded on a set of beliefs have elevated historical experiences and ideology to a prominent role in foreign policymaking. In many cases, culture, the means by which such a vast and often rootless society has managed to retain its identity and global leadership, has been one of the most important determinants of foreign activities, or the lack of them.[3]

The emphasis on the centrality of culture in foreign policy is clearly at odds with "realism," the dominant approach to the study of international relations. Since World War II, the importance of domestic cultural factors in the shaping of a country's external behavior has been downplayed by scholars. Anthropology as a tool of foreign policy, with its focus on culture, has been superceded by political science, which largely avoids the nebulous and mushy concept of culture. Vlahos notes that political scientists were more comfortable with the concept of an international system because it could be quantitatively defined and precisely understood and managed. Human behavior, according to political scientists, could be analyzed and predicted by mathematical models.[4] This depreciation in the relevance of the domestic sources of foreign policy helps to explain why the vast majority of scholars, academic think tanks, and government agencies—despite their sophisticated methods of analysis—failed to predict the disintegration of the Soviet Union in the late 1980s and the escalation of ethnonationalism in the 1990s. Realists assume that the international environment determines a country's foreign policy. From their perspective, factors such as a state's position in the international system, its participation in alliances, and the balance of power "are vastly more important than national variations in domestic political institutions and values" in determining that country's foreign relations.[5]

Functioning in a hostile environment, governments are perceived by realists as being primarily concerned with defining and protecting their countries' interests. The dominant view among foreign policy analysts, which is the essence of realism, is that national interests are closely identified with national security. Given the anarchic nature of the international system, military might is regarded as the principal means of achieving foreign policy objectives.[6] From most realists' viewpoint, the moral values or impulses of a particular country's citizens are largely irrelevant. Foreign policy decisions are viewed as neither moral nor immoral. As George F. Kennan puts it, "the interests of the national society for which government has to concern itself...have no moral quality."[7] But the absence of morality does not necessarily mean the absence of culture. Hans J. Morgenthau, a leading proponent of realism, emphasizes that how the national interest is defined "depends on the political and cultural context within which foreign policy is formulated."[8] Generally, however, realists stress military and economic factors in international relations to the virtual exclusion of ideational considerations.

Although the international environment is clearly an important determinant of how nations behave, most policymakers are attentive to the domestic ramifications of international relations. In many cases, domestic politics drives national security policies and frequently brings Congress into conflict with the Executive branch. Whereas the former tends to be more concerned with domestic implications of foreign policies, the latter has to be sensitive to external as well as domestic factors. Presidents sometimes initiate external activities to obtain domestic support. President Jimmy Carter's grain embargo against the Soviet Union following its invasion of Afghanistan, and President Ronald Reagan's decision to lift it, had more to do with domestic considerations than with attempting to alter Soviet behavior. Contrary to the realists' assumption that the international environment is the most important restraint on U.S. foreign policy, domestic constraints are often stronger than external constraints. To a much greater degree than is the case in other democratic societies, American policymakers are sensitive to domestic pressures, partly because they operate in a more open and accessible political system.[9] Americans expect the government to be responsive to their concerns. Pressure groups, citing the latest public opinion polls on issues that interest them, are a visible and powerful component of political life. Consequently, the national interest, which is essentially subjective, is ultimately rooted in the people's fundamental values and beliefs. American policies toward South Africa during the 1980s, and U.S. humanitarian intervention in Somalia in late 1992, emanated from domestic pressures and moral impulses.

Culture and Foreign Policy

It may be argued that nations are primarily cultural entities and secondarily geographic areas. This is manifested by numerous late-twentieth century developments in Europe, the former Soviet Union, Yugoslavia, and elsewhere. Nations have traditionally been defined in terms of their common identity, values, languages, and customs. Even as technology and science are instrumental in forging greater interdependence among nations and spreading cultural habits and thought around the world, the rise of nationalism, fueled mainly by cultural claims, is simultaneously fostering disintegration of some countries and exclusivity in others. The United States itself faces tensions caused by the unraveling of the dominant culture and the rising influence of rival subcultures. Although Americans have held differing opinions on what defined them as a nation, there has always been general agreement on core values and symbols. The emergence of a more pronounced ethnic consciousness and a greater emphasis on multiculturalism are widely perceived as challenging the view that the United States possesses a consensual political culture.[10]

Furthermore, demographic changes in the United States have helped to reinforce the perception that the dominant culture and the nation itself are disintegrating. Even though roughly 75 percent of Americans still trace their roots to Europe, those origins are becoming distant in the country's memory. Recent immigrants from Asia, Africa, Latin America, and the Middle East are demanding that America refocus its priorities and move away from Europe and what many racial and ethnic minorities regard as a Eurocentric culture.[11] As the population center of the United States shifts from the East Coast to the West and the Southwest, areas in which the newer immigrants are most numerous, foreign policy is directly affected. Europe becomes relatively less important, while Latin America and Asia are elevated. Clearly, trade and other factors are helping to change the country's international relations.

Michael Lind, for example, discusses the foreign policy implications of the unraveling of the cultural fabric, and what he perceives to be cultural decline. From Lind's perspective, internal tensions divert energies, destroy America's ability to compete in world markets, and drain the country's financial resources. "As the decay spreads at home, the country's power and prestige decline abroad."[12] Domestic cultural clashes, in his view, are inextricably linked to foreign policy. The angst generated by cultural upheaval is evidence of the power of culture and its centrality in the lives of individuals, groups, and nations. In addition to weakening the realists' assumption that developments in the external environment rather than domestic factors determine a country's foreign policy, post-Cold War conflicts underscore the importance of cultural reservoirs in international relations.

A cultural reservoir may be defined as an accumulation of goodwill and understanding that stems from a set of values, beliefs, attitudes, historical experiences, and racial and ethnic links that two or more countries have in common. Similarities are strengthened by international exchanges, military alliances, and economic interdependence. However, as John A. Kroll argues, the link between interdependence and increased cooperation is not automatic.[13] When disputes between countries occur, cultural reservoirs, or the lack of them, play a pivotal role in how differences are resolved. Leaders can draw upon their cultural similarities to diminish international tensions. Conversely, as developments in Bosnia, Rwanda, and elsewhere have demonstrated, leaders can draw on accumulated cultural differences and hatreds to promote conflict. Cultural reservoirs strengthen the perception that friendly relations between culturally similar countries are the norm, and that a particular disagreement is a deviation from an otherwise peaceful relationship. America's policy toward the Palestinian-Israeli conflict demonstrates the importance of cultural reservoirs in foreign affairs. Cultural similarities between the United States and Israel, as Chapter Five shows, influenced Washington to patiently negotiate an end to the conflict. On the other hand, the absence of strong cultural links and significant economic interaction between states may facilitate indifference (as the case study of Bosnia clearly indicates) or hostility.

Even where there are strong economic links between countries, as is the case between the United States and Japan and the United States and the Arab states, cultural factors appear to be dominant, and economic dependence may engender hostility. Cultural differences, as well as ignorance of other cultures, tend to exacerbate difficulties that arise in interstate relations and diminish the chances of such problems being resolved peacefully. Whereas cultural distance is conducive to using coercive methods to terminate conflicts, cultural proximity is likely to encourage the negotiated settlement of disputes.[14] Even if actions taken by countries that are culturally similar to the United States are essentially the same as those of states that are culturally distant, the American response is likely to be different. Samuel P. Huntington believes that "a world of clashing civilizations is inevitably a world of double standards: people apply one standard to their kin-countries and a different standard to others."[15] While most nations tend to find ways to justify kin-countries' behavior and avoid imposing punitive measures against them, they often condemn and attempt to punish culturally distant "others."

Although many political scientists attribute the fact that democracies rarely fight each other to structural constraints that encourage leaders to resolve disputes peacefully and to democratic norms that emphasize compromise, persuasion, peaceful competition, protection of minority rights, and so on, it could be argued that democracies do not fight each other because their cultures are very similar.[16] Yet culturally similar countries have clashed militarily and culturally distant countries have been allies when significant interests were perceived to be at stake. For example, Russia cooperated with the United States during the Napoleonic Wars in an effort to keep the rising new American power from formally joining France, and again during both World Wars. On the other hand, Britain and the United States fought each other in the American Revolution and in the War of 1812, with Russia acting as a mediator in the latter.[17] Despite the two Anglo-American wars, however, Rostow contends that strong kinship ties and a pervasive sense of a shared civilization militated against the likelihood of America's becoming Britain's potential enemy.[18]

The concept of culture is nebulous, complex, and divergent in its various applications. Anthropologists, sociologists, political scientists, and others define culture in different ways. The distinction can be made between material culture--the tangible products of human society, and nonmaterial culture--the intangible products of society, such as values and rules of right and wrong behavior. Nonmaterial culture is the learned ideational aspects of human society.[19] The two are intertwined, however. In most of Western Europe, the United States, and Canada, culture is generally equated with civilization and refers to political, economic, religious, technical, moral, or social facts. In the German intellectual tradition, by contrast, the concept of *Kultur* is almost exclusively concerned with levels of excellence in the fine arts, literature, music, and individual personal perfection. Reference to human behavior, to the value which a person possesses by virtue of his or her mere existence and conduct, without any meaningful accomplishment, is very minor.[20]

In this book, culture is understood to be a set of shared learned values, beliefs, perceptions, attitudes, modes of living, customs, and symbols. Culture is usually defined as a way of life. According to Clifford Geertz, "the concept of culture denotes an historically transmitted pattern of meanings embodied in symbols, a system of inherited conception expressed in symbolic forms by means of which men communicate, perpetuate, and develop their knowledge about and attitudes toward life."[21] Although there exist discrete and often contradictory aspects of culture, they function together to form an interrelated and integrated whole. The connections among different components of culture give the culture meaning.[22] They also contribute to the ambiguity, dynamism, and complexity that are essential characteristics of culture. Certain aspects of a culture are so divergent that they appear unbridgeable; not everything is connected to everything else with equal directness. Geertz notes that cultural discontinuity is as real as cultural integration.[23] In his view, "culture moves like an octopus—not all at once in smoothly coordinated synergy of parts, a massive coaction of the whole, but disjointed movements by this part, then that, and now the other which somehow cumulate to directional change."[24]

While the analysis of the role of culture in foreign affairs focuses on the dominant culture, it does not overlook the variations within American culture. Indeed, the concept of culture is understood in a pluralist sense, as differentiation within a collectivity. Subcultures are the bedrock of a pluralist view of culture. According to Chris Jenks, "a subculture is the way of defining and honoring the particular specification and demarcation of different interests of a group of people within a larger collectivity."[25] To some extent, culture varies from one group to another, from region to region, and so on. Emile Durkheim, in Division of Labor, articulated the view that as societies become more complex cultural consensus is weakened. Divergent attitudes and values develop, and beliefs and attitudes are modified, in ways that are significantly different from those prescribed or proscribed by the conscience collective or strongly defined moral consensus.[26] By promoting skepticism and innovation, pluralism challenges established traditions, values, and beliefs.

But pluralism does not eliminate a shared core culture that is largely assumed. Pluralism and tradition coexist in what Peter L. Berger and Thomas Luckman call "a state of mutual accommodation."[27] Despite America's ethnic, religious, and racial diversity, and its plethora of subcultures, there is widespread agreement that an American culture exists, and there is consensus on its fundamental attributes. Often, many of the cultural differences associated with various subcultures are downplayed or temporarily overlooked when our society confronts distant cultures. But international conflict may also highlight these differences, many of which are often expressed in antiwar protests.

Culture, as defined by Geertz and others, is a historically transmitted pattern of meaning embodied in symbols. The social functions of symbols depend to a great extent on their cognitive meaning. Meaning is understood in two different ways. It may be utilized in a cognitive sense, as when one asks for the explanation of a natural occurrence, a historical development, or a sociological fact. But meaning is also used in a semantic-affective sense, as when one inquires about the meaning of unequal life-fates, frustration, or death.[28] Symbol means any object, word, gesture, or sound to which cultural traditions have given meaning as representing something. The omnipresence of the American flag and the frequent recitation of the Pledge of Allegiance underscore the centrality of symbols and the meanings attached to them in American life.

These meanings are socially constructed. Individuals attach subjective meanings to their actions, which become objectified in the artifacts of culture—ideologies, belief systems, moral codes, and institutions. According to Berger and Luckman, "these meanings are reabsorbed into consciousness as subjectively plausible definitions of reality. Culture, then, is at base an all-embracing socially constructed world of subjectively experienced meanings."[29] Edward T. Hall and Mildred Reed Hall emphasize that all cultures have hidden codes of behavior which are largely unintelligible to outsiders, inasmuch as approximately 80 to 90 percent of the significant features of a culture are reflected in its nonverbal messages.[30]

Values, a component of culture, are widely shared abstract assumptions about what is right and wrong, desirable and undesirable, good and bad, or just and unjust. Values help shape attitudes toward particular situations and provide both justifications for, and guides to, the policies designed to cope with them.[31] Attitudes may be defined as "general evaluative propositions about some object, fact or condition: more or less friendly, desirable, dangerous, trustworthy, or hostile."[32] Values and attitudes directly influence our perception of others. Erroneous judgments about another country and its leaders often distort reality and engender conflict. As Jack S. Levy observes, "in the external case, perceptions of unmitigated hostility generate belief in the inevitability of war, possibly triggering a preemptive strike in a crisis situation in order to gain benefits of the initiative."[33]

Beliefs are largely unexamined assumptions upon which national policies are constructed. Beliefs help organize perceptions into a meaningful guide for behavior. The belief system has the function of establishing goals and ordering preferences. "It tells us what ought to be."[34] In other words, beliefs set broad parameters and guidelines for action. Douglas W. Blum maintains that "whereas the actual implementation of policy depends on situational factors, core beliefs set tentative limits on the kinds of policies that can be pursued. Policy outcomes then feed back into the system. Desired outcomes reaffirm the validity of the beliefs that produced them, whereas problematic outcomes have the opposite effect."[35] For example, America's failures in Vietnam undermined the validity of some of its beliefs, which, in turn, weakened national consensus on foreign policy matters. The Gulf War was perceived by President Bush and others as "kicking the Vietnam syndrome," an obvious effort to restore the validity of the beliefs that undergird national consensus. Beliefs help determine how nations interact and how they perceive themselves, their allies, and their adversaries or potential enemies. While belief systems are extremely stable, external shocks or the emergence of new leaders and generational change help to facilitate changes in the prevailing belief system.[36] This explains, in part, some of the differences between Bush and Clinton in the area of foreign policy.

Although clashes between perceived reality and objective reality result in modification and reinterpretation of some beliefs, values, perceptions, and behavior, cultures tend to be relatively stable. Most Americans' preoccupation with change and newness, and our general predisposition to ignore the past, obscure obvious continuities in the dominant culture. The tenacity of American values is due principally to their workability and the enormous and unprecedented economic, political, and social success the nation has experienced, based on its fundamental beliefs and attitudes. In other words, most of us believe that America's political-economic creed is the cause of its material wealth and political stability. Consequently, fundamental values and beliefs remain essentially unaltered.

Michael Vlahos contends that throughout history the American reaction to change has not been to tear down existing structures, but rather to reinterpret the national pantheon.[37] As the country developed, adjustments were implemented within the framework of accepted customs and beliefs. Examples of these major changes are the inauguration of Jacksonian democracy, the New Deal, the civil rights movement, and the equality for women movement. Many of these changes occurred because the majority of Americans benefited from the resulting economic progress and political stability. Cultural stability is reinforced by the very process by which dominant values, attitudes, customs, and beliefs are transmitted from one generation to another. Agents of cultural transmission include parents, schools, religious institutions, the media, political and social organizations, friends, and peer groups.

Enculturation, no matter how thorough, does not create complete uniformity of behavior. This is due to several reasons. First, human beings are strongly influenced by biological as well as cultural factors. Biological factors will invariably promote innate variations in mental, physical, and behavioral capabilities. Consequently, individuals are likely to respond differently to enculturation. Second, information transmitted through enculturation varies from family to family and from institution to institution. Third, enculturation is an ongoing process, some of which occurs outside one's culture. For example, to what extent did Clinton's experiences at Oxford shape his crime and health care policies? Finally, individuals tend to maneuver within their cultures, choosing actions to meet their personal interests as well as the demands of their society.[38]

Personal qualities such as empathy, which is the ability to put oneself in another person's shoes, as it were, are likely to militate against simple stereotypes, which are transmitted through enculturation. The empathetic person is apt to perceive motivational complexity and decisional differentiation when dealing with conflicts with distant cultures.[39] This tendency will probably be reinforced by a cosmopolitan socialization, international travel, friendships with individuals from foreign countries, membership in international organizations, and so on.

Because schools are products of culture, and because their principal function is to teach society's values, they reinforce culture, even as they educate students to challenge it. If education is inseparable from culture, then religion is at the heart of it. Max Weber argued in *The Protestant Ethic and the Spirit of Capitalism* that even in the most secular Western countries religion and culture are intertwined.[40] Religion and religious beliefs may also reinforce nationalism. By elucidating a broader worldview, religion infuses the symbols of public and private cultures with universal significance.[41] Religion is clearly the fountainhead of many cultural values, perceptions, and concepts of justice, morality, and humanitarianism. This is particularly true of the United States, a country founded upon religious freedom and one in which religious issues continue to dominate political and social life. America is the most insistent of all industrial countries on separating church and state, and, as will be discussed, is simultaneously the most religious Western nation. In politics or education, war or peace, foreign or domestic policies, religion predominates. Will Herberg concludes that "America seems to be at once the most religious and the most secular of nations."[42]

The media's importance as a transmitter of cultural values is obvious. In a society in which dreams are so often transformed into reality, where one can achieve extraordinary success relatively quickly, television's and Hollywood's fictional happy endings and actual life are often blurred. Television also reinforces stereotypes of those considered as different, and glorifies violence. For many Americans, television programs are reflections of reality. As Chapter Four shows, negative stereotypes of Arabs facilitated the use of force by the American-led coalition in the Gulf. Does television manufacture the predominant values of success, winning, fame, and the use of force to resolve conflicts? Successful television shows are products of the general culture and, in turn, play a pivotal role in shaping and highlighting certain aspects of that culture. Television portrays other cultures in favorable or unfavorable ways for American audiences, thereby influencing our perceptions of them. Haynes Johnson, for example, maintains that in this context television's impact on American foreign policy is significant.[43]

Domestic factors in general, and cultural values in particular, interact with external stimuli to shape a country's foreign policies. When America faces challenges from abroad, its culture often influences how it responds to them and is, in turn, modified by those developments. This connection contributes to the culture's dynamism and its ability to deal with inevitable changes in the international system. But the effects of external stimuli on culture are neither uniform nor consistent. For example, America fought for democracy and freedom in Europe during World War II, but in the war's aftermath, it found itself facing the reality that democracy at home was not enjoyed by many citizens, particularly those of African descent. Greater international involvement subsequent to the war underscored the need for significant changes in many of the country's racial attitudes and practices. Widespread racial discrimination undermined America's credibility as the world's champion of democracy. Recognition of discrepancies between ideals and practice, underscored by foreign policy issues, had a major impact on the success of the civil rights movement in the United States.

The Cold War's advent fostered an anti-communist consensus, a widespread and exaggerated fear of military conflict with the Soviet Union, suppression of domestic dissent, and visceral patriotism. Superpower competition for global dominance influenced Americans to interpret their history in a way that was consistent with the perceived threat. American exceptionalism, the belief that the United States is unique and morally superior to other nations, was rejuvenated, and a stark simplicity of confrontation between good and evil was accepted by most Americans.

While the East-West struggle suited U.S. cultural approaches to problems, it also profoundly affected virtually all aspects of the culture. Morton H. Halperin and Jeanne M. Woods point out that political authority became more centralized in the Executive branch, government secrecy mushroomed, the national tendency toward paranoia was heightened, and dissent was equated with disloyalty.[44] American business achievements were perceived as a vindication of the cultural values and beliefs. However, Stephen J. Whitfield argues that because materialism was viewed as "the special philosophical province of the enemy, respect for religion also became pervasive."[45] In other words, to differentiate itself from the communist countries that adhered to the doctrine of economic determinism and rejected religious beliefs, the United States stressed its own religious foundations and belief in God. America's response to the Cold War did not radically alter underlying cultural values; it brought into sharper focus contradictions that are inherent in the society.

At a deeper and more important level, however, paradoxes in America's culture and its domestic and foreign policies emanate from the myths upon which the country was founded. Americans, regardless of their group identity, multicultural concerns, or social status, embrace many myths that are the foundations of contemporary culture and which help to define us as a nation. But some of these myths, as is commonly the case, are inconsistent. For instance, viewing itself as an example for all nations, the United States attempts to change the world even as it attempts to avoid being contaminated by it. Louis Hartz observes that "embodying an absolute moral ethos, Americanism, once it is driven on the world stage by events, is inspired willy-nilly to reconstruct the very alien things it tries to avoid."[46] In other words, instead of tolerating differences, the United States tries to transform other countries into its own image when it becomes involved, often reluctantly, in world affairs.

Public Opinion and Foreign Policy

In a democratic society, especially one that is as decentralized, as open, and as politically accessible as the United States, public opinion often, but not always, plays a prominent role in influencing foreign relations. Public opinion's ability to affect foreign policymakers' choices varies from one conflict to another. To obtain support for their policies, political leaders in general, and the President specifically, must appeal to public opinion. Given the ideological nature of the country's underlying values, public opinion has remained a remarkably stable component of foreign policy. This stability is reinforced by cultural habits. John Spanier maintains that Americans' apprehension of external danger has repeatedly led them to insist on an almost dogmatic reaffirmation of loyalty to the "American way of life."[47] This tendency led to the extremism that characterized McCarthyism, which dominated American life during the early 1950s.

Accentuated during the Cold War, pressure to conform to the American creed may have its origins in the very insecurity of the experiment that became the American civilization. While the commitment to freedom of expression in the United States is unmatched anywhere in the world, public opinion tends to be politically uniform, especially when compared to Western Europe. Differences are often variations of the same myths. Alexis de Tocqueville wrote more than 150 years ago that: "I know no country in which, speaking generally, there is less independence of mind and true freedom of discussion than in America.... In America the majority has enclosed thought within a formidable fence."[48] This observation has clearly been modified by numerous changes in the United States and the growing influence of various subcultures.

Policymakers usually pay close attention to public opinion, especially when considering policies that would lead to the use of American troops abroad. Consequently, both immediate public sentiment and the deeper cultural values sometimes constrain policymakers' choices. While the United States Constitution establishes the powers and responsibilities of the various branches of government, and imposes checks and balances so that they will function to safeguard the people's freedom, the authority essential for the realization of constitutional guarantees comes from the political culture in particular and the broader culture in general. Ultimately, the government's legitimacy resides in the people and their political culture.[49] Consequently, foreign policy decisions, whatever their objectives, must be communicated to the public as being consistent with shared values, attitudes, and beliefs.

Too great an emphasis on elite influences on foreign policies leads to the erroneous assumption that those in positions of power are basically free from the culture that binds the rest of society. On the contrary, those who aspire to political office and those who manage to realize their aspirations are, in general, immersed in many of society's fundamental values. They are thus perpetuators of culture, even as they manipulate society's values to achieve their own goals. Even if their own personal beliefs are significantly different from those of most voters, they realize that to be elected they have to operate within the boundaries established by culture.

In a country that often seems to be obsessed with newness, the past provides a constant reference point for the public and policymakers alike. Feelings, images, beliefs, and attitudes can be mobilized for particular purposes, and ordinarily facilitate the achievement of decision-makers' objectives. Presidents constantly refer to the foundations of culture to justify current policies and mobilize public support. A cursory review of political speeches readily reveals the heavy reliance on potent symbols of history. In other words, cultural values are arguably more influential upon America's foreign policies than they are upon those of countries that appear to be less obsessed with newness and are more concerned with preserving the past. In both domestic and foreign policies, public rhetoric is replete with widely understood codewords that are summaries of deeply held values. Because of their explanatory power and popular appeal, codewords are employed by policymakers to simplify complicated problems and to mobilize public support for foreign policies.[50] As will be discussed, Bush, for example, probed the culture to find the right codewords to gain public approval for his military solution to the Gulf crisis.

President Reagan's popularity was due in part to his embodiment of those attributes that represent cornerstones of American culture. These include individualism, optimism, willingness to take risks, physical strength, a clear sense of personal identity, self-assurance, and a reputation as a winner. He constantly referred to history and culture not only to marshal support but also to reassure Americans of their role in the world. In a speech at the annual convention of the American Legion in Salt Lake City in 1984, Reagan pledged to "keep America a beacon of hope to the rest of the world and to return her to her rightful place as a champion of peace and freedom among the nations of the earth." Adding that he was not preaching manifest destiny, he declared that "we Americans cannot turn our backs on what history has asked of us. Keeping alive the hope of human freedom is America's mission, and we cannot shrink from the task or falter in the call of duty."[51] In his final radio address to the nation, Reagan reiterated many of the codewords that resonate in the society: "Whether we seek it or not, whether we like it or not, we Americans are keepers of the miracles. We are asked to be guardians of a place to come to, a place to start again, a place to live in the dignity God meant for his children. May it ever be so."[52] These references to history and specific myths were designed to buttress America's self-image, reinvigorate its culture, and strengthen culture's role in the formulation and implementation of foreign policies.

While it is generally agreed that bureaucratic structures play an important part in shaping the content of foreign policy, the connection between organizational structures and a country's self-perception and beliefs is often overlooked. The values, attitudes, and beliefs of a particular society ultimately help to shape that society's institutions. And institutions lead people to hold certain values, attitudes, and beliefs.[53] In other words, structures and culture are inseparable and are part of a circular process. As national leaders attempt to secure what they regard as their country's interests, their beliefs inevitably enter into the decision-making process. Emphasizing differences between systems in nature and the international system, Robert Jervis concludes that leaders' beliefs influence them to behave in certain ways, and that it is not possible to infer outcomes from the objective situation without considering the decision-makers' analyses and expectations.[54] Furthermore, because policymaking is rarely as rational as is frequently assumed by many political scientists and international-relations specialists, cultural differences matter. Apart from the biases inherent in human judgment, decision-making processes in the real world, as opposed to computer-generated models, tend to be ad hoc and chaotic. In this fluid and ill-defined process, cultural factors have a direct bearing on the outcome.[55]

Culture inevitably influences decision-making because it defines us and distinguishes us from others. Indeed, to define oneself, one must define others. All societies, directly and indirectly, promote their values as positive and desirable while, simultaneously, devaluing those of other societies. This behavior is referred to as ethnocentrism. Positive images of one's society are developed and augmented by rewards for conformity. Ken Booth, Marshall H. Segall, and others contend that each society views itself as the center of the world, perceives and interprets other societies within its peculiar frame of reference, and invariably judges them inferior.[56] The more culturally distinct the other society, the more inferior it is often deemed to be, and thus suitable to be treated differently. This ethnocentrism has serious ramifications for foreign relations, affecting how conflicts are resolved, what military strategies are employed when force is used, and whether Americans are able to empathize with citizens of other nations. U.S. policies toward Iraq following its occupation of Kuwait, and toward the Palestinian-Israeli conflict, demonstrate the centrality of culture, theirs and ours, in determining how disputes are settled.

National self-images, like perceptions of others, are directly shaped by culture and transmitted through the agents of socialization, especially the mass media and schools. A nation's self-image is intertwined with how it perceives its international role, as well as with how it should accomplish its objectives.[57] Bush's decision to demonstrate American resolve in relation to Iraq virtually foreclosed the use of negotiations to end the Gulf crisis. Images, the conscious and unconscious products of culture, serve as organizing devices that enable decisionmakers to simplify complex problems and to filter information to make it consistent with their beliefs, attitudes, and feelings. Information that contradicts the images held by policymakers may be deliberately ignored or inadvertently misconstrued. Leaders' policy preferences are therefore influenced by their cultural backgrounds.[58] With constant repetition, the stereotypes that accompany imaging may be accepted as objective reality.

Ideology, Myth, and American Foreign Policy

The concepts of ideology and myth are closely related. Both function within the broader cultural framework to perpetuate as well as to alter culture. As will be discussed, myth is much broader in scope than ideology. There are dominant ideologies and subordinate ideologies within the same culture, and they are often in competition. Ideology is a system of values, beliefs, and ideas within the larger cultural system. It is defined as a reasonably coherent body of ideas, a framework of political consciousness, by which a people, or at least its dominant, governing element, organizes itself for political action.[59] Stated another way, ideology is concerned with practical questions of how to maintain, change, or reform a sociopolitical or economic order.[60] In a broad sense, ideology is meaning in the service of power.[61] The function of ideology, from Geertz's viewpoint, is "to make an autonomous politics possible by providing authoritative concepts that render it meaningful, the suasive images by means of which it can be sensibly grasped."[62] Ideologies tend to emerge in periods of significant socioeconomic and political strain. For example, the French Revolution generated extreme ideologies. The American Revolution and the integration of people from many different countries into American society were conducive to the emergence of ideologies. Ideologies become crucial as sources of sociopolitical meanings and attitudes.[63]

Ideology often profoundly affects how we perceive ourselves and others; it places some limitations on our ability to comprehend different cultures and political systems, which are also influenced by their own particular ideologies. But ideology does not always play a deterministic role. Some individuals are less restrained than others by ideology. Whatever the drawbacks of a coherent set of values might be, ideology is used by most individuals in virtually all societies, in varying degrees of intensity, to navigate a complex and often confusing world, to facilitate functioning in the international environment, and to take actions to safeguard long-term interests. The concept of ideology is closely related to the symbolic forms through which we express ourselves, understand others, and determine what is real. In this sense, ideology is connected to the concept of a worldview. A worldview is composed of various beliefs about the nature of reality and the world. Thus, a people's ideology usually cannot be separated from its nation's purpose, goals, and its expectations of itself and others.

Ideology affects the formulation and implementation of foreign policy in several ways. Geertz believes that "whatever else ideologies may be, they are, most distinctively, maps of problematic social reality and matrices for the creation of collective conscience."[64] In other words, ideologies help to establish the intellectual framework through which those responsible for making foreign policy observe reality. Information about international developments is given meaning within the categories, predictions, and definitions provided by ideology.[65] This does not mean that ideology usually plays a dominant, direct role in determining solutions to specific, concrete problems. Ideology operates on a more general level. Ideology helps to establish a people's perceptions of their role in the world and their nation's choice of strategies for accomplishing foreign policy objectives. Ideology may exert influence on whether a country decides to emphasize the use of force, as opposed to diplomacy, to achieve its foreign policy goals. Finally, ideology may serve to rationalize and justify the choice of specific foreign policy decisions.[66]

National myths, which are often intertwined with ideology, are stories taken from a country's history that give meaning to a wide range of experiences. According to H. Mark Roelof,

"myth denotes the nationally shared framework of political consciousness by which a people becomes aware of itself, as having
an identity in history, and by which it is also prepared to recognize some governing regime as legitimate."[67]   Richard Slotkin
maintains that myth can be viewed as an intellectual or artistic
construct that bridges the gap between the world of the mind
and the world of affairs, between dream and reality, between
impulse and action. It draws on the content of individual and
collective memory, structures it, and develops from it imperatives for belief and action.[68]

Because myths and ideologies are as durable as the culture that nurtures them, many beliefs and values that were developed by the early Americans retain remarkable power in
contemporary society, despite revolutionary changes in science
and technology. The myths of the frontier and America as a
"City on a Hill" continue to provide the foundation upon which
many U.S. foreign policies are based as well as the justification
of them. According to the myth of the frontier, the conquest of
the wilderness and the subjugation or displacement of Native
Americans have been the means to the achievement of a national identity, a democratic polity, an ever-expanding economy, and
a dynamic and progressive civilization. Conflict and individualism were central to this process.[69] America as a "City on a Hill"
underscored the United States' separation from the rest of the
world as well as its role as a unique model for other countries to
emulate.

Several factors have combined to perpetuate certain myths
in America's internal affairs as well as its relations with other
countries. These myths include the belief that everyone is
equal, that hard work automatically leads to success, and that
America is inherently an exceptional country. The extraordinary success achieved by the United States in virtually all
areas of human endeavor reconfirms the validity of the myths
for most people. Unlike Europe, with its feudal aristocracies
and difficult economic conditions, the United States did not develop a rigid class system. The country expanded rapidly
enough to allow Americans, especially those of European descent, to amass large fortunes relatively quickly, and to perpetuate the myth that anyone with ambition and the determination
to work hard could become wealthy.

Generally, Americans have subscribed to a common ideology of Lockean liberalism.[70] John Locke, having articulated a direct connection between the possession of property and political and social freedoms, was embraced by the Founding Fathers and subsequent generations of Americans. The availability of economic opportunities for most Americans made other ideologies unattractive and useless. Furthermore, despite the presence of a rigid, dogmatic ideological strain in the United States, most Americans were, and remain, hard-headed realists in business affairs.

Another important factor that helps perpetuate national myths is nationalism. Unlike most European states, where nationality is generally still synonymous with ethnicity and common ancient historical experiences, the United States was, and remains, largely a country of immigrants. Uniting such diverse people in a new country required their willingness to adhere to common symbols and myths. The immigrants embraced the broader and more nebulous set of values and beliefs that comprised the American creed. Given the centrality of religion in both private and public life, American patriotism is infused with a degree of religious fervor not usually found in Western Europe or Japan. Consequently, when America gets involved in conflicts with countries that are culturally distant and whose leaders can be easily demonized, the messianic aspect of the culture is likely to prevail.[71]

Another factor which contributes to the relative durability of ideology in American life is that the United States has left its ideology implicit and informal. Michael Hunt argues that some ideologies assume a formal, explicit, and systematic form precisely because there is resistance to them within the culture, whereas an ideology left implicit rests on a consensus and therefore exercises a greater, albeit more subtle, power.[72] In other words, the lack of self-consciousness about an ideology actually strengthens its power in helping to shape both domestic and foreign affairs.

Further augmenting ideology's influence in society has been the remarkable political and social stability of the United States. Relatively isolated from the turbulence of European troubles, unthreatened by its neighbors, and enjoying widespread consensus, America has never been forced to seriously examine most of its fundamental values and beliefs. While the Civil War, the civil rights movement, the Great Depression, and other major upheavals have led to an examination of certain values and beliefs, adjustments have been made largely within the existing political and cultural framework. Growing prosperity has dampened desires for social revolutions. Consequently, virtue and institutions have become interchangeable. Most Americans believe that the extraordinary economic and political success of their country demonstrates the virtue of its institutions. This success buttresses an important national myth, namely, American exceptionalism.

American Exceptionalism and Foreign Policy

An underlying assumption which inevitably shapes American foreign policy is that the United States is inherently different from and morally superior to other countries. Unlike ordinary nations, America was divinely chosen and set apart from the evil Europeans and others to be an example for the world to follow. The early European settlers in America, perceiving themselves to be the new Israelites in the promised land of the New World, regarded their experiences as having cosmic significance and believed, like the South African Boers who defeated the Zulus at Blood River in Natal in 1838, that evidence of their special relationship with God would be demonstrated by their ability to resist more numerous foes and by the success of their economic endeavors.

Virtuous and unique among the nations, America was not subject to the standards by which other countries would be judged. Americans had to be more righteous. They were destined for economic and political dominance. This view, articulated by John Winthrop and other Massachusetts Bay settlers, is still strongly embraced by Americans today, regardless of whether they label themselves conservative or liberal. As Winthrop put it, "we must consider that we shall be a city upon a hill; the eyes of all the people are upon us."[73] More recently, President Ronald Reagan asserted: "I have always believed that this blessed land was set apart in a special way, that some divine plan placed this great continent between the two oceans to be found by people from every corner of the earth—people who had a special love for freedom and the courage to uproot themselves, leave their home land and friends to come to a strange land."[74]

The belief in exceptionalism has played a major role in the development of great civilizations. Such myths, often supported by tangible evidence of economic, social, or military superiority, strengthen the tendency of countries to define themselves through differentiation from others. Britain, for example, from the early seventeenth century until its empire crumbled in the aftermath of World War II, believed that it was exceptional and that it was another Jerusalem. Indeed, William Blake's popular poem, "Jerusalem the Golden," specifically addressed the issue of building Jerusalem in "England's green and pleasant land." Akin to the United States, Britain perceived itself as Israel and regarded its adversaries as Satan. Britain distinguished itself from others, particularly Catholic France, through its adherence to the Protestant religion. Linda Colley argues that Britain, the result of joining England, Scotland, and Wales, remained united and perpetuated the belief in its exceptionalism "by maintaining prosperity at home, by means of recurring wars with the Catholic states of Europe, and by means of a frenetic and for a long time highly successful pursuit of empire."[75]

Depicting their own behavior as humanitarian and above criticism, even as they destroy those they are purportedly saving from sinister forces, powerful countries have generally perceived themselves as being exceptional. For example, few Americans have accepted responsibility for the suffering of ordinary Iraqis that was caused by the Gulf War and the continuation of sanctions after the country was reduced to what a UN report termed "a preindustrial age." The greater the geographical distance between a people and others they regard as inferior, the more likely they are to believe in their own exceptionalism. Britain and the United States, similarly separated from Europe—America clearly more so—believed that they were morally superior to continental Europeans, a view not evidently shared by France.

Yet America is exceptional in significant ways, the most important of which is that the country was started from a revolution and consolidated by adherence to the American creed.

Americans deliberately attempted to create a unique country, and developed myths that reinforced society's belief in that uniqueness. Not surprisingly, America's history and many of its assumptions and attitudes are quite different from those of the European societies that gave it birth.[76]

The war for independence from Great Britain served to confirm the United States' uniqueness among nations. The religious fervor of prerevolutionary America was integrated into a broader national ideology. Victorious against the world's most formidable imperial power, Americans concluded that God had intervened on their side. This view continues to dominate the United States' thinking when it engages in conflicts in which its victory is seen as a step toward building God's kingdom on earth. Many Americans perceive themselves as that Kingdom's architects. The U.S.-led war against Saddam Hussein and the extraordinary military victory, for example, was perceived by Bush as heralding in a new world order which the United States is destined to lead. God not only blessed Americans but also expected them to be paragons of virtue. America would be a beacon to nations that remained in darkness. Loren Baritz believes that the war for independence transformed the idea of American exemplary morality and mission into a necessary ingredient of the national belief system.[77]

Unlike Europeans, who established overseas colonies for economic gain, strategic superiority, and to exercise physical control over people regarded as uncivilized and in need of European guidance, most Americans are more likely to concentrate on correcting the way other people think and act.[78] Consequently, while we boast of a past free of European-style imperialism, our belief in our exceptionalism enables us to deny what others regard as our own imperialism, beginning with westward expansion and the Indian wars, not to mention American activities in Cuba, Latin America, Puerto Rico, the Philippines, and Hawaii which have been perceived as imperialistic by many of those areas' inhabitants.

From America's perspective, the troubled histories and intractable problems of other countries are amenable to its designs when it decides to intervene. The words echoed by Thomas Paine still resonate in contemporary American society and in many of its foreign policies. When the first shots of the American

Revolution were fired at Lexington and Concord, Americans believed that they were heard around the world, thereby giving them universal significance. Thomas Paine stressed that the cause of America was in great measure the cause of all mankind. Moreover, Americans could annul history and all previous human experience because, from Paine's perspective, "we have it in our power to begin the world over again. A situation similar to the present has not happened since the days of Noah until now. The birthday of a new world is at hand."[79] Historical experiences combined with religious beliefs to strengthen the assumption that through destruction of the enemy, new worlds might be created. Violence is viewed as an unpleasant but essential part of the regeneration process. This component of American exceptionalism was evident in U.S. involvement in both world wars and in the Persian Gulf. Out of the destruction of war would emerge a new international order, an opportunity for the United States to begin the world all over again.

Exceptionalism is embraced by conservatives and liberals alike. When the United States intervenes in foreign conflicts, whether under Democrats or Republicans, morality and the righteousness of American power become cornerstones of the enterprise. The difference between various groups is only a matter of degree; they do not really challenge the ideology and myths that undergird U.S. international behavior.[80] Most American policymakers, not content to accept the world as it is and to deal realistically with problems that defy easy solutions, fashion policies designed to save the world, only to be disappointed when the world refuses to participate in its own salvation. The fact that leaders emphasize divergent themes of U.S. ideology does not mean they do not adhere to American exceptionalism. The moralism of former President Jimmy Carter's human rights policies represented an important aspect of American utopianism as well as an attempt to treat people in other states with greater respect. With Ronald Reagan as president, America rediscovered, in a more profound way than under the Carter administration, other guiding myths, particularly those that emphasized America as a politically rejuvenating phenomenon. Garry Wills contends that "Reagan did not argue for American values; he embodied them. He renewed our past by resuming it."[81]

A Religious Nation: Church and State Inseparable

American foreign policy is characterized by a tendency toward crusades and the humiliation and complete destruction of regimes and individuals designated as enemies on the one hand, and deep, unsurpassed humanitarian instincts toward those who are non-threatening on the other. An underlying reason for this paradoxical approach is the centrality of religion in American culture. Another is the need to galvanize public support for policies that would otherwise lose out in the competition for scarce resources. Although predominantly Protestant religious views push Americans toward compassion for victims of natural disasters and other short-term crises, these same religious beliefs also influence Americans to view material success as a reward for goodness, and poverty as punishment for sin. Whereas churches in Europe, Canada, and Australia generally accept the inherent weakness of human beings, their inability to escape sin and error, and the importance of forgiveness, American Protestants in particular are more inclined to emphasize the perfectibility of humanity, and more determined to inflict severe punishment on sinners.[82] Those branded as evil must be destroyed, because compromise and coexistence with them is unacceptable. This attitude has played a role in America's refusal to recognize China, North Korea, Vietnam, and Castro's Cuba long after Europeans, Canadians, and others did. It also helps to influence U.S. policy toward Iraq.

Despite what appears to be a largely antagonistic attitude toward any connection between religion and the government, the United States remains far more religious than the rest of the industrialized world. Numerous national research surveys consistently and unambiguously indicate that the vast majority of Americans perceive themselves to be very religious. Whereas 17 percent of the Danes, 27 percent of the French, 50 percent of the Spanish, and 57 percent of the British believe in Heaven, an overwhelming 84 percent of Americans do. Similarly, while only 18 percent of the Germans, 29 percent of the French, 54 percent of the Spanish, and 31 percent of the British say they never doubt the existence of God, approximately 60 percent of Americans never doubt that God really exists. Furthermore, more than 87 percent of all Americans say that religion occupies a central role in their own lives, and 79 percent of them be-lieve there are clear guidelines about what is good or evil.[83]

Yet the religiosity that distinguishes Americans from Europeans does not mean that Americans subscribe to biblical teachings in the traditional sense. Extensive surveys done by George Gallup and Jim Castelli show that American religious life is marked by a series of gaps. First, there is an ethics gap between expressed beliefs and actual behavior. Second, though religion is extremely popular, it is also very superficial. Most Americans don't believe much of what they verbalize. And fi-nally, there is a knowledge gap between their stated faith and what they know about that faith.[84] It is not uncommon to find in America, especially among college and high school students, a surprising lack of biblical knowledge, despite widespread refer-ences to the Bible. How, then, can religion influence U.S. cultur-al values in general and its foreign policies specifically?

Obscured by public debates on separation of church and state in America is the reality that the United States is a reli-gious nation. Samuel P. Huntington states that: "Americans give to their nation and its creed many of the attributes and functions of the church."[85] Instead of having prayer in school, the whole nation often prays collectively, as it did during the Gulf War. Unlike Britain, where the Anglican church is recog-nized as the official church of England, the United States was formed as a reaction to the excessive controls that European states attempted to exercise over the religious beliefs of private citizens. But even as freedom of worship was jealously guarded, sometimes unsuccessfully, the early European settlers in America believed that their responsibility was to build a society in which people would live according to God's will.

America developed various myths that consolidated the role of religion in political life. The nation at war against Britain became our Israel; George Washington was an American Joshua.[86] Thomas Jefferson and Thomas Paine articulated the view that sovereignty resided not in the King but in the people, who were ultimately given their freedom by God. By relying heavily on John Locke's philosophy, the Declaration of Independence augmented the connection between religious free-dom and democratic values. The Lockean approach to govern-ment embraced the assumption that democracy and the belief in God are interwoven. If European Christianity was despotic, American Christianity was democratic and republican. Alexis de Tocqueville asserted that "from the start politics and religion agreed, and they have not since ceased to do so."[87] This observation remains essentially valid.

The emergence and rapid spread of popular sovereignty following the American Revolution helped to fuse political ideas and religious beliefs. Given the country's strong religious roots and the active role of churches in promoting and justifying the Revolution, a rigid separation of church and state was virtually impossible. American popular culture was further Christianized by the conjuncture of evangelical fervor and popular sovereignty.[88] Precisely because the impetus for welding religious values and democratic freedoms together was a grassroots phenomenon, religious influences on public life and policy were accepted by successive generations of Americans. Alexis de Tocqueville believed that "for Americans the ideas of Christianity and liberty are so completely mingled that it is almost impossible to get them to conceive of one without the other; it is not a question with them of sterile beliefs bequeathed by the past and vegetating rather than living in the depths of the soul."[89]

Whereas church and state are separate in terms of protecting individual freedoms, within the political system politics and religion are intertwined. To a much greater extent than is the case in other industrialized countries, America has a vibrant civil religion which influences almost all aspects of political life, including foreign policy. Civil religion is part of the larger system of beliefs, symbols, and rituals that unifies a diverse people into one nation. It draws upon religious ideologies and historical experiences to provide a common frame of reference. As a component of culture, civil religion is instrumental in rejuvenating culture, affirming it, and justifying international and domestic activities by referring back to culture-building and culture-affirming processes.[90] Civil religion, like religion in general, can be mobilized for destructive as well as humanitarian purposes. It can serve to fuel holy wars against foreign and domestic enemies; or it can buttress arguments for respecting the individual's fundamental freedoms and human rights, as it did in relation to the treatment of African-Americans. Borrowing selectively from religious traditions, civil religion created powerful symbols of national solidarity without causing any significant conflict with religious organizations.[91] Although some basic conflicts reflect religious differences, which are perpetuated by the existence of so many different religions and the composition of political parties and their regional bases, most Americans strongly support civil religion. The majority accept the view that their country is a moral society that was created "under God."

National leaders, especially presidents, have historically invoked religion to mobilize public support for or against particular international and domestic activities. Whatever their own personal religious beliefs might be, they realize the importance of religion in the United States. Both the North and the South used religion to support their cause during the American Civil War. In most presidential campaigns, Republicans and Democrats compete on the basis of their adherence to religious values. However, efforts by the Republicans to focus on God in the 1992 presidential campaign were rejected by the nation, partly because the Republicans were perceived as attempting to use religion for purely political gain and to divide the country. During the Cold War, when the nation was preoccupied with fighting "godless communism," no presidential candidate could be successful if he or she was perceived as disregarding religion. In the public's mind, God and freedom are too closely intertwined for a candidate who embraces only secular values to be elected to public office. Atheists do not fare well in American politics. Recent presidents, particularly Ronald Reagan and George Bush, cast themselves as holy warriors in the tradition of President Woodrow Wilson. An ultimate crusader, Wilson believed that America's participation in World War I would not only make the world safe for democracy, but would also redeem the Old World. Wilson expressed yearning for the Kingdom of God on earth in his definition of American foreign policy.[92]

During the Reagan administration, the religious component of America's foreign and domestic policies was pronounced, partly because of the power of fundamentalist Christians. Mobilizing their followers for political influence, many church leaders, particularly Southern Christian fundamentalists, exerted significant pressure on the government to adopt an extremely conservative social and political agenda. From many fundamentalists' perspective, only religious people are good people. Emphasizing God and the country, traditional values, American morality, and the Judeo-Christian ethic, fundamentalists strongly supported Reagan's foreign policy agenda, especially his crusade against communism and leftist regimes.[93] Both communism and radical regimes represented evil, in the fundamentalists' view.

Asserting that American traditional values had eroded, Reagan argued that they should be promoted and preserved by permitting children to start their days the same way members of the United States Congress do—with prayer. He asserted that the public expression of our faith in God, through prayer, was fundamental—as a part of the American heritage. In his message to Congress that accompanied his proposed constitutional amendment on prayer in school, Reagan made a strong case for civil religion in American society by stating that he joined the people "in acknowledging this basic truth, that our liberty springs from and depends upon an abiding faith in God. This has been clear since the time of George Washington."[94]

Echoing many of Reagan's views, President Bush underscored the linkage between politics and religion in America. In many ways, Bush seemed to be simultaneously extremely pragmatic and religious. The latter characteristic was clearly on the ascendancy during and after the Gulf War. In addition to conducting international diplomacy by phone, Bush also prayed with Edmond Browning, the Bishop of the Episcopal Church of the United States of America, on the telephone. However, prior to the war against Iraq, Bush, instead of praying with Bishop Browning—who staunchly opposed the war—turned to Billy Graham to lead the nation in prayer and to pray with him.

Apart from reiterating the view that from the very beginning we have relied on God's strength and guidance in war and peace, Bush stated that one cannot be president of the United States without faith in God and without knowing with certainty that we are one nation under God. "God is our rock and salvation, and we must trust Him and keep faith with Him."[95] Enjoying the highest public approval of any president in recent history, approximately 89 percent, Bush proclaimed that by the grace of God, America had won the Cold War, and that the teachings of Jesus Christ were the moral force behind the stunning military victory in the Gulf. Bush thanked members of the National Religious Broadcasters organization for "helping

America, as Christ ordained, to be a light unto the world."[96] And after Bush ordered the bombing of military installations in the "no-fly zone" in southern Iraq the week before leaving office, he declared that the pilots involved had done the Lord's work.

Race, Culture, and American Foreign Policy

Race has profoundly affected the character of American society, its institutions, self-perception, and, significantly, its foreign relations. A nation that presented itself as a paragon of virtue and a beacon of freedom, equality, and democracy was, at the same time, a country that embraced many negative attitudes toward Native Americans, African-Americans, and Mexicans, among others. Obvious contradictions between an extremely strong commitment to liberty and individualism on the one hand, and the existence of slavery and the categorization of individuals into groups on the other, ultimately divided the nation, a development that had unparalleled ramifications for virtually all aspects of American life, including foreign policy.

While the economic and political success of racial minorities in the United States is unmatched by any other European-dominated society, race remains one of the most explosive issues in America. The relative success experienced by a growing number of minorities, and their entrance into the American mainstream, have generated contradictory attitudes and behaviors that are supportive of progress, on the one hand, and resistant to what is often viewed as competition for positions white Americans had essentially monopolized, on the other. Thus, as Americans begin to achieve their long-held objective of an egalitarian society, a significant number seem reluctant to accept the realization of a cherished myth. Many minorities, with access to the nation's best universities and some of its most prestigious public and private bastions of power, seem uncomfortable with being integrated into the mainstream of society.

Although the relationship between domestic racial practices and attitudes and the formulation and implementation of foreign policy is not always direct, there are many examples of connections between them. The dominant cultural values often influence many Americans to adopt positive attitudes toward most Europeans and negative attitudes toward non-Europeans.

U.S. generosity toward and understanding of Europeans are sometimes matched by its hostility or indifference toward non-Europeans. Because culture conditions Americans to be color-conscious, they continue to perceive other countries and peoples through the prism of race, a reality reflected in the language used to describe behavior of Europeans and non-Europeans. While most Americans can "sympathize with" and "understand" behavior by Europeans that they find difficult to ignore, they tend to label similar behavior by non-Europeans as "barbaric," "uncivilized," and "savage." Extreme cases such as World War I and World War II are obvious exceptions to this general tendency. Dehumanization of non-Europeans is sometimes followed by the use of force against them when U.S. interests are percieved to be threatened. This aspect of America's foreign policy behavior is linked to the close relationship between race and nationalism. Michael Hunt contends that "Americans used race to build protective walls against the threatening strangeness of other people and to legitimize the boundaries and terms of intergroup contact."[97]

Americans believed in the concept of a racial hierarchy in which Europeans occupied the top and Africans were relegated to the lowest positions. Social, economic, and political rights were allocated according to one's place in the system of racial stratification. Although the origins of this concept are complex, racial differentiation was highlighted by the technological revolutions that facilitated and expanded with European colonization of the Third World. Like Europeans, Americans subscribed to the view, clearly at odds with Judeo-Christian beliefs, that human worth could be measured in terms of the scientific and technical progress of a particular society. General assumptions about the correspondence between the mastery of nature and overall social development frequently determined how Americans and Europeans treated Africans, Native Americans, and Asians.[98]

Perceptions of Native Americans as primitive peoples who lacked technology enabled various American presidents, especially Andrew Jackson, to subjugate and destroy many of them. Development of the country and respect for the native inhabitants were regarded as virtually irreconcilable. Loren Baritz points out that only when the forest and Native Americans were subdued and the latter removed to remote locations did some Americans attempt to ennoble "the savage" and glorify the virgin land.[99]

Darwinism's emergence in the late nineteenth century strengthened the racial beliefs that were already influencing U.S. policy toward Native Americans, enslaved Africans, and Mexicans. Darwinism added credence to theories of racial superiority that were accepted throughout the American society. Richard Hofstadter and others argue that both the enslavement of Africans and the near extinction of Native Americans had been used as evidence of European superiority long before Darwinism.[100] Racial assumptions have been so deeply ingrained in the fabric of the culture that, despite major social, economic, and political changes, most Americans still perceive Europeans to be at the top rungs of the social ladder and African-Americans and other non-Europeans to be at the bottom. Within the European groups, those who came to America first, the British and Protestants, are assigned the highest social standing.[101] The high esteem in which British culture is generally held in the United States attests to the durability of ethnic loyalties.

According to Alvin Rubinstein and Donald Smith, many Third World elites view most Americans as a people who assume that they are racially and culturally superior, who are ignorant and disdainful of other civilizations, and who are eager to teach but disinclined to learn from others.[102] They perceive U.S. behavior to be characterized by cultural arrogance, which is manifested in the general assumption that others must interact with it on its terms. Not having to negotiate as equals with enslaved Africans, Native Americans, and neighboring countries, the United States often finds it difficult to compromise with non-Europeans in particular or anyone who is not regarded as an equal in general, as the case studies in this book suggest. Thus, while U.S. foreign policy is based, to a large extent, on protecting national interests it is also influenced by the idea of a racial hierarchy that is interwoven in American culture and institutions. Cultural fears of nonwhites directly influence the United States to respond forcefully when countries such as Panama, Grenada, Iran, and Iraq take, or threaten to take, Americans hostage. Charles William Maynes, the editor of *Foreign Policy*, argues that "the idea of innocent Americans in the hands of savages has been a powerful one since whites first arrived on these shores."[103] Yet President Carter, a product of that same culture, negotiated to obtain the release of American hostages in Iran.

Racial images and the attitudes they spawned have had an impact on American foreign policy. Just as the Europeans sought to justify their control over nonwhites by emphasizing their own cultural superiority and innate goodness, most Americans also believed in manifest destiny and the white man's burden. But unlike the vast majority of Europeans who governed their colonies from afar and with the assistance of the colonized, many Americans viewed the existence of Native peoples as a direct threat, and were therefore convinced that their removal would advance American civilization. This historical experience contributes to Americans' relative lack of understanding about and empathy for the Third World, which, according to Howard Wiarda, is at the heart of U.S. policy failures.[104] It is also at the root of America's tendency to use force to resolve conflicts with distant cultures.

Chapter Two

Cultural Roots of Force in American Foreign Policy

Responding to growing domestic and international pressures to end widespread starvation in Somalia, President George Bush decided to launch a massive humanitarian relief effort, known as Operation Restore Hope, in December 1992, a month before leaving office. Hailed initially as an example of how American military forces could be used for humanitarian purposes in the post-Cold War period, and as a dramatic departure from previous military practice, six months later Operation Restore Hope degenerated into another violent conflict involving the United States. U.S. gunships attacked the military compound of Somalia's principal warlord, Mohamed Aidid, to punish him for his alleged participation in orchestrating ambushes that resulted in the deaths of twenty-three Pakistani soldiers who were serving with the UN. Although several objective factors contributed to the outbreak of violence, cultural differences between the United States and Somalia, America's tendency to employ force to terminate conflicts, and the fact that U.S. troops are not trained for peacekeeping but for using massive firepower played a significant role.[1]

To a much greater degree than is generally acknowledged, a nation's decision to resolve international problems with force is influenced by its culture. Quincy Wright observes that "a culture may give preference to particular modes of dealing with conflict situations. These may be classified as renunciatory, conciliatory, dictatorial, or adjudicatory."[2] In other words, cultures may be predisposed, to varying degrees, to yield to pressure, to compromise, to dominate opponents, or to submit to group decisions and demands. Cultures that emphasize aggressiveness are more likely to favor military solutions than those which promote passive resistance. This point is accepted as valid by most Americans when they analyze the behavior of other countries. Yet most of us tend to overlook it in relation to U.S. foreign policy. Remembered historical experiences, which directly shape culture, help to determine a country's choice of instruments for resolving conflicts. Specifically, methods utilized to promote nationalism strongly influence a country's tendency to go to war.[3]

Cultural beliefs, attitudes, and the values of ordinary citizens help to shape the decision to go to war, the objectives of war, the way war is fought, how it is terminated, and postwar relations between combatants. While developments in the international environment may precipitate war, it is difficult for a democratic society's leader to initiate a major conflict without persuading the general public to accept the decision to fight and its possible consequences. To accomplish this objective, leaders appeal to emotions embedded in the culture, as President Bush did at the onset of Operation Desert Storm. After examining several variables to determine which ones are the most significant in a president's decision to commit the United States to war, Charles W. Ostrom and Brian L. Job conclude that "the absolute and relative levels of popular support turn out to be the most important influence on the political use of major force."[4] Consequently, America's cultural values, the foundation of politics, are inextricably linked to American decisions to engage in military conflicts abroad.

Political leaders tap into their cultures to dehumanize and demonize those designated as enemies. The greater the distance between cultures in conflict, the easier it is for leaders to mobilize public support for war and to dehumanize those designated as enemies. Dehumanization of others is designed not only to destroy their humanity but also to reassure those who dehumanize of their own presumed goodness. Dehumanization facilitates justification of the inhumane treatment of those regarded as enemies by diminishing empathetic faculties.

Empathy, viewed as the emotional cornerstone of moral judgment, enables us to feel with other human beings, to cognitively and effectively put ourselves in their place, and to become more aware of others' needs and concerns.[5] Empathy is inconsistent with simplistic divisions of the world in terms of good versus evil, right versus wrong, and heroes versus villains. Empathy reduces a person's will to harm others, who are perceived as ordinary human beings. Personalizing the injurious effects experienced by others makes their suffering much more noticeable and troubling. It is therefore difficult to kill people we do not dehumanize without risking personal distress and self-censure.[6] President Carter's success with negotiations in the Middle East, Panama, the Horn of Africa, North Korea, Haiti, and elsewhere was due to some extent to his ability to empathize with others from distant cultures.

Dehumanization is closely related to moral exclusion, a concept and practice that is intertwined with cultural values. Culture significantly determines which groups we perceive as being outside the boundary within which moral values, rules, and considerations of fairness apply. Culture also creates perceptions of connectedness and alikeness, which, in turn, engender empathy and positive behavior toward those who are viewed as belonging within our culturally delineated circle. Because those who are morally excluded are regarded as expendable, subhuman, threatening, and undeserving, harming them often appears acceptable, appropriate, and just.[7]

Like many other great powers, the United States is inclined to equate physical force with strength. Senator J. William Fulbright argued that even peaceful nations often believe that force engenders respect and recognition and that violence is the most concrete proof of superiority—that a country with a powerful military has better people, better institutions, better principles and values, and a superior civilization.[8] While it is relatively easy for such powers to conclude that other countries and cultures are evil, it is far more difficult for the former to see their own shortcomings. President John Adams was clearly aware of this problem. Writing to President Thomas Jefferson, Adams asserted that "power always thinks it has a great soul and vast views, beyond the comprehension of the weak; and that it is doing God's service when it is in violation of all His laws."[9]

The Link Between Internal and External Violence

Attempting to mobilize public support for Nicaragua's Contras, Angola's Jonas Savimbi, and so-called "freedom-fighters" elsewhere, President Ronald Reagan constantly linked American values to U.S. foreign policy objectives and the instruments needed to accomplish them. Presidents Franklin D. Roosevelt and John F. Kennedy, among others, articulated domestic as well as foreign policy issues in military terms. Most American presidents use war metaphors when dealing with diverse problems. President Lyndon B. Johnson declared a war on poverty at home while America was fighting in Vietnam; President Jimmy Carter viewed the energy crisis and his conservation efforts in terms of "the moral equivalent of war"; President George Bush declared a war on drugs, a commitment that was largely abandoned to conduct the war against Saddam Hussein; and the "war room" of Bill Clinton's campaign was transferred to the White House. Because of the importance of public opinion in American democracy, political leaders appeal to the country's cultural values to communicate effectively with the general public. The linkage between domestic values and foreign policies is assumed. But is there a link between internal violence and the use of force to settle disputes abroad?

Partly due to the dominance of realism as an approach to the study of international relations since World War II, the linkage between internal violence and international conflicts has been largely discounted. Realists, emphasizing external threats to a country's security, tend to ignore the significance of domestic factors in shaping the foreign policy process. However, by viewing international relations in Hobbesian terms, realists inadvertently create a strong link between internal and external violence. From their perspective, the international system closely resembles the "state of nature" which Thomas Hobbes articulated. Similarly, the Kantian view that democratic societies rarely fight each other, which is accepted by most scholars and foreign policymakers, suggests a link between internal conflict resolution strategies and international behavior. As William J. Dixon puts it, "if political leaders are accustomed to nonviolent procedures of conflict resolution in domestic affairs, then it is likely that such methods will also prove useful in settling international disputes."[10]

But given the fact that democracies fight undemocratic states, it could be argued that many democracies also have norms that sanction using force to deal with international problems. Clearly, democracies are not inherently peaceful. Bruce M. Russett argues that "empirically speaking, democracies are about as likely as any other type of state to fight conflicts."[11] The absence of war among democracies does not mean that norms within democratic societies that support violence are lacking. The United States, the most democratic nation in the world, is also very violent, both at home and abroad. While America does not fight other democracies, U.S. history is replete with violence against societies that are culturally distant. James Meernik, for example, estimates that since World War II, American presidents have employed the armed forces short of war over 200 times. Rather than engaging in full-scale wars to impose their will on adversaries, presidents have attempted to influence nations, leaders and world events with limited military action.[12]

A society that is plagued with violence and which glorifies violence generally responds forcefully to outside threats to its perceived interests and status. The domestic environment, including cultural values, directly affects national security policies designed to address perceived threats in the external environment. A culture immersed in violence is likely to engage in external conflict, depending on objective domestic and international constraints. But the relationship between internal and external conflict cannot be precisely measured, partly because several different causal mechanisms are required to explain the linkage.[13] Focusing on various narrow aspects of the association between internal and external violence, most empirical studies support the view that internal conflict is not strongly related to external conflict.[14] Charles W. Kegley, Neil R. Richardson, and Gunther Richter reach a more ambiguous conclusion about the relationship between conflict at home and abroad. They find that in militarized countries, "the higher the level of civil strife, the lower the level of external conflict and, conversely, militarized nations experiencing low levels of domestic turmoil tend to be more conflictual in the behavior they direct toward foreign targets. Only in highly militarized societies does a patterned relationship between civil strife and foreign conflict exist."[15] Although there are several possible exceptions, historical evidence, as well as contemporary cases, suggests that internal conflict is a reliable predictor of the level of external conflict, and vice versa. It seems reasonable to conclude that societies that are psychoculturally predisposed toward violence tend to behave more aggressively both internally and externally.[16]

In addition to the militarization of society, factors such as interpersonal violence, high crime rates, norms which support violent behavior, and the structure of society may also contribute to external violence.[17] Clearly, these connections are not always direct and unambiguous. Individual aggression does not necessarily lead to group warfare or vice versa. Societies which are nonviolent may be governed by norms that discourage internal conflict but promote external violence against others perceived to be culturally different.

Countries that are as diverse racially, ethnically, and religiously as the United States, may use force internationally to consolidate domestic cohesion and to sharpen the national sense of identity. In Vietnam and the Persian Gulf, decisions to either initiate or continue fighting were clearly intertwined with national identity, as American leaders often stressed. Lewis A. Coser argues that "group boundaries are established through conflict with the outside, so that a group defines itself by struggling with other groups."[18] The United States' diversity predisposes it to resort to violence to maintain the cohesion of the dominant group domestically, and the nation as a whole internationally. Historically, African-Americans were portrayed as a threat to preserve solidarity among European-Americans.[19]

Foreign enemies were also instrumental in consolidating American nationalism, which has largely been defined in terms of opposition to others. Because internal solidarity is often perceived by many leaders to be endangered by the absence of an enemy, "disappearance of the original enemy leads to a search for new enemies so that the group may continue to engage in conflict."[20] Following communism's demise and the disintegration of the Soviet Union, the Pentagon began to identify potential new enemies, a list that included an already militarily and economically devastated Iraq. This effort was also motivated by concerns within the Pentagon about post-Cold War budget cuts. While some Pentagon officials searched for new rationales and threats, others, including former Secretary of Defense Les Aspin, agreed with the need for a leaner defense budget, and have been reluctant to play the game of threat inflation. Clinton's own desire to focus on domestic issues and to trim defense spending has reinforced the latter approach.

Linkages between internal violence, or the cultural values that glorify violence, and external conflicts can be demonstrated by examining specific societies' behavior. Greece, Rome, Britain, France, Germany, Japan, and the Yanomami of South America will be briefly discussed, to put the connection between violence in America and our tendency to militarize conflicts in a broader, comparative perspective.

Ancient Greece embodied values and practices that were reflected in its external relations. Whereas peace, Eirene, was represented by a subordinate female deity, war was portrayed by Ares, a powerful and dominant male god. Greeks perceived war to be a natural state, the basis of society and the "father" of all things. Courage was demonstrated by participating in war and activities related to war. Men who refused to fight became slaves. The founding Greek myth was that the gods themselves had achieved power through a victorious war against the Titans.[21] Women and slaves were treated as inferior persons. Different standards existed for warriors on one hand and women and slaves on the other. Whereas justice governed relations between Greek citizens, violence was routinely used against those designated as "others." Although Jean Bethke Elshtain concludes that "internal relations between dominant citizens and lesser persons were not a perfect mimesis of external relations ruled by force and existing in a kind of ethical twilight zone,"[22] the ancient Greeks' domestic behavior bore striking and unmistakable resemblances to their external behavior. The warrior culture nurtured at home was essentially indistinguishable from the Greeks' external use of force.

Perhaps the Roman Republic best exemplifies the link between internal and external violence. Force was an integral part of virtually every aspect of Roman life. Crimes against individuals and property were commonplace. Violence was made routine, and the culture of violence became deeply entrenched in Roman society.[23] The Romans mobilized their army every spring and went to war with surrounding states more out of habit than in response to military threats. This yearly event was part of Rome's religious calendar. The gates of the temple of Janus, the custodian of the universe, were closed in peacetime and opened during war. William V. Harris estimates that "during the first 86 years from 327 (B.C.) onwards there were at most four or five years without war. It was probably in 241 (B.C.) that the doors of the temple of Janus were closed for the first time after a very long interval, to be opened again almost at once because of the rebellion of the Falerii."[24] This warrior culture was strongly supported by ordinary Romans, with the people often urging war when the Senate favored peace. Popular support for violence was evidenced by the importance ordinary Romans attached to their soldiers' acts of valor. Battle honors, highly prized by civilians and soldiers alike, were conspicuously displayed in homes.[25] Candidates for public office, and those who aspired to join the Roman aristocracy or maintain their position in it, had considerable military experience. Participation in war was a prerequisite for most positions in Roman society.

Public support for external aggression was matched by the sanctioning of widespread domestic violence. Romans were among the cruelest slaveholders. Slaves were treated like animals, and many were worked to death in state mines. Violent entertainment became a normal component of Roman life. People amused themselves by watching men, who were forced to fight animals, die in the most gruesome ways. Private individuals kept large numbers of trained gladiators to fight each other for public entertainment. War prisoners and condemned criminals were forced to fight and die for popular amusement.[26] Societal acceptance of extreme forms of violence was reflected in the brutality of the Roman legal system. Barbaric penalties like burning people alive became common, and methods of torture atrocious beyond description were used on everyone except the highest classes. Elias J. Bickerman's conclusion that this brutality was probably due to the cumulative effect of torture through the centuries in popular entertainment echoes debates on the impact of television violence in the United States on the country's growing crime epidemic.[27]

Strongly influenced by both Greece and Rome, Britain also promoted values and behavior that undergirded its efforts to consolidate a national identity and create a global empire. Linda Colley contends that "Britain was an invention forged above all by war. Time and time again, war with France brought Britons, whether they hailed from Wales or Scotland or England, into confrontation with an obviously hostile other and encouraged them to define themselves collectively against it."[28] Cultural differences between the Welsh, Scottish, and English that were natural barriers to the national unity of Britain were rendered less potent by conflict between Britain and other countries. National cohesion was tenuous without a well-defined external enemy, usually the French.

To maintain this external aggression, British authorities promoted cultural values that supported violence as an instrument of foreign policy. Public schools encouraged children to celebrate Britain's military successes overseas, and the academic emphasis on courses dealing with the Greek and Roman civilizations ensured that boys in particular received a steady diet of stories about war, empire, bravery, and sacrifice for the state. By separating boys from their families for long periods of time, by instilling the values of fortitude and survival through playing tough sports, and by inculcating a special sense of responsibility, British schools prepared boys for military or colonial service.[29] Excessive corporal punishment helped reinforce acceptance of physical coercion as an appropriate method of achieving compliance and maintaining power within and outside the country.

Britain's expansion of its empire was accompanied by rising crime rates within the country. Nineteenth-century London was not only Europe's largest city and the commercial and political center of the world's most powerful and richest empire, it was also an extremely dangerous, crime-ridden place. Akin to Rome's, the British legal system was extremely harsh. Believing that severe punishment was the most effective deterrent to crime, according to Ted Robert Gurr, British authorities specified the death penalty for more than 200 offenses.[30] Conflict with other nations seemed to have exacerbated domestic violence in Britain, and vice versa. And Britain's culture, shaped to a large extent by Protestantism and wars with others, predisposed British settlers in Australia and America to resort to widescale violence against the native inhabitants.

Britain's rival, Catholic France, provides another example of the linkage between internal and external violence. As with the United States, France's view of its position in the world has been strongly influenced by its revolution. The violence that accompanied the French Revolution began to spread beyond the country's borders in various forms, primarily through colonizing non-Europeans. The Revolution was consolidated at home and it was aggressively exported. French institutions were used to reduce the vast conquests to order and submission.[31] Like Britain, France promoted values at home that supported violence against Africans, Asians, and others who became part of the French empire. However, France's Catholic tradition and its revolutionary experiences also facilitated the development of better relations with indigenous peoples in North America and Africa than was the case in the British colonies.

Perhaps Germany provides the clearest and least controversial example to support the thesis that there is a connection between internal and external violence. Although West Germany renounced military involvement overseas, and has emerged as a leading economic power and a democratic country, many Europeans, Americans, Israelis, and others remain apprehensive about the resurgence of German militarism. These fears arise primarily from the widespread assumption that norms supportive of violence are deeply embedded in German culture, and the apprehension that these norms might fuel German aggression abroad. Many Germans also subscribe to this analysis. Concerns about German militarism are caused largely by that country's founding values and its subsequent reliance on force to achieve its foreign policy objectives.

Created by Otto von Bismark in 1871, the German state was a partnership between the Prussian military and authoritarian state on one hand and the industrial and commercial leaders on the other. Fritz Fischer, who directly links Germany's internal violence to its international aggression, argues that "the Germans were the only people who did not create their state from below by invoking the forces of democracy against old ruling groups, but accepted it gratefully at the hands of those groups in a defensive struggle against democracy."[32] Prussian militaristic values were embraced by the general population, and the liberal component of the German national movement was dominated by military influences.

Furthermore, in the process of attempting to eliminate liberalism and socialism, the Germans reinvigorated strong anti-Semitic sentiments. The national consciousness embodied the view that Germany resulted from victorious wars and that Germans were a superior race. Militaristic and racial aspects of German nationalism were intertwined with Germany's imperialism and brutality in East Africa and Namibia, its initiation of two world wars that devastated Europe, and its responsibility for the Jewish Holocaust. Referring specifically to Germany's aspirations in World War I, Fischer concludes that "both German public opinion and Germany's leaders were fully resolved to overthrow all their enemies and dictate peace to them."[33] Germany's internal cultural values and its external behavior were strongly linked, a reality not overlooked today by Germans and others who are troubled by growing racial and ethnic violence in Germany.

The relationship between cultural values that support violence and the use of force to resolve conflicts both domestically and internationally is more complex in Japan than in Britain, Germany, or the United States. Despite the existence of a culture of violence in Japan, interpersonal crime is extremely low. Furthermore, Japan also has a strong tradition of nonviolence, a situation which accompanied Japan's long period of isolationism. However, to a much greater extent than is the case in other cultures, the Japanese belief that suffering and deprivation are purifying experiences leads them to accept violence that is self-inflicted.[34] Suicide has long been part of Japan's warrior spirit. It was an integral component of the Samurai tradition. From around the tenth century to the modern period in Japan, the Samurai warriors ruled the country, and their values strongly influenced aspects of its culture. A Samurai was obligated by custom to commit suicide, principally by disembowelment, under certain conditions. Whereas Europeans did not regard an opponent's surrender negatively, Japanese did. H. Paul Varley and others have stressed that the Japanese held few things in greater contempt than capture or capitulation, and warriors were expected to destroy themselves to avoid falling into enemy hands. If taken alive, they could only anticipate inhumane treatment.[35] These cultural values were externalized during Japan's wars with other countries. British, American, and other Allied troops who were captured by or surrendered to the

Japanese during World War II were brutally treated, basically because they allowed themselves to be taken alive, in sharp contrast to Japanese soldiers who rarely capitulated.

Japan's culture of violence is reflected in art, movies, and television programs. Samurai warriors blended art and violence, aesthetic and killer instincts. Military leaders recited poetry or danced gracefully in front of their troops before fighting.[36] Contemporary Japanese society continues to promote "aesthetic cruelty" in popular entertainment. Violence is choreographed and bloodshed is aestheticized in a way that is unimaginable in the United States. Most Japanese do not wrestle with questions of morality in relation to widespread bloodshed on television. Ian Buruma asserts that Japanese tolerate gratuitous cruelty because their culture stresses the arbitrariness of fate and does not contain absolute moral rules against portraying sadistic behavior.[37]

Even though brutality permeates many aspects of Japanese culture, interpersonal violence is extremely rare, especially when Japan is compared to Western Europe and the United States. Unlike American culture, which encourages impulsiveness, individualism, assertiveness, and gun ownership, Japanese culture promotes harmony, self-control, group rights, and a sense of community. Loyalty to the group is paramount. Thus, while cultural norms allow Japanese to accept extremely violent entertainment, a strict sense of hierarchy and a rigid system of etiquette effectively prevent frequent confrontation between individuals.[38] Generalized cruelty would indicate a lack of self-restraint, which is inconsistent with the dominant values of a group-oriented society. Nevertheless, Japan's hierarchical system facilitated the rapid mobilization of its citizens to fight non-Japanese, a realization that is at the heart of domestic and international debates about changing the provision in Japan's constitution which prohibits that country's use of force to settle international disputes or to allow it to play a greater role in UN peacekeeping. The Japanese' reluctance to get involved in international disputes also emanates from that part of Japan's culture that favors nonviolence.

A final example of the connection between cultural beliefs and belligerency toward others is the Yanomami of South America. Anthropologists and social psychologists have accepted the view that a group's norms determine, to varying degrees, how it will respond to external threats.[39] The Yanomami have, by almost any standard, an extremely violent society. Women, almost routinely seriously abused by men, accept harsh treatment as normal behavior. In fact, Napoleon A. Chagnon points out that "women who are not too severely treated might even measure their husbands' concern in terms of the frequency of minor physical reprimands they sustain."[40] Violence pervades the entire society. Although formal and informal rules mitigate the severity of violent behavior, men are expected to fight regularly. Just as force is an acceptable method of resolving domestic disputes, war is regarded as an appropriate response to problems with neighboring villages. The link between fighting within and between villages is very strong. Men wear their scars proudly, and many shave their heads and apply a red pigment to highlight their war wounds.[41]

America's Historical Experiences and Its Use of Force

Although most countries have been shaped by violence, to greater or lesser degrees, the United States was the first modern nation to obtain its independence through revolution. Violence therefore became an integral component of nation-building and undergirds America's self-definition. Almost every major aspect of political, social, and economic development in the United States was accompanied by officially sanctioned, as well as unofficial, violence. Expanding westward, maintaining slavery, preserving national unity, emancipating enslaved Africans, and securing various political, social, and economic freedoms were accomplished through force. If violence is generally viewed as the lifeblood of freedom in democratic societies, that idea has been constantly rejuvenated in the United States and maintains a potency that is rare elsewhere.

Arguably, the American Revolution was the most significant event that contributed to the glorification of violence in the United States and to the embrace of guns as symbols of national freedom and personal autonomy. The success of the revolutionaries against the world's most formidable empire accounts for the enshrinement of the Revolution in American tradition and history. Richard Maxwell Brown believes that "the example of violence associated with that great event served as a grand model for later violent actions by Americans in behalf of any cause deemed good and proper."[42] Despite protests against military intervention abroad and increasing support for negotiation as a method for settling disputes, American presidents continue to employ military might in areas where U.S. efforts are virtually guaranteed to succeed. Popular acceptance of successful actions is influenced not only by factors specifically related to the conflict but also by the popular view of war as "the supreme expression of American values."[43] Military success in American society is widely regarded as incontrovertible proof that "our cause is just." While many other countries have been far more brutal than the United States, violence in American history has assumed special mythical importance. As Richard Slotkin puts it, "what is distinctly American is not necessarily the amount or kind of violence that characterizes our history but the mythic significance we have assigned to the kinds of violence we have experienced, the forms of symbolic violence we imagine, and the political uses to which we put that symbolism."[44]

An important aspect of American political thought is the belief that force engenders peace. Consequently, while Americans proclaim their dislike of violence, they often justify utilizing force to bring about harmony and "new world orders." This paradox is rooted in U.S. history. A country that was made by war offered its vast resources and abundant economic opportunities to immigrants who had escaped poverty and cruelty that pervaded much of Europe. In that connection, America's existence became a monument against war and represented a rejection of Europe's problems. To accommodate immigrants from diverse places, many of which had been at war with each other, it was essential that the newcomers reject their old ideologies and embrace consensus. Faced with a fundamental conflict of ends that endangered consensus at home, Americans resorted to force—which we have always considered to be the most decisive and compelling way to terminate such disputes.[45] The righteousness of the objective has had to be stressed to justify behavior that is obviously inconsistent with America's belief in peace and harmony. Thus, wars generally become moral crusades in which there can be no compromise with evil and no partial victory. While biblical language has been largely replaced by sophisticated technical jargon, the perception that as God's "Chosen People" Americans have to eliminate their enemies and to cleanse with fire what is regarded as evil remains ensconced in the culture. Operation Desert Storm exemplifies this approach to conflict resolution. Stanley Hoffmann argues that America's external experience has corroborated its domestic experience with using force as the ultimate problem solver.[46]

As has been the case in all European settler societies, violence against non-Europeans was an integral component of the process by which the United States was created. Europeans who emigrated to North America, South America, Australia, and South Africa employed different strategies, which included varied levels of violence, to subjugate the native inhabitants. The latter faced extermination, confinement to reservations, or incorporation into the settler society. In virtually every case, Europeans used violence to accomplish their objectives. Coexistence between Europeans and non-Europeans on an equal basis was perceived to be basically impossible. The significance of cultural distance as the dominant factor in these conflicts has been extensively examined by Louis Hartz. Referring specifically to settler societies, Hartz stresses that "for all of the tension between the English and the Dutch which resulted from the racial issue in South Africa, the underlying fact about the attitude of the fragment toward the non-European is that he is outside a consensus of values, European in character, which, despite their limited social circumference, all of the fragments share. And under these circumstances, a common European violence in relation to the non-European is almost inevitable."[47] This collision of cultures continues to influence contemporary international relations.

To a much greater degree than Spain or France, the United States viewed its struggle with Native Americans as symbolic of progress and as an essential ingredient of its self-definition. Neither the Spanish nor the French felt a need to define themselves in terms of violent opposition to Native Americans and what they purportedly represented. Both countries were relatively confident of their own durability, superior civilization, and identity. In sharp contrast to the French and Spanish, Americans were creating a new country based on beliefs that were significantly different from those prevalent in Europe. The tendency to view our own particular experiences in global terms was extended to confrontations with Native Americans. Richard Slotkin argues that these wars were perceived to be "representative of a general and universal principle."[48] The most important aspect of that principle was that violence is closely linked to progress. Alexis de Tocqueville's observations support the notion that violence and America's development were inseparable. Referring to Native Americans, de Tocqueville wrote that "these savages have not just drawn back, they have been destroyed. As the Indians have withdrawn and died, an immense nation is taking place and constantly growing. Never has such a prodigious development been seen among the nations, nor a destruction so rapid."[49]

Whereas English Protestants in America sought to displace the original inhabitants, Spanish Catholics focused primarily on converting them to Christianity, in addition to pacifying them and occupying their lands. Spanish conquistadors, landowners, entrepreneurs, and others caused the deaths of millions of Native Americans. Bartholome de las Casas, the Dominican friar, Bishop of Chiapas in Guatemala, and a leading advocate for the humanitarian treatment of the inhabitants of Spain's colonies, believed that the Spanish killed more than fifty million Native Americans, a claim that is widely disputed.[50] Nonetheless, it is clear that large numbers of inhabitants perished. On the other hand, Spanish monarchs and the Roman Catholic church retained significant control over the colonies and attempted, with varying degrees of success, to protect Native Americans. King Ferdinand and Queen Isabella stressed that "the natives" were to be treated well and converted to Christianity. Admirals were charged with the responsibility of selecting settlers who were likely to comply with this objective. In Royal Orders Concerning Indians, Ferdinand and Isabella instructed admirals to "give them graciously various presents from their highnesses' merchandise and to honor them highly. And if it should happen that any persons treat the said Indians badly in any manner, the said admiral as their highnesses' viceroy and governor, is to punish them severely."[51] Similarly, Pope Paul III strongly emphasized that "the Indians are by no means to be deprived of their liberty or the possession of their property, even though they be outside the faith of Jesus Christ."[52]

In addition to Spain's control over its colonies, the Spanish zeal to Christianize native peoples also contributed to significant differences between how the latter were treated in Protestant North America and Catholic South America. Unlike English settlers, especially those who expanded westward and viewed Native Americans as threats to their existence, the Spanish perceived their new subjects as ripe for conversion. Whereas English settlers regarded themselves as the instruments through which a New Jerusalem would be established in North America, the Spanish believed that Protestantism had eliminated the possibility of building the New Jerusalem in Europe and that it was essential to win the souls of Native Americans to create it in the Americas. Consequently, the Spanish developed a much closer relationship with indigenous peoples. Lewis Hanke points out that Spanish missionaries learned their languages, lived with them, paid attention to their culture, and attempted to make Christian doctrine intelligible to Indian mentality.[53] Spanish monarchs controlled missionary activities in the colonies, thereby minimizing the gratuitous violence that characterized the United States' development. Instead of relying principally on coercion, the Spanish sent several investigating groups to the colonies to find ways of bringing the inhabitants under Spanish rule peacefully. Persuasion, not force, was emphasized.[54] To ensure compliance with Spanish policy, and to punish heresy and sins against God, Ferdinand and Isabella transferred the Inquisition, which they had established to purge Spain of Jews and other non-Christians, to the Americas. The tribunals were not granted jurisdiction over Native Americans, however, a fact that reinforces the view that Spain sought to deter Spaniards from violating the numerous laws by which the colonies were governed,[55] although Spanish policy and practice often diverged significantly. Nevertheless, Spanish rule in America was theoretically committed to protecting the indigenous peoples, a goal that Protestant America essentially eschewed.

Like Spain's, France's treatment of Native Americans was influenced by the combination of the Jesuits' religious tolerance and the mutual economic, political, and military dependence of the colonizers and the colonized. Unlike English Protestants in America, whose exaggerated sense of cultural, racial, and religious superiority basically precluded close ties between them and Native Americans, French Catholics not only believed that indigenous peoples could achieve salvation, but that they could become French citizens. In Africa as well as in North America, the British were more inclined than the French to emphasize racial and cultural differences and to encourage segregation. Whereas Native Americans in New England could do little to alter their status in relation to the British, the Company of New France's charter provided equality for anyone attaining a certain level of French civilization and embracing Catholicism. Native Americans with these qualifications were "to be accepted as French subjects with all the rights and privileges appertaining, including the right to settle in France whenever they wished and to acquire and dispose of property there as would a subject born in the kingdom."[56] Strongly influenced by the Jesuits, the French were also determined to establish a New Jerusalem in North America that would include anyone who became a Roman Catholic. The racial exclusivity that characterized Protestant America's vision of a New Jerusalem mirrored the inclusive nature of Catholicism in New France.

Political, economic, social, and military expediency undoubtedly influenced France to develop close alliances with various Native American peoples and to treat them more humanely. Given the traditional hostility between Protestant Britain and Catholic France, as well as the numerical superiority of English settlers in North America, New France's very survival depended on France's ability to develop alliances with Native Americans through adroit diplomacy. The small number of French settlers, fur traders, and other entrepreneurs developed a keen sense of appreciation for their dependence on Native Americans. Consequently, the French did not antagonize their allies by occupying their lands. On the contrary, as James Axtell observes, they respected the inhabitants' sovereignty, encouraged them to preserve their lands, attempted to give them the best trade goods at reasonable prices, and drew them tightly to the Catholic faith.[57] This approach sharply contrasted with rapacious British policies that deprived many Native Americans of their land, their humanity, and their lives. The French were less reluctant than the highly ethnocentric British to marry Native Americans. While France's small and overwhelmingly male population may have been a crucial factor in such interracial relationships, cultural factors appear to account for critical differences between French and British social interaction with indigenous North Americans.

The French transplanted many aspects of their culture to the New World, prominent among which was the paternalism of France's political institutions. The "benevolently" paternal royal governor of New France was portrayed as the father of his "Indian children," just as King Louis XIV was the father of his "French children" in France. But Native Americans, in J.H. Elliot's view, skillfully exploited this perception. Elliot maintains that "the Indians were less interested in the paternalism of the father than in his potential for being a mediator between competing groups."[58] Yet it was the convergence of what appeared to be divergent interests that consolidated alliances between the French and Native Americans. While France's role as a mediator strengthened its position in North America, the British, by contrast, had relatively little use for mediation or negotiation and were more determined to destroy or forcefully subjugate people from distant cultures and different races. Despite military conflicts between the French and Native Americans, alliances between them were so strong that, according to Axtell, "cultural descendants of the English colonists still speak of the French and Indians in the same breath."[59]

Although commercial, strategic, and social considerations contributed immensely to France's comparatively enlightened and harmonious relations with Native Americans, Jesuit missionaries played a crucial role. Departing from their previous endeavors to convert and "civilize" Native Americans by bringing them into French settlements, the Jesuits made long and hazardous journeys into the interior. Like the Spanish in America, the Jesuits compromised to achieve their overriding objective of spreading the Roman Catholic faith and saving souls. Consequently, the Jesuits learned Native American languages and adopted many of their customs, thereby improving communications and building trust with them. Partly because of their considerable experience in other parts of the world and their extensive missionary training, the Jesuits successfully adapted their lifestyle, methods, and message to local conditions. Axtell concludes that although the Jesuits articulated and practiced what could be viewed as cultural relativism, the fundamentals of Catholicism were preserved, and the Jesuits continued to be confident of their own ethical and cultural superiority.[60]

America's Historical Experiences and the Rule of Law

In their effort to eliminate threats from Native Americans and enslaved Africans, European-Americans permitted violence to be legally employed against them. The ethnocentrism of a majority of English Protestants in North America strengthened their view that the rule of law protected them but did not extend to non-Europeans. The latter had few legal rights that had to be respected by the former. Westward expansion complicated the general view of the rule of law. Development of the frontier was accompanied by vigilantism, which reflected the absence of effective law and order. In addition to dealing with horse-stealing and counterfeiting, Richard Maxwell Brown notes that vigilantism was often used against those perceived to be different and threatening: Native Americans, African-Americans, Jews, Catholics, labor union members, advocates of civil liberties, and nonconformists in general.[61] Law enforcement agencies embraced and condoned violent behavior by vigilante groups, thereby sanctioning the use of force by ordinary Americans.

Differences between the United States and Canada in relation to violence and law and order were, and continue to be, striking, despite the two countries' geographic proximity and similar historical roots. Canadians occupied the western provinces without fighting the equivalent of the American Indian Wars. Relatively harmonious relationships that were established between the French and Native Americans early in Canada's history served as a model for future encounters between the two peoples. British settlers in Canada, many of whom were refugees from the American Revolution, were more like the French than the Americans in their relations with Native Americans. Furthermore, slower Canadian expansion diminished the possibility of conflict. The Mounted Police were able to accompany the settlers and were given unprecedented responsibility for establishing "peace, order, and good government." Kenneth McNaught contends that the six-shooter never became the symbol of Canadian freedom.[62] Instead, Canadians relied primarily on negotiations to conclude agreements with the native inhabitants that permitted settlers to occupy fertile lands. Although Canadians put Native Americans on reservations, they generally avoided the widespread and ruthless confiscation of their lands that marked much of U.S. history.

Unlike many Americans, most Canadians regard the individual as part of a community that provides protection for its members. As part of the bargain, greater deference is accorded to the government, the law, and people in positions of authority. Seymour Martin Lipset points out that, by contrast, Americans are far more predisposed to redefine or ignore the rules and are more inclined to employ aggressive, informal, and sometimes extralegal means to correct what they perceive as wrong or unfair.[63] After slavery was abolished, by means of the most violent war America has ever fought, whites in the South continued to resort to brutal methods to maintain control and to perpetuate the myth of white supremacy. Vigilante activities by the Ku Klux Klan and other groups were routinely condoned by most Southerners. Gunnar Myrdal attributed the acceptance of such behavior to a culture of lawlessness, conservatism, and illegality. Myrdal stressed that "white people are accustomed—individually and in groups—to take the law into their own hands and to expect the police and courts to countenance this and sometimes to lend their active cooperation."[64] Belief in the rule of law as it has been shaped by historical experiences helps to determine the conduct of American foreign relations, especially toward countries that are culturally distant.

Although the United States has from its inception been committed to upholding international law and has been instrumental in building international institutions to promote the rule of law, in the process of demanding that other countries obey international norms America has sometimes taken the law into its own hands to enforce compliance. This tendency toward taking unilateral action and circumventing the rule of law was apparent under President Ronald Reagan, who emphasized traditional values at home and militant internationalism abroad to demonstrate America's power and the resolve to use it. In some cases, the United States disregarded international law, purportedly to advance democracy and the rule of law in other nations.[65] Reagan's decision to illegally mine Nicaraguan harbors,

Bush's invasion of Panama and the subsequent arrest of Manuel Noriega, the U.S. Supreme Court's 1992 decision upholding the government's claimed right to kidnap people in foreign countries who are suspected of violating American laws, Bush's attack on Iraq in early January 1992, and Clinton's decision to launch twenty-seven cruise missiles against Iraq in June 1993 "to send a clear don't tread on us message" are all recent examples of the United States' taking the law into its own hands and calling on the concept of self-help to justify actions that many of America's closest allies have condemned. On the other hand, Bush's diplomatic efforts to build a broad international coalition against Saddam Hussein's occupation of Kuwait and to obtain UN Security Council resolutions to enforce international law demonstrate American pragmatism as well as a commitment to the rule of law.

However, there were divergent views among coalition members on the relatively hasty application of force to make Hussein comply with international law. These views reflected the various countries' historical experiences, goals, interests, power capabilities, and approaches to conflict resolution, among other factors. A New York Times/CBS/Tokyo Broadcasting System poll conducted in 1991 found that whereas 72 percent of Americans believed it was appropriate to use military force to maintain international justice and order, 70 percent of the Japanese people said that force was inappropriate.[66] Although most Americans have generally been ambivalent about war, evidence suggests that they expect presidents to take strong action when the nation's interests or its citizens are threatened. Meernik concludes that "while the American public has been swift to punish presidents who do not take forceful action, it has also generally rewarded them with greater approval rating for prominent displays of military force."[67] This willingness to militarize conflicts stems in part from the culture of violence.

A Culture of Violence

Even though America's political institutions have been remarkably stable, and despite the country's relatively low levels of political violence, the United States is generally regarded as an extremely violent society. Contemporary debates on lawlessness and crime in America tend to focus excessively on current reasons for the increasing savagery in American cities, streets, schools, and homes. This short-term view obscures historical roots of the present crime epidemic, and suggests that most Americans remain unwilling or unable to confront those aspects of the culture that perpetuate high levels of interpersonal violence. Richard Maxwell Brown argues that Americans have relied on violent solutions to various national and international problems for so long that violence has become "part of our unacknowledged or underground value structure," despite the rhetorical rejection of violence.[68] Hugh Davis Graham believes that democratic individualism, which often results in repudiation of restrictions imposed by tradition, the family, church, and state, demands a self-restraint that puts a tremendous psychic burden upon the individual, in an unending and often elusive quest for material equality. Graham states that: "Persistently faced with a social reality that denied such equality, the frustrated American democrat became particularly vulnerable to seizures of violent aggression."[69] Given the United States' unparalleled racial, ethnic, and religious diversity, finding scapegoats against whom this frustration could be vented was, and remains, relatively easy.

U.S. murder rates are much higher than those in Western Europe and Japan. In 1988, there were approximately 8.4 homicides per 100,000 Americans, 5.5 in Canada, 4.2 in Germany, 3.9 in France, 2.0 in Britain, and 1.2 in Japan.[70] Differences between the United States and Western Europe are even sharper when intentional homicides are compared. According to figures compiled by the United Nations Development Program in 1987–88, the intentional homicide rate per 100,000 persons was 9.0 for the United States, 2.1 for Canada, 1.1 for West Germany, 1.2 for France, 1.0 for Britain, and 0.8 for Japan.[71] Mass murder increased dramatically in the 1980s and early 1990s, both in frequency and in the number of persons killed in each instance. A troubling aspect of the rise of violent crime is the seemingly uncontrollable escalation in casual killing, killing simply for amusement, and drive-by murder.

Contrary to public rhetoric about the safety of the family, evidence indicates that the American home is extremely dangerous. According to the former United States Surgeon General Antonia C. Novello, more than a third of the women murdered in America are killed by their husbands or male companions. Domestic violence causes more injuries to women than automobile accidents, muggings, and rapes combined.[72] The American Medical Association, the National Organization for Women, and other groups support the Surgeon General's conclusion that domestic violence is a public health problem of epidemic proportions.

Schools in some parts of the country continue to rely on physical punishment to enforce conformity. Consequently, these schools, according to Irwin A. Hyman, reinforce the culture of violence by teaching children that force, violence, and humiliation are legitimate ways to change another person's behavior.[73] Increasingly, American schools are integrating conflict resolution methods into their curricula in order to encourage students to talk things out instead of resorting to force to settle problems.

At the root of violence in America is a culture in which guns are virtually sacrosanct. American heroes are usually experienced gunmen, and presidents have often been war veterans as well as members of the National Rifle Association, the main proponent of unlimited access to some of the most lethal weapons. These include semi-automatic assault rifles and guns with a range of almost one mile—to keep burglars away from one's home. In a society that equates force with security and problem-solving, there are more than two hundred million guns. The conflict between the Branch Davidians and the Bureau of Alcohol, Tobacco, and Firearms (ATF) in Texas in early 1993 and the Oklahoma City bombing in April 1995 focused, once again, the nation's attention on how readily ordinary citizens can obtain a wide variety of firearms and ammunition. Under current law, the ATF grants a license to sell guns to any applicant who is over twenty-one years old, has never been convicted of a felony, and has $30 for the licensing fee. In 1990, of 34,336 applicants, only seventy-five were denied licenses by the ATF. Consequently, over a quarter of a million Americans can legally sell weapons, and approximately 80 percent of them conduct business from their homes. The ease with which licenses are obtained has resulted in the United States' dubious distinction of having more gun dealers than gas stations.[74]

Reflecting a cultural self-help approach to fighting the U.S. crime epidemic, more women are buying guns and learning how to use them. Many women have abandoned their reluctance to kill in self-defense. To keep from being passive victims of violent crime, women are rejecting the traditional psychology of helplessness that makes them easy targets for both criminals and male companions. Many women assert that only by arming themselves can they avoid being victimized. Like men, they believe that guns provide security.[75]

According to a survey published by Harvard University's School of Public Health, more than sixty-six million loaded firearms are kept in American households.[76] But instead of serving their intended purpose of protecting the family, guns are frequently used against family members. Supporting the view that murder is primarily a societal problem, the Federal Bureau of Investigation (FBI) found that nearly three out of five murder victims were related to or acquainted with their assailants, and that gun owners kill themselves and family members forty-three times more often than they shoot a criminal in their home.[77]

More than 400,000 children carried guns to school in 1987, underscoring societal values that support the notion that force equals power in domestic and international relations, and that power entitles one to take what one wants. It is increasingly common in the United States for children to kill each other because of petty arguments that children in other cultures accept as a routine part of growing up, or for children to be murdered for their shoes or leather jackets. In 1990, more than 2,160 children were killed by firearms.[78] At Thomas Jefferson High School in Brooklyn, New York, about half of the 1900 students have puncture wounds at any given time, and seventy of them were killed or seriously injured over a four-year period. The school established a fund to assist families with burial expenses and has a grieving room for traumatized students. Overall, homicide is the second leading cause of death among Americans between the ages of fifteen and twenty-five, and more teenage boys die from gunshots than from any other cause.[79]

Television and the Culture of Violence

Television has been cited by government officials, the American Academy of Pediatrics, the National Institute for Mental Health Initiatives, parents, and others as a major contributor to violence in the United States. What is often overlooked, however, is that violence on television and the culture of violence in America are symbiotic: television reflects societal values even as it helps to mold them. The success and longevity of television shows depend on the public's willingness to watch them. Consequently, any attempt to address television violence must, despite the difficulty involved, examine the cultural context in which such violence flourishes. By the age of sixteen, the typical American child has witnessed approximately 200,000 acts of violence, including 33,000 murders. A.M. Rosenthal asserts that "we live in a cultural nut house, a mad world of blood, torture, and murder that surrounds us in the movies and follows us home when we turn on television entertainment."[80]

Throughout the 1980s, toughness, a quality that has long characterized American heroes on screen as well as in real life, was revivified on television and in movies. Simultaneously, the country's foreign policy became increasingly militaristic, defense expenditures escalated, U.S. involvement in regional conflicts in which the Soviet Union and Cuba participated intensified, and the Soviet threat was often exaggerated to justify huge military outlays. Popular culture conveyed the message that American warriors could accomplish anything if sufficient force was used. In an effort to "kick the Vietnam Syndrome," expressed in terms of Americans' reluctance to use force to resolve Third World conflicts, movies such as Rambo suggested that America's defeat in Vietnam had resulted from politicians' unwillingness to fully support the military.

Children's toys, games, and television cartoons also became more violent, aggressive, and militaristic. Music videos, and music in general, increasingly portray cruelty as acceptable behavior. It is estimated that the average hour-long children's program contains twenty-five acts of violence, and that roughly 95 percent of all children's television cartoons have violent themes.[81] The vast majority of these television programs reinforce fears, stereotypes, and prejudices that are deeply ingrained in American culture and foreign policy. The heroes conform to an image of what society regards as the ideal person: a blond, blue-eyed male whose mission is to save the world from inferior people. The villains also conform to America's values: they are dehumanized, animal-like creatures, frightening, foreign, and with darker skins.

The messages in these cartoons are essentially the same as those communicated by many American political leaders about foreign countries, particularly those that are culturally distant. They are perceived as threatening, untrustworthy, and cruel to everyone, including their own friends. Their behavior serves to justify the destruction we inflict not only on them but also on those who suffer from their cruelty. Just as the extremely popular war movies and video games of the 1980s were barely distinguishable from Operation Desert Storm, so too are the attitudes and values transmitted by television indistinguishable from those of the larger society. The underlying message is that the world is divided between good and evil, and that these two opposing factions cannot coexist. Deborah Prothow-Sith and Michele Weissman contend that instead of preparing children for the increasingly complex global society of the 21st century, television perpetuates destructive mistrust, anger, intolerance, frustration, and a sense of hopelessness.[82]

Sports, Violence, and Foreign Policy

Links among sports, nationalism, and war have always existed in most societies, with less aggressive people tending to focus on games that are less violent than those played by more warlike groups. However, violent sports alone are not a reliable predictor of how a country will resolve its problems with others. The broader cultural context of sports, the historical experiences of the country, its current concerns and military capabilities, and the worldviews of the majority of citizens combine to either moderate or exacerbate sports' impact on foreign affairs. Virtually all facets of American life, including foreign policy, are influenced by sports and understood through sports metaphors, many of which come from war and the military.

In a country as diverse as the United States, sports play an integrative role and serve as vehicles of upward mobility. Baseball, for example, has been instrumental in Americanizing immigrants. Since baseball and other sports embody many cultural values, immigrants who participate in sports generally embrace the political system, in essence declaring a form of allegiance to the country's institutions and creed. The relationship between sports and patriotism is evident. Presidents throw out the first pitch of the baseball season and welcome winning teams to the White House, the national anthem is sung at the beginning of games, and U.S. flags are everywhere. Moreover, anyone who aspires to high political office, particularly the presidency, is required to be athletic and interested in a variety of sports.[83] Ronald Reagan, the oldest American president and an avid equestrian, projected an image of athletic prowess that symbolized national strength. George Bush, a former baseball player, fished and raced around in his speed boat, especially on the eve of the Gulf War. Presidential candidates also conspicuously demonstrate their physical stamina by jogging, swimming, and engaging in other strenuous activities.

In an extremely competitive society, where victory is widely seen as the ultimate determinant of what is right, just, and good, defeat is tantamount to evil. How Americans play sports can be compared to how the United States conducts foreign relations, and vice versa. By pursuing victory, Americans understandably attempt to avoid being humiliated and victimized.[84] While few cultures praise the losing side, defeat in America is made more painful because so many of our competitive sports are zero-sum, and schedules all point to getting to the bowl game. Most sports in the United States ensure that only one clearly defined victor emerges, by the use of overtime periods, extra innings, and sudden death.[85]

Operation Desert Storm might be compared to a football game. The last major war, Vietnam, had at best an ambiguous outcome, and the troops returned to a country that seemed unwilling to recognize their sacrifices partly because they were not victorious, despite the war's length and expense. But the Gulf War was short and filled with suspense, American casualties were low, the other side was dominated and defeated militarily, President Bush declared victory, parades were everywhere, and returning troops received a tumultuous welcome. David D. Newsom, a former Undersecretary and Acting Secretary of State, observes that, as with a football game, America collected its equipment immediately after winning and went home.[86] The other side's injuries and humiliation, the environmental destruction, and the dangerous war litter were not the United States' responsibility. But the war's aftermath dampened our enthusiasm and muddled the outcome of what had been perceived as a decisive victory. Americans who once cheered the President joined those who had opposed the war to condemn him for allowing the other side's leader to claim victory for having survived a crushing military defeat. Saddam Hussein was not playing by America's rules, a reality that continued to frustrate both Bush and Clinton.

Just as lower-class Americans were over-represented in the Persian Gulf War, they are generally more willing than upper-class men and women to sacrifice their bodies in football and other sports, particularly boxing. The physical violence frequently used to achieve position and power in poor neighborhoods is often transferred to playing fields. By participating in sports, lower-class Americans can acquire money, fame, position, power, and a degree of acceptance by the larger society. Upper-class men and women can use their wealth to obtain dominant positions and respect. While Ivy League universities value winning as highly as other universities, their athletes play amateur sports, and usually avoid the excessive violence that tends to characterize sports at non-Ivy League colleges and universities.[87] However, upper-class individuals, especially men, who aspire to high office are expected to have demonstrated a willingness to sacrifice their bodies in war and in sports.

The Government: Reinforcing the Culture of Violence

Responding to an astronomical crime rate and pervasive violence in society, federal, state, and local governments focus on punishing individuals as a deterrent to committing crime. The Sentencing Project, a private research and advocacy group, has concluded that the United States imprisons a larger proportion of its population than any other nation. U.S. incarceration rates are about ten times higher than those of Japan, Sweden, Ireland, and the Netherlands. Almost one in four African-American men between the ages of twenty and twenty-nine is either in prison or on parole or probation on any given day. Compared to South Africa, the United States is five times more likely to imprison males of African descent. The United States' incarceration rate for African-American males in 1991 was 3,370 per 100,000, compared to roughly 681 per 100,000 for black males in South Africa. The overall cost of imprisoning more than a million Americans was approximately $20.3 billion a year.[88]

The United States was surpassed only by China, Iraq, and Iran when its execution rates were compared to those of other countries. In contrast with the United States, Western European nations have outlawed capital punishment. Despite the United States' dubious reputation of being in the same category as China, Iraq, and Iran as far as executions are concerned, 76 percent of Americans continue to favor capital punishment, not only because they think that it deters crime, but also because they believe in the biblical adage: "An eye for an eye."[89]

The ascendancy of militaristic thinking during the Cold War strengthened the culture of violence. The government played a crucial role in changing national priorities, and strongly influenced the emergence of cultural values that favored preparation for war. Military expenditures grew significantly, and many leading universities and research institutes were awarded large grants to work on military-related projects. Government agencies that had been created to confront Soviet expansionism, such as the National Security Council, competed with organizations that were principally concerned with diplomacy and the peaceful resolution of conflict, such as the State Department.[90] This opposition, evident throughout the Cold War, was highlighted on the eve of Operation Desert Storm. Whereas the Defense Department and the Joint Chiefs of Staff were deeply involved in efforts to remove Iraq from Kuwait, the State Department, except when it participated in the fund-raising drive for the war, was essentially silent. However, since Vietnam, high Defense Department officials, including the Joint Chiefs, have often opposed U.S. military intervention in Third World crises, a fact underscored by the number of former Secretaries of Defense who opposed Bush's rush to use force in the Gulf.

Constantly preparing for war, the United States has nourished attitudes that are intertwined with a culture of violence. Men in particular have been expected to defend their country from an attack that could occur at any moment. The Cold War helped to reinforce the idea that America must always be vigilant. This vigilance was heightened by a Selective Service system that required all healthy American males to register for the draft. Even in 1992, amid rhetoric proclaiming the end of the Cold War, improved relations with the individual countries of the former Soviet Union, and greater preoccupation with domestic issues, young men were still required to register with the Selective Service, and were told by that agency that doing so was an easy way to prove their manhood. Sam Keen observes that in the process of fighting communism for almost forty-five years, a warfare system developed and "formed the eyes through which we see war."[91]

The culture of violence is reinforced by the government's excessive reliance on weapons sales to other countries to safeguard their security. In Somalia, Afghanistan, Angola, Nicaragua, El Salvador, and elsewhere, the United States focused primarily on military solutions, and provided its allies with weapons, while simultaneously rejecting efforts to reach negotiated settlements that might have resulted in partial victories for its friends. As Chapter Five shows, weapons sales became an important component of America's policy in the Middle East.

Instead of seizing the opportunity provided by the decisive military victory over Iraq during Operation Desert Storm to reduce the flow of weapons to the Middle East and the Gulf, the United States embarked on a new effort to sell some of its technologically advanced weapons to friendly countries in the region. Despite President Bush's proclamation of a new world order and his commitment to promoting democracy around the world, the United States continued to export arms to democracies and dictatorships alike. It is estimated that as a result of its concerted efforts to promote sales abroad, the U.S. Government authorized the sale of $63 billion worth of weapons, military construction, and training in about 142 countries in 1991.[92] Because many civilian jobs and important sectors of the economy are directly dependent on arms sales, there is little public opposition to these developments. Furthermore, most Americans believe that, like individuals, countries should have weapons to defend themselves, a belief that has contributed to America's indecisiveness in Bosnia, as Chapter Six shows. But just as the ATF agents faced the deadly consequences of that organization's permissive policies on licensing firearms in the Branch Davidians' compound in Texas in early 1993, the U.S.

government also found itself fighting in Somalia to destroy some of the weapons it had given that country's former dictator, Siad Barre. As if to demonstrate linkages between external and internal violence, some of the men the United States had financed to remove occupying Soviet forces from Afghanistan were found guilty of participating in the 1993 World Trade Center bombing in New York.[93]

Flight from Responsibility

American society's dominant beliefs and values permit the U.S. Government to use massive force against an enemy and walk away from the responsibilities that accompany victory. An excessive concern with materialism leads Americans to judge an individual's or country's worth on the basis of possessions. This makes it easier to mistreat the poor and to inflict severe suffering on them—even as we claim to have absolutely nothing against innocent civilians. In both Vietnam and the Persian Gulf, the United States employed some of the most advanced technology to destroy the enemy and, in the process, caused incalculable damage to civilians. And, after the war, America prolonged their suffering to punish their leaders. In Vietnam, the United States conducted chemical warfare against the Vietnamese people and the environment, drenching more than five million acres of land with approximately eighteen million gallons of Agent Orange and other chemicals.[94] While its opponents argued that the Vietnam War was both unjust and unwise (a view that gained support in light of the United States' failure to win), the conclusion drawn from that experience by some was that America's conduct of the war was not destructive enough, a mistake that Bush vowed not to repeat in Operation Desert Storm.

Believing that violence against others is invited by their behavior, Americans generally eschew responsibility for their own actions. The aftermath of Vietnam forced the nation to wrestle with the consequences of war. In addition to Americans killed and wounded, the United States had to deal with a flood of Vietnamese refugees, children fathered by U.S. soldiers in Vietnam, and lingering questions about missing American soldiers. However, American culture is more supportive of abdicating responsibility, turning one's back on unpleasant realities, and moving on to start over. America's speedy exit from Iraq and the unwillingness to count Iraqi casualties had as much to do with cultural values as it did with military strategy.

Obsessed with individual rights, American society has moved away from the idea of personal, governmental, and corporate responsibility as an integral component of freedom. Arguably, this flight from responsibility is indicated not just by actions, or inaction, but also by the rising inflection that pervades our language, especially among younger Americans. Our speech is marked by uncertainty, a need for others' approval, and a kind of flexibility that enables us to abandon our views, if necessary.[95] Reluctance to accept responsibility is also demonstrated by the growing popularity of high-tech weapons that remove any feelings of guilt and empathy that might accompany closer contact between enemies. The formula for fighting, which grew out of Operation Desert Storm, might tempt the United States to go to war sooner than it ordinarily might, while simultaneously allowing America to walk away from war's devastation without feeling a sense of responsibility.[96]

Americans' Quest for Absolute Security

Reliance on force as an instrument of foreign policy is influenced by the American quest for invulnerability. Improved security is generally seen as solving virtually any social ill. Separated from Europe's wars by the Atlantic and Pacific Oceans, endowed with abundant resources, and unchallenged by its neighbors, the United States strongly believes that peace is its natural condition. But to ensure tranquility the government has sought to acquire absolute immunity from external danger by building a strong national defense system. Although most nations share this objective, the United States believes that its security can be guaranteed only through the unilateral application of military power. America's often exaggerated sense of vulnerability has led to the hasty use of force to preempt any possible threat to national security interests. Compared to the Europeans, who have carefully fashioned alliances to preserve the balance of power upon which much of their security depends, Americans have always been more comfortable with what might be called a "Lone Ranger" approach to security matters, even when the United States has been allied with other countries. America's initial response to Iraq's invasion of Kuwait underscored the U.S. predilection for unilateral actions. James Chace and Caleb Carr argue that Americans have always assumed that absolute security cannot be negotiated; it can only be won.[97]

Foreign Policymaking by Analogy

A country's decision to use force is shaped to a large extent by "lessons of history" accumulated from major international conflicts. The lessons of history play a pivotal role in determining how foreign policy is made, whether or not to consider various options, and how to decide to solve a particular problem. By focusing primarily on the similarities between two situations, such as events leading up to World War II and Saddam Hussein's invasion of Kuwait, significant differences are usually overlooked. The basic assumption is that factors that were essential in the first case must be decisive in the second.[98] Because America's global interaction has been induced principally by the outbreak of major international wars, U.S. policymakers are predisposed to believe that quick and decisive action is essential to prevent history from repeating itself.

Analogical reasoning leads to the kind of rigidity that impedes realistic assessment of a problem and eliminates solutions that might be cost-effective militarily, economically, and politically. Robert Jervis concludes that if the previous outcome depended on the interaction of several factors, the application of the lessons of history without a careful analysis of the two situations will undoubtedly be misleading.[99]

Apart from cultural restraints, a leader's own experiences directly affect how he or she perceives a conflict. Formative experiences, in the absence of dramatic contradictory messages, will influence a leader's worldview. A leader is likely to draw analogies from developments that profoundly affected his or her country and in which he or she participated, thereby acquiring firsthand but largely idiosyncratic experiences. President Bush's quick response to Saddam Hussein's invasion of Kuwait, and his use of the World War II analogy to mobilize support for military action, was undoubtedly influenced by his own experiences in the Second World War. In an interview on ABC, Bush indicated that he wanted to join the U.S. Navy at age seventeen but had to wait. Shot down by the Japanese in the Pacific, Bush concluded that America's isolationist posture resulted in the country's lack of vigilance that led to Pearl Harbor. Believing that America should have been more engaged, Bush made foreign affairs his administration's priority.[100] Similarly, Bill Clinton, influenced by Vietnam, has attempted to focus on domestic affairs, and tried to avoid involving American forces in conflicts abroad, as the case study of Bosnia shows.

Pearl Harbor and Munich are powerful codewords in America's foreign policy, and are two of the most important analogies used to guide the nation's response to international threats. As Bush indicated, the lesson derived from Japan's bombing of Pearl Harbor was that vigilance is essential to safeguard freedom. Munich's impact on American foreign policy was equally profound. The Munich analogy became the cornerstone upon which both America's involvement in Third World conflicts and its anticommunist policy were based. The specific circumstances under which British Prime Minister Neville Chamberlain concluded an agreement with Adolf Hitler in Munich concerning Czechoslovakia, though complex, were reduced to the powerful codeword—appeasement. It was first employed in America during the 1940 presidential campaign by Franklin D. Roosevelt, in an effort to obtain Congressional support for U.S. involvement in the war. American isolationists were castigated as apologists for despotism, and neutrality was equated with defeatism or appeasement.[101] Munich's major lessons are that appeasement results in devastatingly costly wars, and that negotiating with evil leaders is not only useless but dangerous. Only the swift application of massive military force can prevent the spread of evil.

The Munich metaphor, or "the lessons of the thirties," shaped America's response to the rise of communism and Soviet expansionism after World War II. The Communist takeover of Czechoslovakia in 1948 only reaffirmed what had become essentially a blind belief in the Munich analogy. This gave rise to the tendency to accept at face value an adversary's open hostility, particularly its rhetoric, as a true reflection of its present and future intentions. Americans became more receptive to confirming information—hostile statements of intent that were compatible with our preconceived views of the enemy—than to challenging information—conciliatory statements that were inconsistent with perceptions of the enemy.[102] Any questioning of national security policy or suggestion of negotiating solutions to regional crises was viewed as appeasement. America's ideologically driven Cold War foreign policy was generally hostile to proposals that opposed ever-increasing defense budgets and arms sales to allies overseas. But applying Munich's lessons to Cold War conflicts, most of which occurred in remote Third World countries, required ingenuity.[103] A preoccupation with avoiding anything that can be regarded as appeasement exacerbates the American cultural proclivity to use force to settle dispute—if heavy American casualties can be avoided and military victory can be quickly achieved.

Chapter Three

Cultural Barriers to International Negotiations

Negotiation and conflict are inescapable components of relations among individuals as well as nations. Efforts to resolve disputes peacefully are either more or less successful for a myriad of reasons, many of them directly related to cultural attitudes, perceptions, prejudices, interests, familiarity, and interdependence, among others. Countries that are culturally similar are more likely to resolve conflicts through negotiations than countries that are culturally distant. Whatever differences emerge between the United States and Britain, for example, are usually settled without much public debate or hostile rhetoric on either side of the Atlantic. On the other hand, relations between the United States and Cuba have been characterized by tension and hostility, despite the end of the Cold War and the demise of communism. It may be argued that U.S. relations with Cuba are conditioned by cultural differences as well as by deep political differences between the Cuban government and the Cuban exile community in the United States. But the influence of Cuban-Americans on U.S. policy toward Cuba is evidence of the power of cultural links to help shape international affairs. When President Jimmy Carter's administration indicated that it was prepared to negotiate with Cuba, political realities in the United States prevented such initiatives. The influence of ethnic groups with cultural ties to another country, on domestic American politics as well as the broader culture, imposes some limits on diplomatic maneuvering.[1]

Clearly, there are considerations unique to every situation that ultimately help to determine whether or not negotiations may seriously be attempted and, if they are, how effective they will be in settling differences. If countries focus primarily on their underlying interests and objectives, they have a much better chance of resolving disputes than if they allow beliefs about what is right and wrong to dominate their policies. Because the United States and Britain share essentially the same cultural beliefs, they are freer to address substantive issues. Cultural proximity between them engenders perceptions and expectations that are conducive to negotiated settlement of disagreements.

When the various impediments to effective international negotiations are examined, cultural differences appear to be among the most prominent obstacles to working out problems between nations without violence. The internal values, attitudes, beliefs, and feelings of particular societies inevitably help to shape the nature of relations among states. How a country deals with internal conflicts is a good predictor of its behavior abroad, its willingness to negotiate, and the effectiveness of those negotiations. A nation that glorifies violence is likely to use force to address international conflicts. A society that is exclusive rather than inclusive might find it comparatively easy to negotiate successfully with those within its approved circle, but refuse to seriously consider negotiating at all with those perceived as "others," a reality which fuels the adoption of double standards in international relations. A country that recognizes the interdependence of its domestic groups as well as the interdependence of nations is inclined to eschew force when trying to address conflicts. But given the cultural diversity of the world, domestic experience with negotiation might be inadequate preparation for settling disputes with other countries peacefully. For ending conflict, an understanding and appreciation of other cultures is as important as technical negotiating skills.

Cultural values directly influence negotiating strategies, the hierarchy of negotiating objectives, the communication process, and deadlines for concluding negotiations. These factors played a major role in the Gulf conflict. Cultural differences between Iraq and the United States had a direct bearing on the negotiation process, or the relative lack of it. Mannerisms, gestures, and other forms of nonverbal behavior, notions of status, conventions observed during social interaction, and other culturally influenced behavior have a direct and significant impact on negotiations. What is regarded as rational, sane, insulting, polite, timely, or appropriate is defined by culture. Glen Fisher observes that the negotiation process is an interplay of perception, information processing, and reaction, all of which turn on images of reality, on implicit assumptions regarding the issues being negotiated, and on conventional wisdom, beliefs, and social expectations.[2]

Ethnocentric perceptions, as products of culture, profoundly shape how nations approach relations with each other, what they regard as rational behavior, how they select objectives and the means for accomplishing them, how they perceive options available to them, how they evaluate others' behavior, and what they believe to be their opponents' intentions. Many alternatives are foreclosed and many opportunities for peaceful resolution of conflicts squandered or overlooked due to cultural perceptions and misperceptions. On the other hand, misperceptions can also produce an illusion of harmony. It is almost impossible not to project one's cultural values onto the other side, even if one is culturally sensitive. What is rational behavior in the United States is often viewed as irrational by other countries, and vice versa.

A common assumption, and one that is often erroneous and fraught with danger, is that those whose behavior we are attempting to influence are as rational as we are, and that our own actions are rational. But such a conclusion rests on the dubious belief that the other side shares our values, has the same set of objectives, and reasons the way we do.[3] What might appear to be reasonable and appropriate to the United States might be totally unacceptable to other societies and their governments. For example, the Sandinistas could not comply with President Ronald Reagan's demand that they relinquish control of Nicaragua and essentially commit political suicide. U.S. leaders who want to achieve certain foreign policy objectives might take advantage of cultural differences, knowing that foreign leaders cannot agree to demands that may be perceived as logical and fair to the United States.

To a greater or lesser degree, all societies have mechanisms for resolving conflict without routinely resorting to violence. In Sweden, for example, the contemporary political culture emphasizes the importance of consensus, compromise, coalition-building, and negotiation as ways to avoid violent conflict. Unlike Americans, who are generally proud of themselves for being tough negotiators, the Swedes tend to be reluctant to introduce proposals containing harsh demands and conditions. The negotiation situation is viewed as an opportunity to take part in a dialogue between sovereign equals.[4] Within the United States, there is a strong belief in splitting differences when the parties are relatively equal. However, Americans are inclined to mistreat or disregard those who are less powerful, or more culturally distant, and to follow the winner-take-all model. Clearly, there are exceptions to this generalization. Carter negotiated agreements with several distant cultures, both while he was President and after he left office. If the United States' approach to negotiations is somewhat paradoxical, it is due in part to conflicting cultural values that emanate from contradictory historical experiences. For example, only through compromise and skillful bargaining could our country have fashioned a constitution that continues to be a model for many countries. But in the process, the concerns of the powerless (the enslaved Africans) were sacrificed. On an issue that strongly influenced America's character—slavery—there were no negotiations between the enslaved and the free, a reality which still resonates in contemporary American society. Negotiations were reserved for relations among the strong.

It has been argued that as a "masculine" society, one that is characterized by assertiveness and competition, the United States shows greater sympathy for the strong than for the weak, and tends to resolve conflicts by fighting rather than through compromise. By contrast, "feminine" cultures, which are viewed as being characterized by modest, caring values, are more likely to be sympathetic to the weak, and to compromise.[5] Clearly these assumptions are debatable and perhaps simplistic. Despite cultural differences, the United States has been involved in numerous successful negotiations, which include the Panama Canal Treaty, the Camp David Peace Accords and other dimensions of the Israeli-Palestinian conflict, and the Zimbabwe Settlement.

The Negotiation Process

Because negotiation at the international level involves two or more independent countries, the concept of equality of states is implicitly or explicitly recognized as valid by the negotiators involved. In order to maintain international stability and protect their own interests, states engage in back-and-forth communication. Negotiation is an attempt to reconcile contradictory positions and conflicting interests in order to reach an agreement that is acceptable to the various parties. An important impetus for advancing proposals and making concessions and compromises is that there are common interests that can be secured through cooperation.[6] Each side must be willing to make those adjustments that are essential to reaching a compromise. Negotiation is viewed as a foreign policy instrument for resolving conflicts and safeguarding national interests through peaceful means.

But negotiation in particular and diplomacy in general are not entirely separated from the use of coercion or violence. Most conflicts cannot be resolved by reliance on either negotiation or the threat of force alone. Especially when countries have few historical, cultural, economic, and military ties, it is commonly believed that the willingness to use force provides a credible threat to a nation that is reluctant to negotiate seriously. But negotiations that result in war have obviously failed to achieve the principal objective of negotiation, namely, the nonviolent solution of a problem. However, in the Persian Gulf, negotiations were used primarily to form an international coalition whose objective was to compel Iraq to comply with UN Security Council resolutions through the application of military force. The protection of long-term security interests usually requires major countries to combine several foreign policy instruments.

While persuasion and compromise are important tools for resolving conflicts, they are not always effective, and the threat and use of force can be counterproductive and even detrimental to a country's long-range interests. A policy that combines negotiations and the threat of force, with varying degrees of emphasis on each, is likely to be the most successful.[7] In the final analysis, negotiation depends more on the decision of political leaders to change the political environment than on the skills of negotiating teams in finding technical solutions.[8] The breakthrough that ended the Israeli-Palestinian conflict resulted in part from the willingness of Israeli Prime Minister Yitzhak Rabin and Palestinian leader Yasser Arafat to negotiate.

To avoid negotiations, while claiming to be committed to them, political leaders portray the other side as intransigent and as an obstacle to peace. Another sophisticated way of circumventing negotiations is to assert that the situation must be "ripe" for resolution. Ripeness refers to the existence of the right circumstances under which negotiations can occur. These include characteristics of the parties to a dispute, some things about the relationship between or among the parties, and the nature of the dispute itself.[9] While the concept of ripeness is useful for negotiators, it overlooks a more significant factor, namely, the willingness of political leaders to facilitate the negotiation process.

Negotiation is principally concerned with helping the other side make a particular decision. In other words, negotiation is about cooperating to resolve conflicts. Therefore, societies that believe in taking unilateral measures are likely to approach the negotiation process with rigid demands and ultimatums. Such societies usually tend to confuse imposing a military result with influencing a decision. What the other side thinks is often ignored or regarded as irrelevant. Societies that favor unilateralism over cooperation are also inclined to escalate their goals, thus rendering their achievement through compromise and persuasion difficult. Since negotiation is not highly valued, delays in the process occur frequently, and the legitimate interests and concerns of the other side are generally unacknowledged.[10]

To be effective, negotiation must become a joint, coordinated process in which adversaries search for agreements that are mutually acceptable. Our adversaries' problems are in effect our problems, and it is therefore in our interest to help them make the decision we want. How they feel about the choices we ask them to make is just as important to us as how we feel about those options.[11] Concern for their perceived choices is therefore an essential part of successful negotiations. It helps us to understand their dilemma and enables us to create options that are in the interest of both sides. When negotiations are viewed as a test of wills and a zero-sum game, compromise is highly unlikely, because neither side will want to appear weak by backing down or altering its position. Instead of attempting to explore and learn, which are essential elements of successful negotiations, both sides cling steadfastly to their positions, especially if their cultures view compromise as an indication of weakness. Since compromise is generally a reflection of the need for the other's consent, it does imply a certain degree of weakness.

Because a nation's perception of reality is influenced by its historical experiences and cultural values, negotiators specifically, and political leaders in general, who are interested in resolving conflicts peacefully must attempt to understand the broader social, political, economic, and religious environment in which the other side operates. Learning the other party's real interests necessitates a careful and patient probing of the needs, hopes, fears, perceptions, and cultural values that form their sense of what is threatening or vital to protecting their identity.[12] This requires a willingness on the negotiators' part to listen actively to the other side and to put themselves in the other side's shoes, as it were. Active listening involves trying to hear and absorb the other side's view of the facts as distinct from one's own, to seek further clarification through questioning, and to process the information received in terms of the larger context of the situation and the issues of the moment.[13]

Understanding the other side is rendered more difficult by linguistic and cultural differences. Differences in values often result in inefficient communication, and sometimes in noncommunication and termination of the negotiating process. Overall, common cultural values facilitate both domestic and international negotiations. The problem that emerges from differences in values is that countries ethnocentrically use their own values, instead of objective criteria, as the standard by which others are judged.[14] Although it is difficult to detach criteria from values, the problem is exacerbated when people from distant cultures attempt to settle disputes.

Language is often a major barrier to effective negotiations between the United States and nonwestern nations, a reality that was underscored by the passage of the National Security Education Act in 1991. Believing that "our ignorance of world cultures and world languages represents a threat to our ability to remain a world leader," the U.S. government allocated $150 million for scholarships for college and graduate students to learn foreign languages and to study in countries deemed to be potentially crucial allies or enemies.[15]

The openness of American society can create a barrier to effective negotiations with countries that are not as open. Whereas Americans are often painfully blunt and direct in communicating their views, and prefer a plain yes or no for an answer, Latin Americans, Arabs, Iranians, and Japanese, among others, will take a more indirect and ambiguous approach. When Americans deal with individuals from Asia or the Middle East, Americans are often frustrated because of cross-cultural miscommunication. Instead of giving a yes or no answer, Japanese or Latin Americans might prefer to say maybe or even yes, despite the fact that they cannot or will not comply. By employing delaying tactics or euphemisms to convey their meanings, Japanese and Latin Americans avoid having to give a "bald no," which is regarded as insulting and unnecessarily harsh. Americans, on the other hand, construe ambiguity to mean yes. When the real no finally becomes obvious, they may feel betrayed.[16] U.S.-Japan trade relations seem to be plagued with such misunderstandings.

As a country that glorifies individualism and independence, the United States has trouble dealing with cultures that are characterized by collectivist impulses. Compared to Americans, who are extremely mobile and not overly sensitive to being embarrassed, many Asians and Arabs believe that losing face and being humiliated in the eyes of one's peers must be avoided. Because preserving one's reputation is so important, collectivist societies develop mechanisms that diminish the likelihood of anyone's losing face. Dishonor is a fate worse than death.[17] Therefore, any communication interpreted as intended to humiliate will generally be counterproductive as far as negotiations are concerned. Saddam Hussein's refusal to back down in the face of ultimatums from George Bush and the international community, while appearing insane to most Americans, made a certain amount of sense within the context of Iraqi culture. To confront the United States and to survive the most intensive bombing campaign in history was perceived as a victory of sorts for Hussein.

Whereas in the United States, language, lacking much emotion and ambiguity, is designed to inform the receiver of certain facts, by contrast, languages in many parts of Asia and the Middle East tend to be less direct, rich in hidden meanings, and designed to preserve social harmony. Yet many foreigners do not always find American codewords and euphemisms easy to understand. Unlike the United States, where conflicts are resolved through legal confrontation and a businesslike approach, nonwestern societies rely on time-consuming mechanisms of communal conciliation, principally because their close relationships and interdependence render obtaining absolute justice less meaningful than maintaining social harmony.[18] Thus, even though the United States and a nonwestern country might claim to be making an honest attempt to resolve a conflict peacefully, linguistic and cultural differences can derail the entire negotiation process because they create serious misunderstandings and misperceptions. Of course, similar problems sometimes occur between the United States and its European allies, but to a much lesser degree and with less dire consequences.

Because public opinion is so important in the United States, government officials deliberately try to impress Americans with progress made, or the lack of it, during negotiations. And in many cases, both parties talk past each other and concentrate on gaining the approval of their respective audiences. As Roger Fisher and William Ury put it, "rather than trying to dance with their negotiating partner toward a mutually agreeable outcome, they try to trip him up. Rather than trying to talk their partner into a more constructive step, they try to talk the spectators into taking sides."[19] Given the difficulties inherent in cross-cultural negotiations, the temptation to avoid making a serious effort to resolve differences is extremely strong.

Perceptions complicate international negotiations, especially when the cultures of the parties are very dissimilar. The tendency for preexisting images to persist, though widely recognized, is frequently overlooked by decision-makers and the public alike when dealing with international problems. Perceptions, like other cultural habits, are so deeply ingrained that it is very difficult for most of us to be fully conscious of them. Information and facts that contradict our perceptions and images of ourselves and others are ignored or overlooked. New information is evaluated in a way that makes sense within the context of cultural values. Therefore, culture plays a significant role in determining objectivity and reality for policymakers.

When countries and individuals are perceived in a certain manner, their behavior is interpreted in a way that is consistent with existing images. Because images of countries with cultures similar to one's own are more positive than perceptions of one's adversaries, the former are likely to escape severe punishment or disapproval for wrongdoing, whereas one generally demands swift and effective retribution for misconduct by the latter. While one "understands" the behavior of friends, similar behavior by those beyond one's cultural circle is condemned. Perceptions and images influence expectations of others, the selection of objectives vis-à-vis various countries, and the choice of foreign policy instruments for obtaining national goals. Expectations of others greatly affect our assumptions concerning the usefulness of attempting to negotiate with them to reach peaceful solutions to conflicts.[20]

Stereotypes impede the negotiating process with states that are culturally distant, by fostering negative interpretations of motives behind actions that could be viewed as positive developments. In many cases, we firmly believe that our fears are actually the adversary's intentions, and then behave in a manner that is consistent with that belief. Essentially, we help to create self-fulfilling prophecies. While it is prudent to carefully assess what the opponent's underlying agenda might be, putting the worst interpretation on what the other side says or does is often not a product of objective analysis but emanates instead from one's existing perceptions. Seeing the other side's actions or statements in the most dismal light can result in the rejection of ideas that might facilitate agreement.[21]

Preconceived notions about the other side are among the most formidable barriers to resolving disputes nonviolently. Yet such difficulties can sometimes be surmounted if the other side is willing to risk behaving in a way that directly challenges the stereotypical images. This requires the other side to make meaningful unilateral concessions that are surprising precisely because they are contrary to expected behavior and involve significant risk. Anwar Sadat's visit to Israel and Mikhail Gorbachev's bold initiatives on several fronts destroyed negative images held by the United States of both leaders.

National policymakers and the political systems in which they function play an important role in the choice of strategies for resolving disputes among nations. Especially in democratic societies, leaders choose options that are not only familiar but are also consistent with the values and expectations of their constituents. If most citizens believe that force is an effective means of dealing with problems, leaders are likely to consider military action against the opponent. A society that perceives compromise as a sign of weakness or emphasizes winning and "standing up" to the other side is likely to produce leaders who devalue negotiations with adversaries.[22] These leaders' own political survival may depend on the public's perceptions of them as tough. President Bill Clinton's use of force against Iraq shortly after taking office and his decision to send U.S. troops to the Gulf in late 1994 in response to Iraq's troop build-up along the Kuwaiti border may have been influenced in part by such political considerations. During the Cold War, American leaders could not afford to be soft on communism, and negotiations with the Soviet Union were often viewed negatively. Moreover, Moscow's general perception of negotiations not as a way to resolve problems but as a means to advance Soviet political objectives had a profound effect on America's willingness to negotiate Cold War issues, including those in the Third World.

Hardliners, perceiving the world as hostile and conflict-ridden, generally reject conciliatory measures when dealing with the adversary. The hardliner's emphasis on military might as the best way of protecting the country's interests and maintaining peace makes him or her extremely sensitive to power-strategic considerations and to the potential aggressiveness of other states.[23] In the United States and elsewhere, the general assumption that only force provides real security is consistent with the hardliner's approach to international relations. One must be vigilant, always on guard, and determined to demonstrate resolve in relation to actions by one's enemies. Unable or unwilling to believe or admit that the other side has legitimate security needs and concerns, the hardliner interprets his or her adversary's military preparedness as evidence of aggressive intentions.

Conditions inherent in the situation itself might facilitate or impede the negotiation process. The situation determines, to a greater or lesser extent, incentives to take either conciliatory or competitive actions, incentives either to act unilaterally or to wait for others to respond, expectations about the probable behavior of the other side, the ability of each side to affect the actions of the other, the ease of obtaining and honoring agreements, and the balance of individual versus mutual interests.[24] The situation may also impede or altogether exclude a negotiated solution if it influences policymakers to believe that an urgent solution is imperative because of time constraints, or that either the domestic consensus or the international cooperation essential to solving the problem will weaken if the dispute is allowed to continue indefinitely. Uncertainty about the coalition's durability during Operation Desert Shield not only reduced chances for a nonviolent outcome but actually contributed to the decision to use force against Iraq while the coalition was still united. Furthermore, the importance of the Gulf region to Western security interests, the relative weakness of Iraq compared to the coalition, the ability of the United States to persuade others to pay for the war, the belief that the situation made a drawn-out conflict unlikely, and the atrocities committed by Iraq in Kuwait made negotiations less attractive than war.

American Perceptions of Diplomacy and American Exceptionalism

Although Americans profess to believe that almost any problem can be solved if people are willing to sit down and talk about it, they have generally had largely negative perceptions of international negotiations and diplomacy. Even domestically, we seem to contradict ourselves. Despite the view that sitting across the table and working things out is a desirable approach, our society commonly disregards talking as a way of solving problems. Rather than communicating to resolve disputes, we tend to debate issues. As David D. Newsom, Carter's Undersecretary of State, points out, "in our assertive society, diplomats are expected to be salesmen rather than assessors. They are to be advocates. Their task is not to survey the market but to sell the product. To a number of American politicians, the purpose of a diplomatic encounter is to persuade a foreign leader or government of the correctness of the U.S. view of an issue."[25]

America's ambivalence toward diplomacy is rooted in its historical experiences, its distance from European conflicts, and the nature of its democratic system of government. Because America represented a rejection of and an alternative to European societies and their problems, some practices that Europeans embraced were anathema to Americans. Diplomacy and war characterized relations among the European states. Americans perceived both diplomacy and widespread bloodshed as indicative of what was wrong with Europe. From the colonial period onwards, we have viewed diplomacy as being closely intertwined with monarchy, aristocracy, political intrigue and machinations, conflict, and war.[26] While some Americans have embraced diplomacy as an instrument of foreign policy, and have evinced a mixture of contempt for and fascination with it, the vast majority have found it difficult to reconcile essential characteristics of diplomacy with fundamental American values, beliefs, and practices.

Rejecting Europe's aristocratic traditions and firmly believing in equality and other democratic principles, Americans have stressed that government must be responsive and accountable to the people. Apart from the fact that diplomacy's slow pace, meticulous attention to words, and often ostentatious concern with the sensitivities of protocol are inconsistent with the impatience, assertiveness, and action-oriented nature of American society, the openness that characterizes American democracy is clearly at odds with the secretiveness of diplomacy.[27] To a much greater extent than Europeans, Japanese, and others, Americans believe that they should not only know what their government is doing abroad but that they should also participate in shaping the country's foreign policy.

Whereas diplomacy must be subtle, democracy prospers in the rough and sometimes vicious domestic political environment. A majority of Americans are most comfortable with "plain" speaking, and demand it from their leaders, who, in turn, demand it of diplomats. While many Americans generally think in terms of right or wrong, black or white, good or evil, and friend or enemy, diplomacy is conducted in an international environment where ambiguity and nuance predominate, and in which stark dilemmas are more often muted and suspended than resolved. And whereas Americans still expect politicians to be honest and straightforward, diplomacy is nuanced and discreet.[28]

Finally, diplomacy is unfamiliar to many Americans or is not regarded as being very important. War is familiar. Whereas Americans think they can get their way through war, diplomacy, by contrast, is seen as risky and no guarantee that objectives will be achieved. War, more than diplomacy, is also consistent with democracy, partly because unlike diplomacy, which is conducted by an elite group, war is usually widely approved of, and people from across the nation are involved in specific sacrifices. Despite the reality that wars create problems, Americans, like many people, generally believe that wars solve problems and demonstrate decisiveness, resolve, and power. Furthermore, we are more inclined to overlook serious mistakes made by our leaders in wars and less willing to forget their diplomatic failures, due in part to our initial underlying negative assessment of diplomacy as an instrument of foreign policy. However, many Americans are increasingly reluctant to involve the country in foreign conflicts.

When parties to a dispute focus primarily on specific interests, those shared as well as those in conflict, they are likely to be predisposed to make the necessary compromises to protect those interests. However, when countries perceive conflicts in terms of morality, good and evil, right and wrong, or just and unjust, finding a compromise to which each side can say "yes" is almost impossible. Dualism presumes that one side must be right and the other side wrong; one must win and the other must lose; one has God on its side and the other is demonized; and one has a just cause while the other has no legitimate interests. Such a stark, simplistic view is a major barrier to effective negotiations.[29] Yet this is precisely how most Americans tend to view the world.

Even when policymakers attempt to focus primarily on interests, the public's demand that foreign policy be moral and principled and the openness of the American political system often combine to undermine pragmatism in U.S. relations with the rest of the world. This moralistic attitude fosters an all-or-nothing approach to foreign affairs and the adoption of rigid positions that call for unconditional surrender of and total victory over the other side. Such perceptions of conflict resolution influenced U.S. policy toward Bosnia. Both Presidents George Bush and Bill Clinton found it difficult to accept compromises in the Vance-Owen peace proposals that would have allowed the Serbs to retain territory taken by force. Yet neither could offer a suitable alternative to resolve the conflict.

Exceptionalism and its accompanying religious passions are inconsistent and largely incompatible with compromise— the essential ingredient of peaceful diplomatic efforts. When international conflicts are perceived in religious and moralistic terms, compromise is regarded as not only appeasement but also contamination with evil. Because American values are perceived to be natural, universal in application, and superior to those of other nations, compromise with countries that are inherently less virtuous is seen as a violation of American principles and a national humiliation. Consequently, the United States has found it difficult to compromise with enemies. European countries, for example, established diplomatic relations with China, Vietnam, the Soviet Union, and other totalitarian regimes long before the United States decided to recognize them. John Spanier contends that American attitudes toward diplomacy "reinforced the predilection for violence as a means of settling international disputes. War allowed the nation to destroy its evil opponent, but permitted it to keep its moral mission intact and unsullied by any compromises."[30]

However, the realities of the East-West conflict forced the United States to make a significant departure from its general tendency of not negotiating with its enemies and to make wide-ranging compromises with the Soviet Union. Nuclear weapons, particularly intercontinental ballistic missiles, rendered many underlying assumptions of American foreign policy obsolete and influenced the United States to engage in diplomatic behavior that it had once eschewed. Confronted with the reality that the superpowers could destroy each other and that neither country could disregard or remove the other, the United States had to deal diplomatically with an ideological enemy even while constructing alliances to contain it. Yet compromise with the Soviet Union was often seen as morally repugnant, especially by conservatives such as Ronald Reagan. In an effort to regain its invulnerability, America under President Reagan began to develop the Strategic Defense Initiative (SDI), not only to make nuclear weapons "impotent and obsolete" but, equally important, as James Schlesinger, a former Secretary of Defense, puts it, to "avoid the moral tarnishing that comes from negotiations or, even worse, from acquiescing in the unacceptable."[31]

If dominant American cultural values have been hostile to diplomacy, a strong subculture that favors negotiations and compromise has also developed, and continues to have an impact on U.S. foreign policy. If religious beliefs have encouraged the growth of a messianic outlook, religion has also fostered the emergence of pacificism and conscientious objection to participation in war. The Society of Friends, known as Quakers, has been the most prominent religious group to directly oppose war in particular and violence in general. Believing that people of any nationality, gender, race, or social status may experience God directly, the Quakers have rejected the Calvinist doctrine of predestination, developed close and peaceful relations with the Native Americans in Pennsylvania and elsewhere, and played a role in the anti-slavery movement.[32] In addition to the Quakers, several peace societies have been formed to demonstrate their opposition to war. These have included the New York Peace Society and the Massachusetts Peace Society, both founded in 1815. A strong humanitarian impulse, which tends to mitigate the harshness of many American policies, is often reinforced by individual leaders' beliefs.

America's nonviolent tradition was represented by Presidents Richard Nixon and Jimmy Carter, the former a Quaker and the latter a Southern Baptist. While numerous factors combined to motivate them to focus on negotiations, such as the influence of Henry Kissinger's realpolitik views on Nixon, it might be argued that their personal beliefs enabled them to transcend myopic nationalism and to relate to foreign countries pragmatically. Nixon's Southeast Asian bombing campaign was accompanied by negotiations. His China policy and his willingness to pursue détente with the Soviet Union marked a sharp departure from previous American practice. Accepting the reality of global interdependence, Nixon stressed that peace requires a willingness to negotiate. He emphasized that all nations have important national interests to protect, and stated that, "in partnership with our allies, secure in our strength, we will seek those areas in which we can agree among ourselves and with others to accommodate conflicts and overcome rivalries. The insecurity of nations, out of which so much conflict arises, will be eased, and the habits of moderation and compromise will be nurtured."[33] Similarly, Carter, believing that many national objectives could be secured through diplomacy, consolidated Nixon's policies toward China and the Soviet Union, worked diligently and skillfully to achieve the Camp David Accords between Israel and Egypt, negotiated the Panama Canal treaties, played a pivotal role in Zimbabwe's transition to majority rule, and improved U.S. relations with many parts of the Third World.[34]

But Nixon's and Carter's willingness to compromise with the Soviet Union, especially as Moscow increased its military involvement in Angola, Ethiopia, Afghanistan, and other Third World countries, ultimately led to the ascendancy of more traditional American values that rejected compromising with evil. President Ronald Reagan, who embodied those values, renewed the anti-Communist crusade and relied primarily on military pressure to win the contest with what he called the "evil empire." Although he initially rejected negotiations, Reagan, paradoxically, helped to facilitate the demise of communism as well as the Soviet Union by accepting Gorbachev's diplomatic initiatives and ultimately compromising with Moscow.

Isolationism, Interdependence, and Negotiations

Misperceptions and misunderstandings that grow out of limited interaction and communication among states exacerbate cultural tendencies to employ military force against countries that are culturally distant. Countries that are isolated from each other are likely to develop feelings of mistrust, a factor that undoubtedly helps to shape their response to each other when they believe they are threatened. In other words, the degree of isolationism or interdependence that exists among states and their people determines, to a large extent, whether they decide to rely on persuasion, negotiation, compromise, or military actions to settle their problems. Since we generally fear what we do not understand, the greater the perceived differences are between two countries, the more likely it is that force will be used to resolve their arguments.

Having no reservoir of trust from which to draw, culturally distant states become even more isolated from and hostile toward each other as conflicts intensify. Instead of attempting to understand each other by encouraging greater communication and interaction, adversaries assume the worst about each other's intentions, escalate hostile rhetoric and actions, demand that third parties abandon their neutrality, and discourage constructive communication. With few nonconflicting relations between them and lacking the constraints of crosscutting cultural, economic, and family links, they have few incentives to refrain from using violence against each other. In fact, efforts by either side or third parties to decrease the magnitude of conflict behavior might be perceived as a trap, or as weakness and therefore an invitation for exerting additional pressure and eschewing compromise. Failure by the other side to respond to efforts to de-escalate tensions is often regarded as evidence in support of the view that defusing the conflict by peaceful means is impossible. But this only enables the side that has rejected conciliatory gestures to believe that it was prudent to maintain a hardline policy in the first place.[35]

The complex interdependence of states and their problems, the growing links between nongovernmental actors from various countries, and the globalization of markets, capital, technology, and communications directly challenge isolationist policies and the methods used to implement them. Ironically, the United States, which continues to have a strong isolationist strain, is the country that has played the leading role in the emergence of complex global interdependence and the growth of a global culture that, at least superficially, is influenced by American values. This interdependence challenges traditional American ways of resolving international conflicts. As more Americans become aware of the reality that their lives and domestic policies are affected by developments elsewhere, the need to communicate and interact with others will increase. This dialogue between states is the substance of diplomacy.[36]

In addition to sharing common values and being interdependent, if the countries involved in a dispute are themselves culturally, racially, religiously, ethnically, and ideologically diverse, then the likelihood of violent conflict will be reduced. Diversity within each country improves the chances that a particular course of action will not enjoy widespread unquestioning consensus. Not only will foreign policymakers have to reconsider their approach to the problem and their objectives, they will also have to weigh the domestic consequences of failure to achieve their goals. Unsuccessful pursuit of objectives is likely to result in a noticeable decline in support. Similarly, diversity facilitates responsiveness to the other side and consideration of a wider range of alternative courses of action than would be the case in a more homogeneous country. Because the feelings of anger and fear that accompany any intensification of conflict tend to influence decision makers to consider fewer options and to rigidly adhere to their positions, if adversaries are characterized by a significant degree of diversity, they may be able to consider new alternatives and be more receptive to overtures and proposals from the other side.[37]

Despite increased interaction among nations, the United States is still reluctant to negotiate differences, at least partly because of its difficulty in accepting others as equals. Recognizing others as equals usually facilitates the negotiation process. Cultures that produce individuals who are predisposed to controlling behavior are extremely unlikely to hold negotiations in high regard. Emerging as a global power due to the power vacuum created by Britain's decline, the United States was unchallenged by its allies and expected them to follow its lead and to cooperate, even if they were not consulted about the common enterprise. This approach reflects the tension between the authoritarian and egalitarian impulses that have always been embedded in American culture. Stanley Hoffmann notes that countries with which the United States has had friendly relations have generally been dependents.[38] Consequently, assertive states or leaders are often perceived as unfriendly and threatening, even though they might share many of America's underlying interests.

Closely intertwined with exceptionalism and a reluctance to accept others as equals is the American obsession with competition, winning, and being number one in everything. Competition pervades every aspect of American life and contributes to abnormally high levels of anxiety among Americans. The constant struggle to surpass others, to be better than friends and neighbors, begins in infancy and continues until death. Life has become an endless succession of contests.[39] This intense spirit of competitiveness has some bearing on America's international relations in general and its approach to negotiations specifically. The United States must win and others must lose. This preoccupation with being superior to everyone is not conducive to fostering cooperation and compromise, the hallmarks of effective negotiations. Despite their relative weakness, few countries and their leaders willingly accept an inferior position at the bargaining table. Excessively concerned with winning, the United States, in many cases, inadvertently sabotages its own efforts to achieve its long-term objectives through negotiations.

Impatience as a Barrier to Negotiation

Despite its myriad of problems, America remains an extremely affluent and efficient society, one in which immediate gratification is a reflection of our ability to produce an almost unlimited range of goods and services at relatively low prices to quickly satisfy consumer demands. Predominantly populated by immigrants determined to improve their lives by taking advantage of the abundant opportunities that were available, the United States has always been characterized by energy, speed, action, and impatience. Restraint and patience have never been encouraged by the country's general culture, which is an embodiment of youth, energy, and impulsiveness. Behind the country's rapid economic development stood values that supported risk-taking, entrepreneurship, competitiveness, a sense of mission, pragmatism, an emphasis on solving problems quickly, and a certain degree of recklessness. Furthermore, the national creed's equation of the pursuit of happiness with the acquisition of material possessions strengthened many of these characteristics, especially impatience and anxiety. Alexis de Tocqueville captured this aspect of American culture, noting that:

It is odd to watch with what feverish ardor the Americans pursue prosperity and how they are ever tormented by the shadowy suspicion that they may not have chosen the shortest route to get it. Americans cleave to things of this world as if assured that they will never die, and yet are in such a rush to snatch any that come within their reach, as if expecting to stop living before they have relished them.

They clutch everything but hold nothing fast, and so lose grip as they hurry after some new delight.[40]

While impatience and the pursuit of prosperity have been positive in many respects, impatience in particular seems to diminish the possibility of resolving crises through negotiations.

Impatience, combined with a relatively short-term view of problems, is more conducive to the use of military force than diplomacy to solve international problems. American culture encourages policymakers and others to focus on the immediate symptoms of problems instead of their underlying causes. Rather than stress preventive measures and address little crises, America tends to wait until a situation has become so dangerous that it can no longer be ignored. When this occurs, substantial resources are mobilized and attention is concentrated on eliminating the obvious aspects of the threat. Just as in medicine, where routine illnesses are often ignored and where the most advanced medical technology is applied to serious emergencies, foreign policymakers allocate significant resources to major crises that might have been alleviated if more emphasis had been placed on preventive measures. While other countries are also inclined to avoid dealing with problems, this tendency is arguably more pronounced in the United States.

Short-term thinking in government, which Secretary of State Henry Kissinger attributed to the fact that the lawyers and business people who dominate the foreign policy making bureaucracy are trained to solve immediate problems, also affects business.[41] Impatience, it is argued, is undermining the long-run viability of American companies because, as Michael T. Jacobs contends, "we cannot develop the technologies, penetrate the markets, or produce the products necessary to compete on a global basis by focusing on results one quarter at a time."[42] These cultural habits diminish America's ability to successfully negotiate peaceful solutions to conflicts, and strengthen its predilection to use military violence to solve problems. Whereas negotiations are generally time-consuming, tedious, and uncertain, war is comparatively more immediate, dramatic, and replete with action familiar to television viewers.

Patience is an indispensable component of successful negotiations. Negotiators must be willing to listen, learn, understand, and empathize—all of which require time and patience.

Because of the complexity of many specific problems and the international environment in general, solutions often arrive painfully slowly. Unlike war, which is a crude instrument even when technologically advanced, precision weapons are employed, diplomacy is a sensitive instrument designed to register and work on the smallest shifts in the attitudes of states toward one another.[43] This reality is inconsistent with American cultural values that regard caution as indecisiveness and protracted negotiation as evidence of incompetence and weakness, especially when the adversary is culturally distant.

Yet there are numerous examples of U.S. involvement in painstakingly slow negotiations. But these have been principally with powerful countries such as the Soviet Union and major allies such as the Western Europeans. Patient, protracted negotiations with the Soviets, which produced the Strategic Arms Limitation Talks Treaties (SALT) and other agreements on nuclear weapons issues, were motivated by the obvious and direct threat that the Soviet Union posed to America's survival, and the increasing disutility of force to deal with the nuclear confrontation. Similarly, patient negotiations produced significant modifications to the General Agreement on Tariffs and Trade (GATT), which Congress approved in late 1994. Apart from the fact that America's major trading partners, with the exception of Japan, share a common civilization and are culturally similar, using force to solve trade disputes is essentially unthinkable because of its obvious drawbacks. But, as discussed in Chapter Seven, there is also a component of American culture, best exemplified by President Carter, that is receptive to negotiations with distant cultures. However, when American interests are directly threatened by distant cultures, and the cost of military solutions is relatively low, the tendency has been to denigrate negotiations and, albeit ambivalently (in many cases), favor using force.

Chapter Four

Operation Desert Storm:
No Negotiations, No Compromise

When Iraqi forces invaded and occupied Kuwait in early August 1990, world leaders strongly and swiftly condemned Saddam Hussein's actions and demanded the withdrawal of Iraqi troops. Although Operations Desert Shield and Desert Storm received unprecedented international support, and were portrayed by President George Bush as international responses to Hussein's aggression against a neighboring Arab state and former ally in Iraq's war against Iran, these military activities were essentially initiated and controlled by the United States and, more specifically, by Bush himself. A careful reading of President Bush's speeches leads one to conclude that he had personalized the conflict and was determined to use force to resolve it. Clearly, Hussein's actions created the crisis. His own serious miscalculations, nurtured by hubris, and his own refusal to seize opportunities presented by the Europeans and others for a negotiated settlement, obviously facilitated America's use of force and its rejection of negotiations. But scholars and practitioners disagreed about how to solve the crisis, and many former American military officials opposed an early embrace of the war option. This chapter attempts to show that cultural factors in general and the cultural distance between the United States and Iraq contributed to the outbreak of the Gulf War.

While Bush's personal preferences helped to shape America's response to Iraq's invasion of Kuwait, his perception of the problem and his selection of policy instruments for resolving the conflict were influenced as well by broader American cultural values, many of which he personified. Opponents of the war tried to mobilize those components of the culture that support the peaceful resolution of conflict. Bush's use of military force to terminate Iraq's occupation of Kuwait and his stated refusal to negotiate a peaceful solution to the dispute were, in part, a reflection of his ability to mobilize public support for his actions by appealing to deeply rooted cultural values.

The war was perceived not only as a defining moment in history but also as a reaffirmation of America's fundamental beliefs and values. President Bush asserted that "in the life of a nation, we are called upon to define who we are and what we believe. Sometimes the choices are not easy. As today's president, I ask for your support to stand up for what is right and condemn what's wrong all in the cause of peace."[1] He reminded the nation of its *raison d'être*. In his State of the Union Address, delivered during the war, Bush pointed out that the conviction and courage we saw in the Persian Gulf was simply the American character in action. He said:

> For two centuries, America has served the world as an inspiring example of freedom and democracy. For generations, America has led the struggle to preserve and extend the blessings of liberty. And, today, in a rapidly changing world, American leadership is indispensable, Americans know that leadership brings burdens and sacrifices. But we also know why the hopes of humanity turn to us. We are Americans. We have a unique responsibility to do the hard work of freedom. As Americans, we know there are times when we must step forward and accept our responsibility to lead the world away from the dark chaos of dictators, toward the brighter promise of a better day.[2]

The massive destruction of Iraq was perceived as symbolizing the triumph of good over evil, and as a reaffirmation of America's perception of itself as a redeemer nation.

Many of the cultural values that are conducive to using force to resolve conflicts, and which serve as barriers to effective negotiations, were predominant in the United States' policy toward Iraq. Emphasis on the rule of law was transformed into rigid demands for Hussein to comply with the various UN resolutions that called upon Iraq to withdraw unconditionally from Kuwait. Instead of seeking a negotiated settlement,the United States embraced the views that it would not compromise with evil and that war was necessary to destroy the enemy and bring about peace. The American preference for doing things quickly, especially when force is involved, was highlighted by what many observers regarded as Bush's hasty march toward war. And the relationship between sports culture and war was demonstrated by comparisons between the clash of rival football teams and the duels between Patriot and Scud missiles, as well as by the language used by the President and Pentagon officials during the war. As long as the war was quick and decisive, Americans would support it. The similarity between how some of us settle conflicts domestically and how the country engages in international conflict was obvious in the President's speech on Kuwait's liberation by the American-led coalition forces. Bush stated that "seven months ago, America and the world drew a line in the sand. We declared that the aggression against Kuwait would not stand. And tonight America and the world have kept their word."[3]

Saddam Hussein's culture also contributed to the clash with the American-led coalition. Despite the certainty of defeat, Hussein refused to lose face by giving in to American pressure. The lack of political diversity within Iraq, combined with the significant cultural distance between the United States and Iraq, militated against the emergence of buffers that might have diminished the negative consequences of confrontation between Bush and Hussein. Americans' lack of familiarity with the Middle East, and the general perception of Iraq as synonymous with Hussein, effectively prevented the development of empathy for ordinary Iraqis. Furthermore, Hussein's ruthless actions facilitated Bush's efforts to demonize him and to portray the conflict as a struggle between good and evil. Within the context of American culture, Hussein was the perfect enemy. He was a brutal, well-armed, and dangerous dictator who threatened to use chemical weapons. His actions exposed America's vulnerability, based on U.S. dependence on foreign oil, and endangered that aspect of American freedom that is widely associated with the automobile. Hussein touched one of the deepest fears most Americans have always had: the dread of being held hostage by people who are perceived as different and uncivilized. Hussein was easily associated with the dark, evil characters that are so prominent in American television cartoons. Furthermore, a strong cultural tendency to engage in analogical thinking enabled U.S. policymakers to successfully portray Hussein as Adolf Hitler.

American Perceptions of Arabs

Geographically and culturally remote from the United States, Arabs generally intrude on America's preoccupation with itself only when there is a particular crisis, such as the oil embargo in 1973–74, war between Israelis and Arabs, or a terrorist threat against U.S. citizens and their property. Relatively isolated from the Arab world, the majority of Americans has developed many negative stereotypes of the area's inhabitants. This general lack of understanding of and prejudice against Arabs was demonstrated by the widespread hostility many Americans evinced toward Arab-Americans, including those who came from countries allied with the United States during Operations Desert Shield and Desert Storm. This prompted President Bush to appeal to the nation to be tolerant and respectful of diversity. Despite obvious differences between Hussein's actions and those of our Arab allies, in the minds of most Americans, all Arabs were essentially the same. During the conflict with Iraq, the FBI interviewed Arab-American business and community leaders. Approximately 53 percent of Americans polled approved the FBI's investigation and 29 percent thought Arab-Americans were unfairly singled out. Despite widespread Arab support for the U.S.-led coalition, 54 percent of the Americans believed that Arab-Americans were sympathetic to Iraq.[4]

Few Americans are aware of the virtues of Arab culture, or believe that they share many cultural values with Arabs. Arab culture is widely seen as distant. Most Americans' cultural perception of Arabs is that they are dangerous, untrustworthy, immoral, undemocratic, barbaric, and primitive. Michael W. Suleiman has concluded that many Americans tend to see most Arabs as either extremely wealthy and immoral or as Bedouins who are indistinguishable from the deserts they inhabit.[5] These negative stereotypes are perpetuated by television cartoons, news stories, and movies. For example, in Walt Disney's popular movie Aladdin, Arabs are portrayed as coming from a land where camels roam, and where "they cut off your ear if they don't like your face." This movie, aimed at children, calls the Arabs barbaric. The editor of the New York Times asserted that, "thanks to current international politics, one form of ethnic bigotry retains an aura of respectability in the United States: prejudice against Arabs."[6]

The views of Arabs held by most Americans are to some extent rooted in the country's religious origins. Despite the United States' unsurpassed tolerance for different religious groups, a large number of Americans still regard Islam, especially Islamic fundamentalism, as a threat to their interests and cultural values. A national poll conducted by the American Muslim Council found that 43 percent of Americans surveyed believed that Muslims are religious fanatics, while only 24 percent disagreed.[7] This fear of Islam may be traced to historical conflict between Christians and Muslims, a confrontation that has been transmitted through generations by literature, folklore, and academic writings. Because strong religious beliefs are more often conducive to crusades than to compromise when conflicts between distant cultures develop, many Arabs and Americans tend to perceive ideological and political clashes in terms of a jihad.

During the Cold War, when some Arab states leaned toward the Soviet Union (to enhance their leverage against the West in general and the United States in particular), the threats of an oil shortage and communist expansion became linked in the minds of many Americans. The Arab alliance with Washington during Operations Desert Shield and Desert Storm momentarily influenced the United States to exhibit greater deference to Arab cultural values and sensitivities, but, following

Iraq's defeat, many Arabs concluded that they were no longer feared or respected.[8]

Furthermore, many Arabs believe that American perceptions tend to foster punitive behavior toward them. Shortly after Iraq was defeated, the United States initiated international sanctions against Libya, to induce Muammar Qaddafi to turn over six Libyans suspected of participating in two 1988 airplane bombings in which 441 people, including several Americans, were killed. Although Libyans are not very popular in many parts of the Arab world, leaders from Egypt, Morocco, Tunisia, and elsewhere attempted to find a negotiated solution to Libya's quarrels with the United States, France, and Britain. The Arab League also endeavored to avert confrontation between Libya and the West, but was ignored by the United States and its Western allies. What the Libyan incident and the continued sanctions against Iraq demonstrated to many Arabs was that the United States was anxious to punish and humiliate them.[9] From the perspective of many Arabs, America's actions symbolize a cultural clash between the Arab world and the West in general.

Perception of the Threat

To mobilize American support for the war, Bush placed developments in the Gulf in a broader international and historical perspective: "Following the invasion, I stated that if history had taught us any lesson, it was that we must resist aggression or it would destroy our freedom. The consequences of our not helping would be incalculable because Iraq's aggression is not just a challenge to the security of Kuwait and other Gulf nations, but to the better world that we all have hoped to build in the wake of the Cold War."[10] The international harmony that many Americans had envisioned after communism's demise and the Soviet Union's disintegration would have to be maintained. The United States was morally obligated to act "so that international law, not international outlaws, govern the post-Cold War world."[11] Within the context of American culture, the term "outlaw" evokes deeply held cultural beliefs and attitudes. But more specifically, American interests were at stake.

While the crisis was often discussed in moralistic terms, a widely accepted view is that the underlying reason for U.S. actions in the Gulf was American dependence on the region's petroleum, a consequence of cultural values that promote excessive consumption and waste. Bush stated that "the Gulf situation helps us realize we are more economically vulnerable than we ever should be. Americans must never again enter any crisis, economic or military, with an excessive dependence on foreign oil and an excessive burden of Federal debt."[12] Higher oil prices would exacerbate American economic difficulties, contribute to the expanding budget deficit, and increase defense costs. Iraq contains approximately 10 percent of the world's proven oil reserves. Its invasion of Kuwait put Hussein in control of another 10 percent of the world's oil supplies. Furthermore, Iraq's occupation of Kuwait would threaten Saudi Arabia and other Middle Eastern states, which have the lion's share of the world's petroleum. From Secretary of State James Baker's viewpoint, the principal issue was whether a dictator who, acting alone and unchallenged, could "strangle the global economic order and decide arbitrarily whether we enter into the darkness of a depression."[13] Pointing out that developing countries in Africa and Latin America were being victimized by "this dictator's rape of his neighbor, Kuwait," Bush admonished those who felt that there was no downside to waiting several months to consider the devastating damage that was being done every day to fragile countries that could afford it least. Yet Bush himself acknowledged that there were significant differences between the conditions that existed in the 1970s and those of 1990.[14]

Unlike the 1970s, when OPEC dominated the international oil market and enforced compliance with the embargo, in 1990 there were several major non-OPEC oil producing states. More importantly, in 1990 all the Arab countries increased their production, thereby offsetting any reductions caused by the cessation of Iraqi and Kuwaiti output. Furthermore, because of their experiences during the 1970s, many countries had accumulated considerable stockpiles of petroleum, from which they could obtain needed oil supplies. The world enjoyed a surplus of about 200 million barrels of petroleum, enough to replace Kuwait's output for roughly 133 days. There was no evidence to support the assumption that Iraq wanted to terminate oil shipments.

Western Europe and Japan, which relied much more heavily than the United States on petroleum from Iraq and Kuwait, were less concerned about the threat posed by Hussein to global oil markets.[15]

A more serious and immediate concern was Hussein's seizure of foreigners, particularly U.S. citizens and West Europeans, to be used as "bargaining chips" and "human shields" to enhance Iraq's leverage vis-à-vis the United States. Influenced by the memory of having endured daily humiliation for more than a year, when American hostages in Iran were exhibited for television audiences around the world, Bush initially refused to acknowledge that Americans were hostages. An estimated three thousand Americans were among the large number of foreigners prevented from leaving Iraq and Kuwait. While stressing that Iraq's behavior was an obvious violation of international law, and contrary to "civilized" ideals, Bush attempted to affect Hussein's decision to hold foreigners hostage by appealing to Iraqi culture and religion. Bush informed Iraq's leaders that "in moving foreign citizens against their will, you are violating the norms of your own religion. You are going against the age-old Arab tradition of showing kindness and hospitality to visitors."[16]

But as both Iraq and the United States prepared for war, the hostage issue became not only increasingly complicated but also a rallying point for U.S. military action against Iraq. Attempting to take advantage of divergent views within the United States and Western Europe on resolving the conflict, Hussein embarked on a policy of releasing hostages to prominent Americans and Europeans who went to Baghdad to negotiate and who openly disapproved of the rapid U.S. military buildup in Saudi Arabia. The Americans who went to Iraq represented that aspect of the culture which encourages individual actions and citizen participation in foreign policy. Prime Minister Margaret Thatcher of Britain and President Bush strongly condemned Hussein's behavior. Bush vowed that America and the world would not be blackmailed by "this cynical and brutal policy of forcing people to beg for their release—parceling out human lives to families and traveling emissaries like so many chattel."[17] The reference to chattel resonated deeply within American culture; it reminded many Americans their own experience with slavery, and may have rekindled

American fears about Europeans being enslaved by ruthless Arabs. If the Iraqis had hoped to avert war by using Americans and other Westerners as human shields at strategic installations throughout Iraq, they clearly misunderstood the dominant aspects of American culture.

To galvanize public support for the war against Iraq, Bush emphasized another threat posed by Hussein, one that Americans had experienced throughout the Cold War. This was the threat of nuclear war. Although the Bush administration seemed unconcerned about Iraq's nuclear potential and had actually helped Baghdad to acquire sophisticated technology that was used for military purposes before Kuwait was invaded, after the New York Times published a poll indicating that Americans would support military action against Iraq to destroy its nuclear weapons program, Bush began to stress the nuclear threat. Bush claimed that "each day that passes brings Saddam Hussein further on the path to developing biological and nuclear weapons and the missiles to deliver them."[18]

Demonizing the Enemy: Hussein as Hitler

Hussein was increasingly viewed as the "mad man" of the Middle East by the Bush administration. He was portrayed as being unpredictable, incomprehensible, extremely dangerous, the "butcher of Baghdad," crazy, and a distant other with whom negotiations would be impossible. Objective observers generally agreed that even though Hussein's isolation from the outside world and his decision to surround himself with sycophants contributed to his tendency to make serious miscalculations, he was first and foremost a judicious political calculator.[19] His survival as Iraq's leader before and after Operation Desert Storm seems to underline both his ruthlessness and his political acumen.

Bush's argument in favor of war also centered around Hussein's evil deeds committed when he was considered a U.S. ally. Both the U.S. Department of State and Amnesty International had documented a wide range of human rights abuses by Iraqi authorities long before Kuwait was invaded. For example, in 1983, more than eight thousand members of the Kurdish Barzani clan were arrested and subsequently "disappeared." In 1988, more than six thousand people, mostly unarmed Kurdish civilians, were killed during large-scale military attacks.[20] As early as 1983, Iraq had used mustard gas and nerve agents against the Iranian army. Eight separate UN investigations had confirmed that Iraq had resorted to chemical warfare against Iran, and Iraqi officials themselves admitted using chemical weapons. Iranian casualties were treated in hospitals throughout Western Europe. Physicians in Belgium, Sweden, and West Germany concluded that the patients were victims of mustard gas. The Iraqi army had systematically attacked Kurdish insurgents who supported Iran, but it was the use of chemical weapons against the city of Halabja in 1988 that attracted worldwide attention. Approximately four thousand people were killed in Halabja alone, and more than twenty thousand Kurdish civilians perished from poison gas. Even after Iran accepted UN Resolution 598, which provided for a cease-fire in the Iran-Iraq War, Iraq launched another chemical weapons attack on Iran, to enhance its bargaining position.[21]

Although the United States was convinced that Iraq had used chemical weapons, and despite its condemnation of that use in the war with Iran, the Reagan administration acted to improve relations with Baghdad.[22] Diplomatic ties between Iraq and the United States were reestablished after a 17-year break. The United States shared intelligence with Iraq about Iran's military strategy and troop movements, and escorted Kuwaiti oil tankers, which were being attacked by Iran. Whereas the United States ignored Iraq's violations of international maritime law, Iran was punished, and was deliberately provoked into confrontations with the U.S. Navy. Finally, America used its leadership in the UN to obtain a resolution to end the Iran-Iraq War.[23]

Both the Reagan and Bush administrations focused on Iraq's contributions to America's objectives, and strongly opposed congressional efforts to impose sanctions against Baghdad. John H. Kelly, Assistant Secretary for Near East and South Asian Affairs in the State Department, testified before Congress that closer U.S. relations with Iraq had led to Baghdad's expulsion of the Abu Nidal terrorist group and the subsequent removal of Iraq from the list of states that support international terrorism. There was improved dialogue between the two countries on issues ranging from the Middle East peace process to Lebanon. Iraq had ended its arms shipments to

General Michel Aoun in Lebanon; had participated in two disarmament conferences on chemical weapons; was discussing a new constitution to provide greater recognition of human rights; and was working with the United States toward a comprehensive ban on chemical weapons.[24] Consequently, when Senators Claiborne Pell and Alfonso D'Amato, among others, introduced bills to impose sanctions against Iraq for its gross violations of fundamental human rights before August 1990, Reagan and Bush strongly opposed them. The Iraq International Law Compliance Act, which sought to withhold U.S. taxpayers' money from Iraq until it improved its human rights record and brought its government into compliance with international law, was opposed by the Bush administration.[25] Nevertheless, in his attempt to demonize Hussein, Bush brought up Iraq's previously ignored human rights abuses. Partly because Iraq is a distant culture, few Americans were aware of either Hussein's violations of human rights or Reagan's and Bush's deliberate policy of ignoring them.

However, following Iraq's invasion of Kuwait, Hussein was regarded as the epitome of evil, Hitler reincarnated. Having assumed global leadership in the aftermath of Hitler's defeat, the United States has been particularly sensitive to aggression comparable to Nazi Germany's. Therefore, Bush's assertion that Hussein was like Hitler resonated in America. Enough similarities existed between Hitler and Hussein to make Bush's claims seem credible. Both leaders ruthlessly invaded a neighboring state; Hussein used chemical weapons against the Kurds and Hitler bombed the villagers of Guernica; Hussein used Scud missiles and Hitler employed V-2 rockets against civilian populations. Both men lacked empathy and disrespected human life. But significant differences also existed between Hussein and Hitler. Whereas Hitler was driven by a socio-political vision based on the concept of racial superiority, Hussein espoused no such ideology. Hussein was not willing to destroy Iraq for an ideology, although his invasion of Kuwait and the American-led coalition's response resulted in widespread destruction and the ongoing devastation of his country. His basic objective was to reach Iraq's top position and to maintain his grip on power for as long as possible. Whereas racial purity was sacred for Hitler, nothing seems to be sacred for Hussein except his own survival.[26] Clearly, these differences did not diminish Iraq's crimes.

Once Bush had demonized Hussein by comparing him to Hitler, he could effectively use the Munich analogy to mobilize public support for war. Most Americans believe that compromise with evil is immoral and inconsistent with their basic cultural values.

Foreign Policy By Analogy: World War II and Vietnam

When British Prime Minister Neville Chamberlain negotiated an agreement with Germany's Adolf Hitler that allowed the latter to occupy the German-speaking Sudetenland border area of Czechoslovakia in 1938, the myth of Munich was born. Munich's lesson is that aggressors must be stopped at the earliest opportunity, with military strength rather than through diplomatic initiatives. The underlying assumption is that negotiation with aggressors indicates weakness, and that it emboldens the leaders of totalitarian regimes to conquer additional countries. For leaders such as George Bush, the belief that aggression must be stopped at its earliest occurrence is deeply ingrained.[27]

Besides overlooking the obvious fact that it was difficult for Chamberlain to know exactly what Germany was planning, those who embrace the Munich analogy as a guideline for American foreign policy conveniently ignore specific details that make comparisons between Germany's actions in 1938 and other developments largely spurious. Just as to the United States was reluctant to get involved in the Bosnian conflict in the early 1990s (as discussed in Chapter Six), Britain was not eager to challenge Germany's decision to incorporate German minorities in Czechoslovakia into the Reich. Furthermore, Britain could not count on support from other countries, including an isolationist America, in a war against Germany. Britain was clearly preoccupied with domestic concerns, and public opinion did not support another war over an area that was not regarded as vital to British interests. And Britain's governing elite believed that another war would weaken the country, hasten its empire's demise, and contribute to the United States' and the Soviet Union's rise as global powers. But as Paul Kennedy observes, "for an overstretched global empire...both appeasement and anti-appeasement brought disadvantages; there was only a choice of evils."[28]

The strategic situation in Europe in 1938 was radically different than conditions that existed in the Gulf in 1990. Germany was a leading industrial country that produced its own sophisticated weapons and had the second-largest population on the continent. Only the Soviet Union's was larger. Furthermore, whereas the world was awash in arms in 1990, not a single European power was prepared to fight even a limited war in 1938.[29] And even though Bush and others in his administration emphasized that Iraq had the fourth-largest army in the world, more battle tanks than Britain and France combined, and more aircraft than Germany, France, or Britain, the one-sided victory in the Gulf War undermined Bush's comparisons between Germany and Iraq. Using its most sophisticated weapons and intelligence-gathering equipment, the United States rendered much of Iraq's military force obsolete.

Bush's formative political experiences in the late 1930s and early 1940s seemed to have influenced him to regard any compromise with an aggressor as appeasement. In his address to the country announcing the deployment of U.S. troops to Saudi Arabia, Bush stated that "if history teaches us anything, it is that we must resist aggression or it will destroy our freedoms. Appeasement does not work. As was the case in the 1930s, we see in Saddam Hussein an aggressive dictator threatening his neighbors."[30] References to World War II can be found in virtually all of the President's speeches on Iraq. In a speech to the Veterans of Foreign Wars in Baltimore, Bush asserted that "throughout history, we have learned that we must stand up to evil. It's a truth which the past eighteen days have confirmed, and its lessons speak to America and the world. The first lesson is vivid as the memories of Normandy, Khe Sanh, Pork Chop Hill. We have been reminded again that aggression must and will be checked."[31] Referring to Hussein as a "classic bully who thinks he can get away with kicking sand in the face of the world," Bush reminded U.S. troops in Saudi Arabia that some pain now would avoid even worse pain later, and that the world had paid dearly for appeasing Hitler. That mistake would not be repeated with Hussein. Iraq's invasion of Kuwait would not stand. Bush called upon Americans to stand united behind his policy toward Iraq, and to respond as they had during World War II. The allied deployment in Saudi Arabia was seen through the prism of World War II. Using imagery and emotion that clearly decreased the chances for a negotiated settlement of the crisis, Bush told the UN General Assembly that "two months ago, in the waning weeks of one of history's most hopeful summers, the vast, still beauty of the peaceful Kuwaiti desert was fouled by the stench of diesel and the roar of steel tanks. Once again the sound of distant thunder echoed across a cloudless sky, and once again the world awoke to face the guns of August."[32]

Another American experience, which has profoundly changed aspects of American culture, also helped to shape the country's response to Iraq's invasion of Kuwait. Like Munich, Vietnam has become deeply embedded in the national consciousness. Failure in Vietnam challenged many American cultural assumptions and national myths, especially the myth of the Frontier. Pledging that the Gulf War would not be another Vietnam, Bush emphasized that "never again will our armed forces be sent out to do a job with one hand tied behind their back. They will continue to have the support they need to get the job done, get it done quickly, and with as little loss of life as possible."[33] In light of these deeply-held views, the possibility of successfully resolving the conflict through negotiations was remote.

Barriers to a Negotiated Settlement

Addressing the nation from the White House at the beginning of Operation Desert Storm, President Bush claimed that the war followed months of "constant and virtually endless diplomatic activity on the part of the United Nations, the United States, and many, many other countries. Arab leaders sought what became known as an Arab solution—only to conclude that Saddam Hussein was unwilling to leave Kuwait. Others traveled to Baghdad in a variety of efforts to restore peace and justice. Our Secretary of State, James Baker, held a historic meeting in Geneva—only to be totally rebuffed."[34] Baker also stressed the "exhaustive efforts" of the United States and other nations to pursue a diplomatic solution to Iraq's occupation of Kuwait, noting that in the 166 days between the invasion of Kuwait and the launching of Operation Desert Storm, he "personally held over 200 meetings with foreign dignitaries, conducted 10 separate diplomatic missions, and traveled over 100,000 miles."[35] Baker was clearly aware of the need to demonstrate to those Americans who believe in the peaceful resolution of conflicts that he had actually pursued a negotiated settlement.

But a careful examination of events leading to Operation Desert Storm, and scrutiny of Bush's speeches, clearly demonstrate that negotiations, defined as back-and-forth communication to achieve peaceful resolution of a conflict, were never seriously tried by the United States. This led former Secretary of State Zbigniew Brzezinski to conclude that "U.S. diplomacy during the crisis often conveyed the impression of being dedicated to the prevention of a diplomatic solution."[36] Determined to control developments, the Bush administration not only tried to block attempts by Europeans, Arabs, and others to achieve a negotiated settlement, but also appeared relieved when such initiatives failed.

The United States embarked on a policy of "principled unwillingness" to negotiate, fearing that flexibility would imply that America was rewarding aggression. Iraq faced a choice between giving in unconditionally or being crushed militarily. However, in his address to the UN General Assembly in late September 1990, Bush appeared to be willing to offer a compromise that would allow Hussein to leave Kuwait without being completely humiliated. Emphasizing that the United States preferred a peaceful, diplomatic outcome, Bush stated that "in the aftermath of Iraq's unconditional departure from Kuwait, I truly believe there may be opportunities for Iraq and Kuwait to settle their differences permanently, for the states of the Gulf themselves, and for all the states and the people of the region to settle the conflicts that divide the Arabs from Israel."[37] In the same UN speech, Bush implied that Iraq's only option was to comply with demands for unconditional surrender. He emphasized that Iraq had been "fairly judged by a jury of its peers, the very nations of the earth. Today the regime stands isolated and out of step with the times, separated from the civilized world not by space but by centuries."[38] Iraq's remoteness from the civilized world would help to justify the use of massive force against it. This was clearly a clash of distant cultures.

Confronted with the dilemma of not wanting to reward aggression on the one hand or to appear overly bellicose on the other, the Bush administration agreed to engage in dialogue with Iraq. But Washington's communications with Baghdad indicated that the United States would not progress beyond making demands for Iraq's unconditional surrender. There is no evidence to suggest that communication between the two governments included discussions about what issues would be on the table following Iraq's withdrawal from Kuwait. When Iraq accepted the United States' invitation to meet Baker in Geneva, Bush stated unequivocally that "this will not be secret diplomacy at work. Secretary Baker will restate, in person, a message for Saddam Hussein: withdraw from Kuwait unconditionally and immediately or face the terrible consequences."[39]

In his letter to Hussein, dated January 5 1991, Bush seemed determined to bully his adversary into submission. While the French, Germans, and others believed that a compromise could be reached that would avert war, Bush's letter clearly implied that he had already committed himself to war: "We stand today at the brink of war between Iraq and the world. This is a war that began with your invasion of Kuwait; this is a war that can be ended only by Iraq's full and unconditional compliance with UN Security Council Resolution 678."[40] Hussein's failure to comply would result in "a certain calamity for the people of Iraq." Bush reiterated that "there can be no reward for aggression. Nor will there be any negotiation. Principle cannot be compromised."[41]

Addressing a Joint Session of Congress, Bush proclaimed that "Iraq will not be permitted to annex Kuwait. That's not a threat, that's not a boast, that's just the way it's going to be."[42] Whether intentional or not, the Bush administration's language of confrontation and the actions it took that humiliated Hussein were not conducive to a peaceful solution to the problem. Indeed, America's approach only helped to stiffen Iraq's own refusal to negotiate. Underscoring the importance of language in cross-cultural negotiations was the fact that a relatively mild vulgarity (by American standards), used by Bush when he promised to kick Hussein out of Kuwait translated into a more humiliating insult in Arabic. And Hussein's rhetoric about making Americans swim in their own blood, and his claim that his army was ready for a showdown with the forces of aggression and infidelity that would result in an unequivocal victory for Iraq, were taken literally by many Americans. Playing to the respective cultures became an important obstacle to effective communication between Washington and Baghdad.

Furthermore, both Bush and Hussein personalized the conflict, thereby reducing it to a test of wills, a development consistent with an important aspect of American culture. Throughout his speeches, Bush emphasized the bilateral nature of the conflict and clearly personalized it. He warned Hussein that he should not doubt America's determination and staying power, that "we haven't blinked," that he would "kick Hussein's ass," that "I'm getting frustrated," and that "I've had it." In an interview with Middle Eastern journalists, Bush recalled that Arab diplomats at the UN would convey their perceptions of Hussein as a bully: "He'll walk into a room with other Arab leaders and swagger in with his—bullying the neighbors. And he had muscle. He had arms, when some of them hadn't gone to the arms route. He had an arrogant swagger that tried to intimidate his Arab neighbors."[43] But Hussein's cultural values also encouraged him to portray the conflict as a contest between himself and Bush. Jerrold M. Post maintains that when the struggle became personalized, it enhanced Hussein's reputation as a courageous strongman who was willing to defy the United States and Bush.[44]

An important barrier to a negotiated settlement was the failure of both sides to try to understand each other's perception of reality, which was shaped to a large degree by their cultures, and to invent options that might have been mutually beneficial. The Bush administration dismissed legitimate Iraqi concerns, which included Kuwait's removal of oil from the Ramaila field, Iraq's war debt to Kuwait, and Iraq's access to the Gulf. An immediate Iraqi concern was Kuwait's exploitation of the oil reserves in the Ramaila field, which straddles the border between the two states. While most of the fifty-mile-long oil field lies beneath Iraq, the Kuwaitis had pumped most of the oil produced. From Iraq's viewpoint, Kuwait was stealing its oil and damaging its economy by overproducing petroleum. Whatever the merits of Baghdad's claims, Washington might have agreed to take them into consideration at a later date, to allow Iraq to make a face-saving withdrawal.

Third-party diplomatic initiatives by the European Community (EC), moderate Arab states, the UN, and others were both feared and resisted by the Bush administration.

Whereas Iraq seemed to be interested in an Arab solution, the United States denied that such a solution existed.[45] The Arabs' cultural willingness to negotiate differences clashed with America's culturally-influenced unwillingness to compromise with distant others. Although fourteen out of the twenty Arab League states voted to condemn Iraq's invasion of Kuwait, even Saudi Arabia initially abstained from inviting American forces into the country, preferring not to appear provocative to Iraq. The Saudis also wanted to see if Arab mediation efforts would be successful in convincing Hussein to withdraw.

Concerned about the possibility of an Arab compromise with Iraq, the United States assured Sheikh Jabir al-Sabah, the ousted Emir of Kuwait, of its strong commitment to Iraq's immediate and unconditional withdrawal and the restoration of Kuwait's legitimate government, as opposed to a puppet government controlled by Baghdad. Administration officials believed that "the natural instinct" of Saudi Arabia and its neighbors to bargain with Iraq would undermine U.S. efforts to force Iraq to leave Kuwait.[46] While it worked at frustrating Arab efforts to achieve a regional solution, the Bush administration enlisted Arab support for military action against Iraq, claiming that Arab cooperation with the United States was evidence that it was the Arab solution that was being implemented. When King Hussein of Jordan, who voted against the Arab League's resolution to condemn the invasion, went to Bush's home in Kennebunkport, Maine, to discuss a peace proposal, his ideas were dismissed by Bush administration officials as a "nothing-burger," a codeword understood by most Americans. Sensing that Saddam Hussein was vulnerable because of his decision to pull his troops out of Iranian territory and to settle remaining issues between Iraq and Iran on the latter's terms, American officials stressed that "this is not the moment for us to be making deals."[47]

Whereas the United States and Britain, united in part by a sense of shared culture, maintained that any flexibility toward Iraq would amount to appeasement and rewarding aggression, continental Europeans believed that a face-saving solution could be found, in which Hussein could withdraw from Kuwait without seriously compromising the overall objectives outlined in several UN resolutions. France and Germany implied that Hussein's withdrawal from Kuwait would open up the possibility of an international peace conference on all Mideast problems, the withdrawal of all foreign forces from the Gulf, and mutually agreed reductions of weapons in the region as a whole.

President François Mitterrand of France and Chancellor Helmut Kohl of Germany believed that they should exhaust "all ways to negotiate" in order to avoid war. In France and Germany, and throughout much of Europe, the general feeling was that the United States' impatience was dragging Europe into a war in a region where its significant interests would be jeopardized. Furthermore, France, in particular, always concerned about maintaining its independence, rejected the view that it should simply follow Washington's dictates. Mitterrand, while stressing his friendship with and respect for the United States and Bush, declared that "I do not feel I am in the position of a second-class soldier who must obey his commanding general."[48] Mitterrand's statement reflected, to some extent, the undercurrent of French suspicion of the Anglo-American alliance, which is undergirded by strong cultural bonds.

But if the Europeans wanted to provide Iraq with a face-saving retreat from Kuwait, Hussein seemed determined to sabotage their initiatives. Instead of taking advantage of the divergence between Europe and the United States, Iraq viewed the European intermediaries as indistinguishable from Americans, and declined an invitation to meet with European diplomats subsequent to the stand-off between its representative, Tariq Aziz, and Baker in Geneva shortly before Operation Desert Storm was launched. Apart from wanting to portray the problems as a cultural conflict between Europeans on one hand and Arabs on the other (despite Arab involvement in the U.S.-led coalition) Iraq seemed to assume that because the Europeans were reluctant to begin a war, they would reconsider their support for the UN resolution authorizing the use of force against Baghdad if the deadline passed with Iraqi troops still in Kuwait. Yet such calculations buttressed the United States' war plans, instead of complicating things for Washington. As one of Bush's senior advisors put it, "Saddam has made it easy for us. He could have jerked us around, turned the Senate vote, and upset the alliance with hints of withdrawal. I am very pleased with the way things are now."[49] Hussein's lack of understanding of American culture clearly contributed to the destruction of Iraq.

Once the number of American troops in Saudi Arabia had been doubled, without the consent of Congress, the United States had moved from a defensive to an offensive position. The absence of a troop rotation policy imposed time pressures that pushed the allies closer to war. Harsh conditions in the desert, concerns about the coalition's cohesiveness, and fears about the complications that might arise for both Saudi Arabia and the United States if a large number of American troops were present in the Gulf during the Islamic holy month of Ramadan, helped reinforce the American cultural tendency to do things quickly, especially when force is involved. Moreover, by obtaining a deadline from the UN after which force could be used against Iraq, Bush pressured Congress into voting for a resolution committing the United States to war. Hussein's own massive deployment of forces in Kuwait, his widespread atrocities against Kuwaitis, and his systematic plundering of the occupied country reaffirmed Bush's view that force should be used quickly.

America's Impatience and Sanctions

Iraq's ruthless invasion of Kuwait was met with the swift and unprecedented imposition of comprehensive sanctions by the international community. The Bush administration severed all economic ties with Iraq. While Japan seemed reluctant to comply with the trade embargo, the West European countries decided to freeze Iraqi assets in their territories, suspend trade and military cooperation agreements, and ordered that measures be taken to protect all Kuwaiti assets to safeguard the interests of Kuwait's legitimate government.[50] The United States allowed Iraq to import medicine and food for humanitarian purposes, provided that distribution could be properly monitored, to underscore the administration's claim that the United States did not wish for Iraqis to suffer.

Despite Bush's emphasis on seeking an international consensus to force Iraq to comply with the UN Security resolution that had imposed trade sanctions against it, the strong U.S. cultural belief in individualism and the tendency toward unilateralism helped influence the United States to order a naval blockade of Iraq and Kuwait. Although Bush may have acted legally under both the UN Security Council resolution that imposed the global boycott and provisions of the UN Charter that allowed Kuwait to defend itself against an obvious aggressor, the speed with which Washington moved to allow U.S. warships to stop, search, and forcibly prevent oil tankers and other cargo vessels from violating the embargo raised serious questions about the United States' ability to work with others. Britain and the other members of the Security Council believed that the UN resolution allowed countries to send naval vessels to the Gulf only to monitor ship movements and report suspected violations to the special Security Council committee on compliance.[51]

Without the political and military complications of the Cold War, and given the widespread and unprecedented international support for sanctions against Iraq, many academic and military experts in the United States believed that the boycott would have succeeded in helping to coerce Hussein to leave Kuwait. Furthermore, Iraq was unique, in terms of both its location and its overwhelming dependence on petroleum for foreign exchange. Unlike previous attempts to use economic measures to induce countries to change their behavior, during which divergent approaches within the international community had weakened the pressures against the target regime, sanctions against Iraq were imposed so swiftly, so decisively, and so comprehensively that, in the view of Gary Clyde Hufbauer and others, there was a very high probability that, combined with a credible military threat and serious diplomatic activity, they could have contributed to the resolution of the conflict.[52] Because more than 95 percent of Iraq's oil was exported by pipelines through Turkey and Saudi Arabia and by tankers through the Persian Gulf, it was comparatively easy to enforce the embargo.

Robert McNamara and several other former U.S. secretaries of defense held the view that Hussein's economic, political, and military strength was declining rapidly. This assessment was shared, at least until early November 1990, by both Bush and Baker.[53] Although some supplies were shipped to Iraq through Jordan, the embargo was the most effective in the history of the United Nations. However, the Bush administration's decision to reject negotiations with Iraq and to rely solely on coercion undermined the power of sanctions to induce

Hussein to leave Kuwait. As Roger Fisher, director of the Harvard Negotiation Project, stresses, "pain creates no pressure unless there is a way to avoid it."[54] America's preoccupation with using the stick, to punish those from a distant culture, prevented it from offering the carrot, to facilitate a negotiated settlement. Without an indication that compliance with U.S. demands would not leave him worse off, Hussein had little incentive to retreat from Kuwait.

Those who opposed sanctions and favored using military power to remove Iraq from Kuwait seemed to believe that war would not only liberate Kuwait but would also spare the Iraqi people the suffering they were experiencing as a result of sanctions. Hussein, it was argued, was willing to make innocent children and civilians suffer, and Americans would not be prepared to watch films of children dying from malnutrition that was caused by our sanctions. Furthermore, sanctions were seen as a blunt instrument that hurt civilians more than military personnel. This was clearly an attempt to manipulate America's cultural values that strongly support humanitarian efforts to assist others, including those from distant cultures. In making the argument against sanctions and for military force, Senator Joseph Lieberman asked: "Is it truly more moral to maintain a strategy that inflicts the most punishment on a civilian population, the most vulnerable in society, the poorest, the youngest, the oldest? If people think that sanctions will work, they must think that they will bring terrible destruction on the heads of the Iraqi people themselves. It is important to consider the morality of that result before decrying the immorality of war."[55] America's postwar policy toward Iraq, especially the continuation of sanctions, has undermined Lieberman's arguments.

Similar arguments were advanced by the Bush administration. Although believing that sanctions were having some effect on Iraq's economy, Baker pointed out that Iraqis were used to suffering, because of Hussein's policies, his costly eight-year war with Iran, and his willingness to impose economic sacrifices on them in pursuit of his own ambitions. Sanctions alone would not impose a high enough cost on Hussein to get him to withdraw. In Baker's view, while Hussein could endure economic sanctions, he understood "more acutely the consequences of military force."[56] From Bush's perspective, waiting longer for sanctions to work would impair the military readiness of American troops, give Hussein more time to brutally suppress the Kuwaitis, and allow Iraqi forces to fortify and dig in deeper in Kuwait. Moreover, he argued that giving Hussein more time to prepare for war meant escalating the costs, both human and material, that the United States might have to bear.[57] What was overlooked in the haste to use military power was that sanctions were weakening Iraq's military capability far more rapidly than the harsh conditions of desert deployment were diminishing America's.[58]

Bush's March to War

Taking advantage of worldwide condemnation of Hussein's flagrant violation of international law, the United States moved quickly to obtain a UN resolution that demanded the immediate and unconditional withdrawal of Iraqi forces from Kuwait. It also called upon Iraq and Kuwait immediately to begin intense negotiations to resolve their differences.[59] In addition to its diplomatic efforts at the UN Security Council, the United States embarked on shuttle diplomacy. To finance the largest deployment of American troops in a foreign country since Vietnam, Baker, Treasury Secretary Nicholas F. Brady, and Deputy Secretary of State Lawrence Eagleburger persuaded Europeans, Japanese, Saudi Arabians, Kuwaitis, and others to contribute substantial amounts of money. Saudi Arabia pledged about $25 billion, Kuwait pledged roughly $21 billion, Japan pledged $13 billion, Germany promised $11 billion, and the United Arab Emirates agreed to give $6 billion. The Gulf Crisis Financial Coordination Group (GCFCG), chaired by the United States, raised more than $16 billion to assist the Frontline States, which included Egypt, Jordan, and Turkey, that were severely affected by conflict in the Gulf.[60] According to the Arab Economic Report, the Iraqi invasion and the ensuing war cost the Arab countries an estimated $620 billion.[61]

The conflict was increasingly linked to America's self-perception, which is intertwined with culture. In his address to the country announcing the deployment of American troops to Saudi Arabia, Bush emphasized that "standing up for our principle is an American tradition," and that "America has never wavered when her purpose is driven by principle."[62] After Operation Desert Storm had ended, the President told returning troops at Andrews Air Force Base that "America rediscovered itself" during the war. Bush's references to aspects of American culture helped to reaffirm American beliefs, an action which is part of the enculturation process. He stated: "First-rate military leaders executed a sound battle plan and delivered a swift victory. Men and women of all races and backgrounds worked together turning blueprints into triumphs. And while we freed a tiny nation, we also regained confidence in America's special decency, courage, compassion, and devotion to principle."[63]

Even as Bush claimed to favor a peaceful solution, he emphasized that Iraq's challenge to America and the "future of our world" would be dealt with militarily: "Simply put, 1990 saw Iraq invade and occupy Kuwait. Nineteen ninety-one will see Iraq withdraw—preferably by choice; by force, if need be. It is my most sincere hope 1991 is a year of peace. I have seen the hideous face of war and counted the costs of conflicts in friends lost...We should go the extra mile before asking our service men and women to stand in harm's way. We should, and we have."[64] Although the general perception of the President was that he had cautiously and skillfully taken diplomatic initiatives to increase international pressure against Iraq and force it out of Kuwait without a major war, it is now apparent that a military confrontation was the only option seriously considered by Bush and his small circle of advisers. According to Bob Woodward, Bush had revealed his real objectives only to this tight inner group which met "with their cowboy boots on the table," in sessions that lacked any clear agenda or conclusion. This group-think mentality had effectively silenced alternatives reportedly favored by General Colin Powell.[65]

Several members of Congress had expressed concern about the likelihood that the President would take advantage of their departure from Washington at the end of the Congressional session, as he did during the Panama invasion in 1989, to move the country toward war. As Senator John F. Kerry put it: "We leave a president who has been known to use force when Congress was out of session. We leave a Secretary of Defense who confided that it was an advantage that

Congress was out of town when he first deployed troops in the Gulf. And we leave an administration, on the verge of midterm elections, the strength of its convictions newly challenged, grappling with a bungled budget, a looming recession, and declining popularity."[66] In other words, Kerry believed that Bush would use force to gain popular support, a strategy that generally works in the context of American culture—as the public opinion polls showed after the war.

In addition to doubling the number of American troops to 430,000 to attain a "credible offensive action," President Bush obtained a UN Security Council resolution authorizing the use of force against Iraq. Resolution 678 called upon Baghdad to comply fully with previous Security Council resolutions by January 15 1991, and permitted member states cooperating with the government of Kuwait to use "all necessary means" to implement all UN resolutions against Iraq and to restore international peace and security in the area. Armed with Resolution 678, the Bush administration effectively altered American policy. The United States clearly embraced military force to remove Iraq from Kuwait. And, as Senator Edward Kennedy observed, because of the "High Noon" atmosphere created by President Bush, the conflict between Iraq and the world was transformed to one between Iraq and the United States.[67] Kennedy's use of codewords indicates that those who opposed the war also appealed to American cultural values.

By obtaining UN Security Council Resolution 678, Bush was able to convince Congress to give him the power to commit American forces to war against Iraq if Hussein failed to withdraw his forces from Kuwait. Bush successfully appealed to the view, deeply ingrained in American culture, that threatening to use force is the best way to achieve peace. The vast majority of the congressional members who supported the resolution authorizing the President to use force argued that a declaration of war was the "last best hope for peace." Senator Orin Hatch stated: "The only way to avoid war in this particular situation is to be prepared to go to war and to show our resolve is for real. The only thing Saddam Hussein and people like him recognize is our willingness to use force."[68]

The linkage between domestic cultural values and foreign policy was articulated by Representative Ronald Dellums, chairman of the House Armed Services Committee. From Dellums' perspective, the President's response to Iraq's invasion of Kuwait confirmed the view, held by many young Americans who are involved in widespread random violence, that resorting to force is the best way to solve problems. Children armed with AK 47s, 9-millimeter semiautomatic weapons, and .357 Magnums were, in Dellums' view, reassured by the President's hasty march to war that "the name of the game is to 'kick butt.'"[69]

War and Religion

Involving God in conflicts among nations has been employed as a venerable custom of war by Christians and Muslims alike. This is understandable, given the religious basis of the modern Western state and much of its culture, and the close links between religion and virtually all aspects of life in many Islamic countries. Both Iraq and the United States appealed to religion, and seemed determined to portray the war in moral terms or as a jihad. The cultural influences in the war were unmistakable.

Even though the United States, like other countries, is primarily concerned with protecting its national interests, unlike most nations, Americans often disguise the pursuit of their interests as a concern for moral purposes, and clothe the instruments of foreign policy in righteousness. This approach is deeply rooted in the culture and is considered to be required to gain public support for military activities abroad.

At the same time that Bush accused Hussein of trying to cast the conflict as a religious war, he himself asserted that Operation Desert Storm had "everything to do with what religion embodies—good versus evil, right versus wrong, human dignity and freedom versus tyranny and oppression. The war in the Gulf is not a Christian war, a Jewish war, or a Muslim war—it is a just war."[70] The concept of a just war is firmly established in Western culture and is an integral component of Christianity. A just war must support a just cause, be just in intent, be a last resort, have limited objectives, be proportional, be declared by legitimate authorities, and must not involve noncombatants. President Bush argued that a just war is one in which "good will prevail"; it is fought for the right reasons—for moral, not selfish, reasons. He maintained that "we seek nothing for ourselves."

America's leadership of the coalition forces was perceived by Bush and others as an inherent responsibility and as part of the national heritage. Only America had the "moral standing" and the means to back it up. As Bush put it: "We are the only nation on this earth that could assemble the forces of peace. This is the burden of leadership and the strength that has made America the beacon of freedom in a searching world."[71] Although Pope John Paul II condemned the war, most Americans (approximately 75 percent) believed that Operation Desert Storm met the criteria of a just war. More than seven out of ten Americans agreed that the good that would be achieved by war would outweigh the harm caused by the conflict.[72] President Bush was strongly supported by the majority of Americans because his actions were consistent with many fundamental cultural values. Furthermore, Hussein's ruthlessness strengthened the case for forcefully stopping aggression.

Many Americans who questioned the view that the war was just and necessary represented another aspect of American culture, one that is largely pacifist. Both opponents and supporters of the war competed for the moral high ground, and relied on religious beliefs to undergird their conflicting positions. While the Moral Majority, the Southern Baptist Convention, and the National Association of Evangelicals endorsed the view that the war met the "just war" criteria, other major religious groups represented by the National Council of Churches, such as the United Methodist Church, the Evangelical Lutheran Church in America, the Presbyterian Church, the Episcopal Church, and the Disciples of Christ, condemned the war. The National Council of Churches criticized the Bush administration for "reckless rhetoric, imprudent behavior, and a precipitous military build up." Its resolution against Bush's policy in the Gulf stated that Christians in the United States "must witness against weak resignation to the illogical logic of militarism and war."[73] Contrary to Bush's view that there was a clear moral justification for war, the representatives of the National Council of Churches emphasized that policy was influenced by the desire to protect American jobs and to insure access to Persian Gulf oil.

Bush and Hussein constantly invoked God's assistance and stressed religion's centrality to the conflict. Whether or not Bush believed what he said, he clearly realized the power of civil religion in American culture. Across the United States, the mood was that of a nation at prayer. The night the war began, Dr. Billy Graham was at the White House with President Bush. Graham spoke of the importance of "turning to God as a people of faith." Bush said that he prayed at Camp David before the air war began, noting that he "had the tears start down the cheeks, and our minister smiled back."[74] Speaking at the National Prayer Breakfast in January 1992, Bush recalled how he and others had been "compelled to pray" for God's wisdom during the war: "And we prayed for God's protection in what we undertook, for God's love to fill hearts, and for God's peace to be the moral North Star that guided us." Bush emphasized that America is "a nation founded under God and that from our very beginning we have relied upon His strength and guidance in war and in peace."[75] Throughout the war, Bush called on God to bless American military forces and their families and to continue to bless the United States of America. In his message on the observance of Passover on March 29 1991, Bush stated that "we are reminded of the triumph of good over evil. We are also reminded that the enduring spirit of liberty can never be crushed by the cruel hand of tyranny and enslavement. This lesson appears time and again in the pages of the Bible; and following the recent coalition victory in the Persian Gulf, it is a lesson all the more vivid to us today."[76] While many Americans probably did not believe Bush's rhetoric, Bush seemed to understand the importance of the nonrational, ideational aspects of culture in mobilizing support for foreign policies.

Similarly, Hussein turned to prayer to manipulate public opinion. He stated that God, "the great divine reinforcement," was the source of Iraq's strength and effectiveness. On September 8 1990, Saddam Hussein informed Mikhail Gorbachev and George Bush that as they met to discuss the crisis "the angels will be hovering above you on one side and devils on the other. Each says his prayer, and each would hope it to be in accordance with his nature and what God has chosen for him. God will be above all."[77] Hussein also seemed to believe that Iraq and the "Arab nation" were blessed by God, and that the region was honored by God to be the "cradle of divine messages and prophecy throughout the ages." The deployment of American and coalition forces in Saudi Arabia was seen in cultural terms, as challenging God, because Mecca and the tomb of the Prophet Mohammed were under the "spears of the foreigner." Hussein called upon Arabs to launch a holy war against the infidels, and assured Iraqis that God was with them. Whether intentionally or not, Hussein evoked images of past clashes between Christianity and Islam. The "candle of light" would snuff out the darkness personified by "the Satan in the White House." Quoting the Koran, Hussein told his nation that "God hath purchased of the believers their persons and their goods, for theirs in return is the garden of Paradise. They fight in his cause, and slay and are slain—a promise binding on him in truth, through the law, the Gospel, and the Koran. And who is more faithful to his covenant than God?"[78] And just as Bush saw the coalition's victory as the triumph of good over evil, Hussein viewed his survival in an "epic duel" which lasted nearly two months as "confirming a lesson that God has wanted as a prelude of faith, impregnability and capability for the faithful, and a prelude of an abyss, weakness, and humiliation which God Almighty has wanted for the infidels, the criminals, the traitors, the corrupt, and the deviators."[79] Neither Bush nor Hussein ignored his culture's religious roots in their respective war efforts, or the power of religion to mobilize popular support in cultural clashes.

The Enemy Must Be Destroyed

Although the Bush administration underscored that America supported the war objectives developed by the international community, many of America's war aims were significantly different from those of the UN Security Council. For example, both the UN and the United States sought to achieve the immediate, complete, and unconditional withdrawal of all Iraqi forces from Kuwait; the restoration of Kuwait's legitimate government; and the protection of the lives of American citizens held hostage by Iraq. But a specific American objective was a commitment to the security and stability of the Persian Gulf.[80] The Bush administration had concluded from the beginning of the conflict that Hussein's army had to be destroyed in order to guarantee that it could not be used again for offensive purposes.

Despite the fact that UN Security Council resolutions on Kuwait did not mention Iraq's nuclear or chemical capabilities, the country's nuclear power plants and chemical production installations were primary targets at the beginning of the intense bombing campaign. Indeed, Bush emphasized this in his address to the nation announcing the start of the war against Iraq: "As I report to you, air attacks are underway against military targets in Iraq. We are determined to knock out Saddam Hussein's nuclear bomb potential. We will also destroy his chemical weapons facilities. Much of Saddam's artillery and tanks will be destroyed."[81]

The United States and its allies attacked Iraq with a vengeance unmatched in any previous war. In the first fourteen hours alone, American and coalition war planes flew more than one thousand sorties against military targets in Iraq and Kuwait. More than one hundred computer-guided Tomahawk cruise missiles were fired from American warships in the Red Sea and the Gulf. It was estimated that the destructive force of the explosives that landed on Iraq and Kuwait in those fourteen hours exceeded that of the bomb dropped on Hiroshima by the United States.[82] For forty-three days, American and allied planes, with virtually unchallenged command of the skies, bombarded Iraq. The list of their targets included Iraq's leadership; command, control, and communications; air defense; airfields; nuclear, biological, and chemical weapons; railroads and bridges; Scud missiles; conventional military production and storage facilities; oil refineries; electrical power plants; naval ports; and the Republican National Guard. Early in the war, there was a concerted effort to kill Hussein. Tomahawk cruise missiles and F-117 Stealth fighter bombers destroyed command bunkers which Hussein maintained in Baghdad. An intensive search for Hussein's American-made "Wanderlodge" motor home was conducted by the commanders of Operation Desert Storm. Although the United States wanted to avoid killing civilians, there were many casualties, euphemistically referred to as "collateral" damage. A civilian shelter, alleged by the United States and its allies to be a military command and control center, was bombed, and approximately eight hundred Iraqi women and children were killed. Mosques and museums were also hit. Hussein and others attempted to show that such actions demonstrated that the West was waging a war against Islam and Arab culture. Allied bombers attacked buses that were transporting civilians who were fleeing the war.

Disturbed by the devastation caused by the relentless bombing of Iraq and the likelihood of a permanent American military presence in the Gulf, several North African countries launched an initiative to persuade the UN to call for a pause in the air strikes. The United States and Britain rejected the proposals. As President Bush put it: "There can be no doubt: Operation Desert Storm is working. There can be no pause now that Saddam has forced the world into war. We will stay the course—and we will succeed—all the way."[83] Despite the intensive bombardment in Kuwait and Iraq, Hussein refused to withdraw unconditionally from Kuwait. In an apparent attempt to save face in his own culture, Hussein added conditions to Iraq's withdrawal from Kuwait in mid-February 1991. News of a possible end to the war was greeted with celebrations in Baghdad. But only an unconditional withdrawal and retreat would satisfy Washington. Within the context of American culture, war with distant cultures is usually total, as opposed to limited.

The Iraqis were confronted with a Hobson's choice: they would be bombed whether they remained in Kuwait or if they decided to withdraw. American commanders did not intend to interrupt the devastating bombing campaign, partly because they believed that the Iraqis might "regenerate" and attack American troops. But the allies had argued throughout the war that their best chances of inflicting damage on the Iraqis in Kuwait would come if they left their entrenched fortifications and drove across the desert.[84] Although Bush claimed to be happy that Hussein had seemed to realize that he had to withdraw unconditionally from Kuwait, he concluded that there was nothing new in the statements from Baghdad, and that Hussein's proposal was a hoax. While stressing that he felt sorry for the people in Iraq and for the families in America who felt that "we really had a shot for peace," Bush pledged to continue the war: "We will pursue our objectives with honor and decency, and we will not fail."[85]

Similarly, efforts by the Soviet Union to end the conflict before the ground war began were rejected by the Bush administration. Iraqi soldiers, thousands of whom had already surrendered to allied forces, were characterized as retreating, not withdrawing from Kuwait, and were trapped between coalition troops, natural barriers, and Iranian territory. Iraq's elite Republican Guards were the main target of "punishing attacks" by American B-52 bombers. It was clear that America's objective was to destroy Iraq's military. Bridges that would have enabled Iraq's forces to withdraw from Kuwait had been destroyed by precision bombing, and cluster munitions which explode on contact were dropped to prevent Iraqis from escaping what amounted to slaughtering sands. When the doomed Iraqi troops crowded on the six-lane highway north of Kuwait City to return to their country, the U.S. Navy's Silverfox bombing squadron destroyed them. Vehicles at the front and rear of the long convoy were disabled, thereby trapping the rest. Iraqis were bombed for hours on what was euphemistically called "the highway of death." Commander Frank Sweigart, the squadron's leader, said the victims were "basically just sitting ducks."[86]

By the time a cease-fire had been implemented, more than 72,000 Iraqis had been made homeless by "collateral" damage caused by the unprecedented bombing. Unconfirmed estimates of Iraqi soldiers killed range from 100,000 to 250,000, compared to about 125 Allied casualties. The United Nations, which had purportedly authorized the war for humanitarian reasons, issued a report that concluded that the people of Iraq had seen their modernized country relegated to a "preindustrial age." The report also predicted the outbreak of epidemics and famine due to the massive destruction of the country's infrastructure, particularly its electrical power plants, sewage systems, and water supplies.[87]

In the same vein, a Harvard University Study Team found that allied bombing was the direct cause of a sharp increase in mortality among infants and children under five years of age. The Harvard Study estimated that 170,000 children would die within a year from the delayed effects of the Gulf crisis. It concluded that food shortages were responsible for widespread infant and child malnutrition, and that throughout Iraq, gastroenteritis, cholera, and typhoid were epidemic. In late 1994 the UN estimated that half a million children had died since the imposition of sanctions by the Security Council in 1990.[88] In June 1993, the United Nations began an investigation of possible health threats to Iraqi and Kuwaiti civilians from uranium-loaded U.S. ammunition littering the war zone. This occurred after Congress had started its own inquiry to determine whether U.S. soldiers had been harmed by toxic, slightly radioactive dust from tank and aircraft cannon rounds made from depleted uranium.[89]

Even though President Bush assured the Iraqis that the war was not against them, his determination to maintain UN sanctions against Iraq after the war, amid widespread suffering among the civilian population, cast serious doubts on his assurances. Moreover, his decision to keep the pressure on Hussein until new leaders emerged in Iraq seemed to disregard the plight of ordinary Iraqis, who had been victimized by Hussein's reckless conduct as well as by massive allied destruction of the infrastructure upon which civilians depended. Preoccupied with destroying Hussein, Bush seemed prepared to hold Iraqis hostage until Baghdad complied with America's wishes. Like Bush, Senator Al Gore, elected as Bill Clinton's vice president in 1992, believed that Hussein could be overthrown by blocking his access to international support, building up his opponents, and depriving him of resources for rebuilding his military machine. Gore, like the majority of Americans, believed that Hussein's very existence and his government were incompatible with the peace and security of the United States.[90] Clinton continued to enforce the policies adopted by Bush.

The United States, in search of total security, regarded what was now a militarily impotent Iraq as a danger to its interests. The enemy, in most Americans' view, had to be destroyed. From the perspective of the dominant culture, there could be no compromise with evil. Indeed, Hussein's survival continued to be viewed by most Americans as evidence of a failed U.S. policy. Concerned about appearing weak during the 1992 presidential election campaign on an issue related to his most important foreign policy victory, Bush allegedly attempted to provoke a confrontation with Hussein over UN inspections in mid-August 1992. The plan, disclosed by the New York Times during the Republican National Convention on the day before it was to be implemented, was to bomb selected Iraqi targets to improve Bush's alarmingly low popularity ratings and enhance his chances for re-election.[91]

Avoiding Responsibility

In a culture where avoidance of personal responsibility seems to be deeply ingrained and where the role of victim is gaining broader acceptance, it was not difficult for the Bush administration to convince most Americans that the United States was not responsible for the destruction that it carefully and systematically inflicted on Iraq. It was solely Hussein's fault. From the beginning of the crisis, Bush and Baker had emphasized that the decision on war or peace was in Hussein's hands; it was his to make. But this approach reflected a cultural habit: that of abdicating responsibility for one's own actions by placing all of the blame on a party that one knows one can destroy. Clearly, Hussein was largely responsible. His invasion of Kuwait and flagrant disregard for international law and human rights played a pivotal role in precipitating the war.

Neither the United States nor Iraq appeared interested in publishing information on the number of civilians killed during the war. In early April 1992, the Bush administration released a three-volume report on the war. However, all references to Iraqi casualties were omitted. Beth Osborne Daponte, a demographer in the U.S. Census Bureau, concluded that 13,000 Iraqi civilians had died as a direct result of the Gulf War. She estimated that another 30,000 people had perished during the Kurdish and Shiite rebellions after the war, and that more than 70,000 Iraqis had died from health problems caused by American and allied destruction of water and power plants. Her supervisor, Barbara Doyle Torrey, called the figures "a deliberate falsification." When Daponte made the unclassified estimates public, she was fired from her job, but was reinstated shortly thereafter.[92]

Margaret Tutwiler, the Department of State's spokesperson, asserted: "Indeed, any civilian casualties are a result of a war that Saddam imposed on the world. Had he complied with the will of the international community, ended his aggression, and withdrawn from Kuwait, there would be no war. Unfortunately and tragically, the Iraqi people are paying the price of that aggression. The United States didn't invade, annex, and destroy Kuwait; Saddam did."[93] This avoidance of responsibility was endorsed by Bush and most Americans throughout the conflict. At the end of Operation Desert Storm, in his address before a joint session of Congress, the President said: "Tonight in Iraq, Saddam walks amidst ruin. His war machine is crushed. His ability to threaten mass destruction is itself destroyed. And when his defeated Legions come home, all Iraqis will see and feel the havoc he has wrought. And this I promise you: For all that Saddam has done to his own people, the Kuwaitis, and to the entire world, Saddam and those around him are accountable."[94]

Similarly, when confronted with evidence about widespread malnourishment and a quadrupling of the death rate of Iraq's children, due in part to their exposure to water-borne diseases such as typhoid and dysentery and the lack of antibiotics and insulin, the Bush administration blamed the dire and inhumane conditions in Iraq on Hussein. Faced with the stark reality that Iraq's children experienced severe psychological trauma from the most intensive air war in history, that most of the water supply was contaminated with feces, and that 25 percent of children under five showed evidence of stunted growth because of malnutrition, Richard Boucher, a State Department spokesperson, said: "The problem has been that there are vulnerable groups inside Iraq that are not getting enough food, and that's not something we have done. That's something the government of Iraq has done."[95]

When American soldiers were cleaning up the carnage caused by the bombing of retreating Iraqi troops on the Kuwaiti highway, many U.S. soldiers were "satisfied that justice had been done." What bothered them was that the Iraqis had stolen virtually everything they could carry from Kuwait. Americans compared the situation to a domestic robbery: "It was like we were the police force, and these guys got caught trying to burglarize a house. They made us come here and do it. They should have listened to the President and left."[96] They seemed to believe that the sanctity of private property, an attitude deeply rooted in American culture, was sufficient justification for what many observers regarded as an unnecessary slaughter.

Another example of avoidance of responsibility was the American response to Hussein's brutal suppression of rebellions by the Kurds and Shiites, whom Bush had encouraged to overthrow the government in Baghdad. The Bush administration simply looked the other way while Hussein massacred about thirty thousand rebels with his helicopter gunships. When more than a thousand Kurdish refugees were dying every day from hunger, cold, and dreadful conditions in refugee camps along Iraq's border with Turkey, Bush not only appeared unprepared to deal with the aftermath of war, but seemed indifferent to widespread human suffering. Al Gore, who had supported Bush's decision to go to war, believed that, "Bush's handling of the postwar insurrection in Iraq revived the most bitter memories of humankind's worst moments."[97] Bush had overlooked his culture's humanitarian impulses in this case.

As the glory of Operation Desert Storm faded, it became obvious that the United States was avoiding its responsibility for having helped Hussein prior to the war. Warnings from officials in the Energy Department about Hussein's determination to build a nuclear bomb had been silenced. Evidence that Iraq had diverted food purchased under a $5 billion American aid program and exchanged it for money and arms from the former Soviet bloc had been ignored by the Bush administration. According to Kenneth R. Timmerman, Iraq had started purchasing arms from Egypt at the beginning of the Iran-Iraq War. Washington had "smiled on the Egyptian-Iraqi arms connection."[98] The Bush administration had also been aware of arms sales to Iraq by Britain and other countries. The Central Intelligence Agency had had information about the Atlanta branch of Italy's Banca Nazionale del Lavoro's involvement in financing an Iraqi project to develop a new missile, the Condor II.[99]

A New World Order: America as a Redeemer Nation

Although President Bush acknowledged that a new world order could not guarantee an era of perpetual peace, the underlying message in many of his speeches was that war would lead to peace and to greater harmony among nations, which is a central belief of American culture. To gain public support for their policies, American leaders often appeal to those cultural values that underscore America's culturally defined role as a redeemer nation. Consequently, Hussein's aggression against Kuwait was viewed as a menace to "the entire world's vision of our future," as a threat to world order and the rule of law, and as a danger to "civilized" standards of international conduct. The myth of the Frontier, discussed in Chapter One, was used to justify the war against Iraq.

Bush saw the Gulf crisis as an opportunity to bring about a new era that was "free from the threat of terror, stronger in the pursuit of justice, and more secure in the quest for peace. An era in which the nations of the world can prosper in harmony. A hundred generations have searched for the elusive path to peace, while a thousand wars raged across the span of human endeavor. Today a new world is struggling to be born. A world where the strong respect the rights of the weak."[100] In the tradition of Thomas Paine, Bush saw America as the instrument through which humankind would begin the world all over again. And, consistent with American cultural values, this new world would be governed by the principles of equality and the rule of law, and America would assume the leadership role. This theme was reiterated during Operation Desert Storm and in the 1992 presidential election campaign. But Bill Clinton effectively made America's economy and domestic problems the main focus of the election.

Bush perceived America as leading the world in facing down a threat to decency and humanity. He stated: "For two centuries, America has served the world as an inspiring example of freedom and democracy. For generations, America has led the struggle to preserve and extend the blessings of liberty. And, today, in a rapidly changing world, American leadership is indispensable. Americans know that leadership brings burdens and sacrifices. But we also know why the hopes of humanity turn to us. We are Americans. We have a unique responsibility to do the hard work of freedom. And when we do, freedom works."[101] The Gulf War was perceived as a universal struggle, just as the shots that began the American Revolution were perceived to be of universal significance. Out of the destruction of Iraq would emerge a new world order.

But as Chapter Six demonstrates, the tragic developments in Bosnia between 1991 and 1995 challenged the assumption that American power had convinced other countries that aggression would not be tolerated in the new world order. The United States has compiled data on the killing and torture of approximately thirty thousand men, women, and children— most of them Muslims—by Serbian forces in Bosnia and

Herzegovina who were carrying out a policy of "ethnic cleans-ing." Under this policy more than 200,000 Muslims were forced from villages where they had lived for centuries. In late 1992, the Central Intelligence Agency informed the Bush administra-tion that more than 147,000 Bosnians might die during the winter if aid deliveries were obstructed by Serbian forces.

While the United States issued statements condemning the atrocities in the former Yugoslavia, it failed to demonstrate the moral outrage that had fueled its policy toward Iraq. The United States continued to emphasize the importance of getting food to the victims in Bosnia, many of whom were subsequently slaughtered by Serbians. The West's response to genocide in Bosnia was to "manage" the problem. When President Bush was asked what the new world order had to offer the people of what used to be Yugoslavia, he replied: "We are not going to use United States troops to solve the political problems. We've got some vigorous diplomacy. We first work the humanitarian question, and then you do what you try to do in preconflict situ-ations or conflict situations and try to use your best diplomatic effort."[102] At the same time, however, the United States, France, and Britain sent warplanes to southern Iraq to enforce a "no-fly zone" they had arbitrarily established to protect Shiite rebels from attacks by Hussein's air force. The conflict in Bosnia was viewed as too complex and dangerous for American military in-tervention. Furthermore, significant U.S. interests were not be-lieved to be at stake in an area perceived to be culturally and geographically distant from the United States. But even the New World Order proclaimed by Bush in the Gulf was under-mined when Hussein amassed about 64,000 Iraqi troops and 700 tanks near Kuwait in October 1994, a development which led to a hasty return of American ships, planes, and troops to the region to deter Iraqi aggression.

Chapter Five

The Palestinian-Israeli Conflict:
Negotiating Peace Patiently

Due in part to a combination of Arab hostility toward Israel and obvious threats to its existence, as well as the refusal of many Israelis to recognize the pain suffered by the Palestinians, the Palestinian-Israeli problem constituted a source of instability and violence in the Middle East, and a threat to American interests in the region, until the Israelis and Palestinians agreed in 1993 to resolve their problems peacefully. The United States patiently pursued a negotiated settlement. Although the United States was generally supportive of Israel, this case demonstrates the complexity of American culture. Presidents Richard Nixon and Jimmy Carter both showed empathy for the Palestinians. Carter's ability to successfully negotiate the Camp David Peace Accords between Israel and Egypt reflected American cultural tendencies that favor compromise and the peaceful resolution of conflicts.

Several factors explain America's emphasis on negotiation as a means to solving the Palestine-Israel conflict. While the

United States perceived Israel as a valuable and dependable ally in its struggle against communist expansion, Washington relied as well on the support of many Arab governments to frustrate the Soviet Union's ambitions. Consequently, America had to mediate between the Arabs and the Israelis, to diminish conflicts between them and quickly end the wars that erupted in order to achieve its own security objectives. Because the Palestinian-Israeli dispute was perceived as part of the broader East-West struggle, the United States was unwilling to do anything that would weaken its alliance with Israel. However, America's economic and military relations with moderate Arab countries influenced Washington to embrace a negotiated settlement and to refuse to accept Israel's occupation of territory seized from the Arabs during the 1967 war. Furthermore, both Egypt and Jordan had important stakes in the peaceful resolution of the broader Arab-Israeli conflict, especially after the 1973 war. Egypt, which had established diplomatic ties with Israel in 1979 and been subsequently isolated in the Arab world, for making a separate peace with Israel without achieving the national rights of the Palestinians and for having recognized Israel's right to exist, had a direct interest in encouraging negotiations between Israel and the Palestinians. And, given the end of the military hostilities that had characterized Egypt's relations with Israel since 1948, the Palestine Liberation Organization (PLO) itself realized that negotiations were the only feasible way to achieve its aspiration of establishing a Palestinian homeland and, ultimately, an independent Palestinian state in the West Bank and Gaza.

Although the complexity of the Arab-Israeli conflict made the threat of force to resolve it less attractive to the United States, Washington's tendency to emphasize the complexity of the problem appeared to be part of a deliberate effort to avoid direct confrontation with Israel over some of the latter's actions that violated international law and were inconsistent with America's commitment to protecting human rights and fundamental freedoms. The Israelis were not demonized, dehumanized, or threatened by the United States. There were no deadlines or ultimatums. Since President Dwight Eisenhower, Democratic and Republican administrations alike eschewed imposing sanctions against Israel.

Despite statements expressing U.S. opposition to various Israeli activities, Washington generally refrained from trying to force Israel to comply with international law. On the contrary, the United States evinced a degree of patience that is reserved for close friends, and continued to allocate approximately one-fourth of its foreign aid budget, or more than $3 billion dollars, to Israel each year. While occasionally disagreeing with Israel, the United States showed respect for its positions and was sensitive to its interests. America seemed willing to try to understand Israel's problems and concerns. Instead of using confrontational language, U.S. officials emphasized cooperation to reach possible solutions. Even though the Cold War was a dominant determinant of U.S. policy toward the Palestinian-Israel conflict, content analysis of speeches and statements of various presidents and State Department officials shows that policymakers found it expedient to appeal to cultural values when seeking support for that policy. An emphasis on culture as an influence on U.S. policy does not overlook the importance of other factors that helped to shape U.S. relations with Israel. The collapse of the Soviet Union made it easier for America to be critical of Israel, and many Israelis understood that the end of the Cold War meant that they could not rely as much on the United States, cultural affinity notwithstanding. But cultural ties still mattered.

Factors such as the democratic nature of Israeli society, the Arab countries' lack of a strong commitment to democratic values, the existence of anti-Semitism throughout much of the world, diverse opinions among American Jews on Israel's behavior, the presence of a strong pro-Israel lobby in the United States, diverse Arab views on the Palestinian issue, and divergent opinions about the conflict within Israel itself undoubtedly made it easier for the United States to encourage negotiations. However, while these factors helped to influence the United States' approach to the Palestinian-Israeli dispute, cultural similarities between America and Israel provided an impetus for Washington's support of a negotiated settlement of the Palestinian-Israeli problem and its patience with Israel. Since Israel's establishment, America's presidents have alluded to cultural and religious links between the two countries, and to Israel's significance to the United States' self-definition. They have credited their own socialization and childhood experiences as factors that shaped their positive perceptions of and strong support for Israel. Arguably, to a much greater extent than security concerns, emotional and cultural bonds have played a pivotal role in the formulation and implementation of America's policy toward the Palestinian-Israeli conflict. These cultural considerations have been reinforced by strong ties between Jewish-Americans and Israel, and the Jewish-Americans' ability to pose an electoral threat. The influence of U.S. presidential politics in particular and national and local politics in general on American policies toward Israel is an example of the impact of cultural links on the formulation of foreign affairs.

American Perceptions of and Cultural Links with Israel

The Puritans who settled America strongly identified with the Israelites of the Old Testament. Fleeing religious persecution, determined to establish a New Jerusalem in the New World, and perceiving America as an alternative to a Europe plagued with evils, the Puritans embraced biblical teachings as guidelines for building their "City on a Hill." Believing that they were a "chosen people," and that the United States was destined to be an exceptional country and a "light unto the nations," the early Americans compared their new nation to ancient Israel. Harvard, Yale, and other leading American universities were founded upon religious beliefs that emanated from the Israelites' experiences. Hebrew was part of the curriculum at both Harvard and Yale. The religious roots of America's major universities and many of the scholars, political leaders, policymakers, and other influential citizens they produced reinforced America's identification with Israel.

Confronted with dangers and uncertainties as they expanded across the continent and developed national institutions to protect their liberties and provide political and social stability, Americans tended to view their experiences in biblical terms. As in Western European societies, the United States' laws and concepts of morality have been strongly influenced by Judaic traditions, a point which American leaders continue to emphasize. The idea that a covenant exists between God and the people became an integral part of our political thinking and behavior. Revitalized by Bill Clinton in his acceptance speech at the Democratic National Convention in 1992, the concept of a covenant is the foundation of our belief in the rule of law. In a proclamation issued during Jewish Heritage Week in 1991, President George Bush underscored the connection between Judeo-Christian values and America's national institutions by stating that: "Our forefathers' declaration of the unalienable rights of individuals was rooted in the biblically supported belief that all people are created equal, in the image of the Almighty. The principles of ethical and moral conduct that form the basis of American civil order and the foundation of any truly free and just society stem from the commandments given by God to Moses."[1] Although the rhetorical aspect of presidential statements cannot be overlooked, America's actual relations with Israel reflect many views articulated by U.S. national leaders.

Psychological bonds between the two countries have been consolidated not only by America's religious and cultural identification with Israel of the Old Testament but also by America's self-perception today. The establishment of the modern state of Israel confirmed America's faith in itself and its traditions. To a greater extent than any other nation, (with the possible exception of Britain), Israel acquired a special meaning for the United States. Israel's pioneering spirit, its youth, its quest for freedom, its technological achievements, and its existence as a monument to resistance against the historical and pervasive oppression of Jews worldwide remind most Americans of their own cultural heritage and commitment to preserving freedom. The symbiotic relationship between the two countries is best articulated by Peter Grose: "As the Judaic heritage flowed through the minds of America's early settlers and helped to shape the new American republic, so Israel restored adopted the vision and the values of the American dream. Each grafted the heritage of the other onto itself."[2] These cultural ties appear to make it difficult for the United States to confront Israel when the latter violates those values, partly because such a confrontation might be viewed as a challenge to America itself. However, leaders from both countries can draw upon the cultural reservoir established between them to work out their differences.

Religious considerations strengthen the psychological connections between Israel and the United States. Like the majority of Americans, U.S. leaders treat religion as a central component of national life and often refer to the impact of their religious education on their attitudes toward Israel. As President Lyndon Johnson put it, "the Bible stories are woven into my childhood memories as the gallant struggle of modern Jews to be free of persecution is also woven into our souls."[3] Israel's creation in 1948 was seen by many Americans as a new Exodus, a return to the Promised Land, and the fulfillment of biblical prophecy. Later, quoting the prophet Isaiah, President Johnson stressed that Israel's existence was evidence of God's promise to "assemble the outcasts of Israel and gather together the dispersed of Judah from all corners of the earth."[4]

Many fundamentalist Christians, particularly Southern Baptists, believe that the "ingathering" of the Jews in Israel is a precursor of Christ's Second Coming and the end of the world. But they also subscribe to the idea that Jews will be converted to Christianity in the process. Most Christian fundamentalists advance the view that the United States is a Christian nation, a precept some Americans find disturbing, given the increasing religious diversity of the United States. For other Southern Baptists, including President Jimmy Carter, Israel's existence has created opportunities for Christians to worship in Jerusalem. In his memoirs, Carter recalls that prior to the 1967 war there were no assurances that Christians would be granted access to holy places or that these sites would not be vandalized.[5] But, as will be discussed, Carter represented the component of American culture that strongly favors religious tolerance. His empathy for the Arabs was obvious.

Centuries of Jewish suffering, culminating in the Holocaust, have appealed to the humanitarian impulse that is an integral component of America's culture, and have sensitized most Americans to Jewish concerns. As a refuge for persecuted Jews, Israel shares with America the distinction of being an immigrant country, one whose borders are open to those, albeit primarily Jews, who seek religious and political freedom. For American postwar presidents, the Holocaust, like World War II itself, was a defining moment in their own lives as well as in American history. The atrocities inflicted upon Jews helped shape these leaders' perspectives on Israel, and strengthened their determination to insure its survival. Carter, for example, considered a homeland for the Jews to be compatible with the teachings of the Bible, hence ordained by God. His moral and religious beliefs made his commitment to the security of Israel, in his words, "unshakeable."[6] Familiarity with Jewish suffering, and the personal relationships that many non-Jewish Americans have with American Jews, combine to engender strong empathy for Israelis. But many American presidents and some ordinary Americans have also empathized with the plight of the Palestinians.

As a democratic society in a region characterized by a general disregard for human rights, the personalization of power, and authoritarianism, Israel is widely regarded by U.S. officials and many ordinary citizens as reinforcing American culture. In his address before the annual policy conference of the American Israel Public Affairs Committee (AIPAC) in April 1985, Secretary of State George Shultz asserted: "When Lincoln spoke at Gettysburg of rededication to the cause of freedom, he was saying that the survival of liberty depended on people's faith in liberty. Israel's success as a thriving democracy helps sustain our faith in the democratic way of life not only in America but throughout the world."[7] Other American leaders and Israeli supporters have reiterated the significance of a democratic society in the Middle East to America's self-definition and foreign policy objectives.

Consequently, helping the small state of Israel defend itself against less democratic, more numerous, and larger adversaries has been regarded as America's responsibility. During the Cold War, Israel was seen as a bastion against communist expansion and an essential American ally in a volatile area. Moreover, because most Arabs rejected the United Nations' vote to partition Palestine, attacked the fledgling Jewish state, and for more than three decades refused to recognize its right to exist, most Americans favored giving military assistance to Israel. A militarily strong Israel was perceived as helping to protect U.S. interests by preserving the balance of power in the Middle East. President Richard Nixon stressed that "we will do what is necessary to maintain Israel's strength vis-à-vis its neighbors, not because we want Israel to be in a position to wage war, but because that is what will deter its neighbors from attacking it."[8]

Activities of the pro-Israel lobby in general, and AIPAC in particular, help perpetuate the politics of sentiment that undergird the special relationship between Israel and the United

States. The pro-Israel lobby is widely believed to be an extension of Israel itself, because of its tendency to publicly support positions and policies adopted by the Israeli government. Congressman Paul Findley, who felt that he was a victim of the lobby in his bid for re-election to the U.S. House of Representatives, claimed: "It is no overstatement to say that AIPAC has effectively gained control of virtually all of Capitol Hill's action on Middle East policy. Almost without exception, House and Senate members do its bidding, because most of them consider AIPAC to be the direct Capitol Hill representative of a political force that can make or break their chances at election time."[9] Numerous members of Congress, including Senators Carl Levin, Paul Simon, Tom Harkin, Rudy Boschwitz, Claiborne Pell, and Bill Bradley, and Representatives Mel Levine, Sidney Yates, David Obey, Howard Wolpe, Les Aspin, and Richard Gephart have accepted significant financial contributions from pro-Israel Political Action Committees (PACS) and individuals to fund their political campaigns.[10] However, the power of the Israel lobby is debatable.

Many members of Congress, diplomats, and ordinary Americans have quietly expressed concerns about AIPAC's power in Washington. When David Steiner, AIPAC's president, boasted about his organization's access to the incoming Clinton administration, the American Jewish community regarded his claims as exaggerated and called for his resignation. Steiner's successor, Steve Grossman, not only downplayed AIPAC's influence but adopted a more conciliatory approach to ending the Arab-Israeli conflict. Like many American Jewish leaders, Grossman supported territorial compromise in the West Bank and Gaza in exchange for credible guarantees of peace, and criticized extremists within the Israeli government who were guided by "religious chauvinism."[11] This view was consistent with those of Secretary of State James Baker and other Bush administration officials. Although conventional wisdom is that AIPAC and other pro-Israel groups are powerful because of their access to members of Congress and administration officials, perhaps a more compelling reason for their perceived influence is that shared cultural values and the affinity between the United States and Israel predispose policymakers and the general public to be generally supportive of and to empathize with Israel. Although difficult to measure, these cultural similarities undoubtedly helped to shape American perceptions and policies.

American Perceptions of Palestinians

When the Soviet Union began to disintegrate, and it was obvious to even the staunchest anti-communists that the Cold War had ended, some American policymakers concluded that militant Islamic fundamentalists posed the next most serious threat to our interests. While fundamentalists of any religious affiliation can threaten both individual well-being and national security, many Americans appear to have a special fear of Muslims which seems to be rooted in our historical experiences with, and our cultural and geographic distance from, countries in which Islam predominates. From Michael W. Suleiman's viewpoint, this fear of Muslims engenders negative stereotypes of Arabs in general and of Palestinians specifically, which are then perpetuated by the mass media and other agents of socialization.[12] Those sterotypes have influenced American policy on the Palestinian-Israeli conflict.

The terrorist activities carried out by some Palestinians against Israel in the late 1960s, and the Arab oil embargo of the early 1970s, which heightened our awareness of Arabs, helped to engender both hostility toward and a sense of dependence on people to whom many Americans could not relate culturally. Many Americans seemed reluctant to try to understand the Palestinians and the causes of their violent activities. Instead, Palestinians were dismissed as troublemakers determined to destroy Israel and to undermine U.S. interests in the Middle East. America's involvement in the creation of and continuing commitment to Israel convinced many Palestinians that there was little difference between the two countries' policies and concerns. Consequently, PLO guerrillas attacked American citizens and property as part of their anti-Israel campaign, and were deeply suspicious of and hostile to U.S. initiatives to resolve the broader Arab-Israeli conflict. Believing that proposed negotiated settlements were designed to diminish their organization's significance as a legitimate representative of the Palestinian people, many PLO members responded with increased violence against both Israel and the United States.[13]

On the one hand, the Palestinian terrorist operations heightened international awareness of the plight of the Palestinian people and their demands for a homeland. On the other, they deepened America's determination to protect Israel. Increasingly, the link between Palestinian suffering and terrorism was cited by policymakers. In his detailed report to Congress on U.S. foreign policy, President Richard Nixon observed that the Arab-Israeli conflict had condemned "to squalor and to soul-searing hatred the lives of Palestinian refugees, who include not only those who originally fled their homes upon the establishment of Israel, but a whole generation born and reared in the hopelessness and frustration of the refugee camps. They are the material from which history creates the tragedies of the future."[14] Nixon's empathy for the Palestinians reflected a strong American cultural tendency to identify with victims and to offer them humanitarian assistance.

Compared to the Israelis, prior to the peace talks between Israel and the PLO, Palestinians were perceived in America as foreign and threatening. They have not been well-represented in Washington. On the whole, pro-Arab groups are faced with a culture that is not receptive to their message. In addition, many Arab-Americans are too preoccupied with their own personal adjustments to their adopted country to focus on the Palestinian-Israeli conflict. Arab-Americans come from diverse national backgrounds and have different perspectives about the Palestinians and their problems. Furthermore, violent attacks by some Palestinian groups on American citizens made it extremely difficult for Arab-Americans to clearly articulate a unified and unambiguous position on the Palestinian-Israeli conflict.

Two developments in the late 1980s combined to change American perceptions of the Palestinians on the West Bank and in Gaza: the first was the PLO's decision to renounce terrorism and to recognize Israel's right to exist; and the second was the Intifada, or the Palestinian uprising in the West Bank and Gaza Strip, and Israel's response to it. By reversing its policy of nonrecognition of Israel, in February 1989, and accepting UN Security Council Resolutions 242 and 338, the PLO acted in a manner that was inconsistent with American expectations, thereby facilitating American attitudinal changes and generating some American empathy. Perhaps a more important reason for the increased support of the Palestinians was that television coverage of Israel's responses to the uprising on the West Bank and in Gaza forced many Americans to confront their prejudices, and enabled them to evaluate the situation for themselves without the filters of Israeli censorship, the pro-Israel lobby, and policymakers. The suffering of Palestinian children elicited a strong American humanitarian impulse. This component of American culture directly affected how Americans perceived Israel. Public support for Israel declined from 61 percent before the Intifada to around 34 percent by 1990. However, as attention shifted from the Palestinian uprising to other areas, the percentage of Americans expressing support for Israel increased to 59 percent. Only 21 percent sympathized with the Palestinians.[15] When all factors are considered, cultural affinity between the United States and Israel appears to have been one of the most important determinants of Washington's approach to the Palestinian-Israeli problem. But the inconsistencies inherent in culture are demonstrated by the variance in American foreign policy under different presidents.

Ignoring UN Resolutions and the Rule of Law

President Bush's insistence on Saddam Hussein's unconditional compliance with numerous UN resolutions drew attention to the UN's role in conflict resolution, the extent to which countries have complied with Security Council resolutions, and the selective inconsistencies in American policies in relation to enforcing international law. Iraq clearly violated its international obligation to respect another state's sovereignty and territorial integrity by invading Kuwait. Given the dramatic and destructive nature of Iraq's military activities (in a region where the United States and its allies have vital interests), the international community had no difficulty reaching a consensus on the measures necessary to punish Iraq and to remove its occupying forces from Kuwait. But Hussein's decision to link his withdrawal from Kuwait to Israel's withdrawal from Arab territories seized during the Six Day War in 1967 drew attention to the divergence in American approaches to Iraq and Israel. Although the circumstances under which the respective occupations occurred are not comparable, both Israel and Iraq violated international law.

Cognizant of America's "unshakeable commitment" to its security and confident of its own military superiority over its neighbors, Israel has consistently defied the UN and ignored Security Council Resolutions. Indeed, Israel has counted on the

United States to frustrate UN efforts to compel its compliance with international law. In many cases, the United States has stood alone in the Security Council in opposing resolutions against Israel. Israel has refused to apply the Fourth Geneva Convention, which details the responsibilities of the Occupying Power to the Civilian Persons in the Occupied Territories; denied Palestinians their right to self-determination; annexed territories seized in armed conflict; arbitrarily deported Palestinians from their homeland; and adamantly opposed UN involvement in the dispute. But the United States has remained supportive. Gabriel Sheffer observes that "Israel appears to enjoy almost endless patience on the part of its patron, relying on the United States to ward off diplomatic attacks in the UN."[16] At the root of America's policy appears to be a historical tendency to apply the rule of law selectively, usually punishing those outside its cultural circle while generally condoning the behavior of those within.

Although it is perhaps coincidental, President Dwight Eisenhower, who sought to enlarge America's cultural circle by expanding equal rights for African-Americans, took the strongest measures against Israel ever adopted by an American president. Even though other American leaders have been concerned about the implications of Israel's actions for U.S. security objectives, they have been unwilling to impose punitive sanctions against Israel to safeguard those interests, thus challenging the assumption that foreign policy is primarily concerned with protecting national interests. Eisenhower, who believed in an evenhanded approach to the Arab-Israeli conflict, briefly imposed sanctions against Israel in 1953, when it ignored an order from the head of the UN Truce Team to terminate work on a hydroelectric plant in the Israeli-Syrian demilitarized zone. Syria opposed the project because it would have diverted water from the Jordan River to Israel. U.S. Secretary of State John Foster Dulles suspended American economic assistance to Israel until it abandoned the project. Eight days later, Israel complied and aid was restored.[17]

Similarly, when Israel, Britain, and France invaded Egypt in 1956, to neutralize the *Fedayeen* who had been attacking Israel, to overthrow Egypt's President Gamal Abdul Nasser, and to prevent the closure of the Suez Canal, Eisenhower opposed the allies' actions, partly because they undermined American efforts to keep the Soviets out of the Middle East. The United States supported a UN resolution that called on Israel, Britain, and France to withdraw their forces from Egypt, and Eisenhower publicly condemned the invasion, thereby humiliating Britain and France and disabusing them of their pretensions to great power status. Whereas Britain and France complied with American and UN demands, Israel refused. However, five months after the invasion, Eisenhower forced the Israeli government to obey the UN resolution by threatening to irreversibly terminate all American assistance to Israel.[18]

Unwilling to confront Israel, and determined to demonstrate their commitment to their ally and friend, subsequent American leaders abandoned Eisenhower's efforts to pursue an evenhanded and objective approach to the Middle East conflict and induce Israel to comply with the rule of law established by the international community. European support of the Arabs following the 1967 war, as well as increased terrorist attacks on Israeli and American citizens by some Palestinian groups, reinforced America's tendency to overlook most of Israel's violations of international law and strengthened relations between the two countries. With a few exceptions, among them Jimmy Carter's pressures on Prime Minister Menachem Begin, between 1967 and 1991 the United States avoided publicly doing or saying anything that might have been construed as a major departure from its commitment to Israel. For example, when the U.S. government concluded in 1991 that Israel had violated the Convention for the Limitation of the Spread of Missile Technology—adopted by the United States and other nations in 1987—by sharing ballistic missile technology with South Africa, President Bush waived congressionally mandated sanctions against Israel in exchange for its pledge to stop violating the law.[19]

Following the 1967 Arab-Israeli war, in which Israel captured Arab territory, including the West Bank and Gaza, Britain was responsible for drawing up UN Resolution 242, which passed unanimously and became a milestone in the history of the broader Arab-Israeli conflict. Resolution 242 called upon Israel to withdraw its armed forces from territories occupied during the war, and reiterated the view that all states in the region had a responsibility to respect and acknowledge the sovereignty, territorial integrity, and political independence of every state in the area and their right to live in peace within secure and recognized boundaries free from threats or acts of force.[20] Despite its approval of UN Resolution 242, the United States refused to take decisive action to obtain Israel's withdrawal from the Occupied Territories. This was due in part to the Arabs' failure to simultaneously comply with their obligations under Resolution 242, as well as to persistent threats to Israel's security. When Prime Minister Menachem Begin defied Resolution 242 by declaring Jerusalem Israel's eternal capital, annexing the Golan Heights, and expanding Israeli settlements in the West Bank and Gaza, the United States issued diplomatic protests but failed to impose punitive measures against its ally.

Concerned about deteriorating security conditions along its border with Lebanon, Israel ignored the UN and international law, and decided to invade Lebanon in mid-1982. Palestinian factions had attacked settlements in the northern part of Israel, and the Israeli government bombed the PLO's headquarters in a heavily populated area of Beirut. Violence was escalated by both the Palestinians and the Israelis. The attempted assassination of the Israeli ambassador to Britain by a Palestinian group in London on June 3 1982 was used by Israel to justify a large-scale invasion of Lebanon on June 6 1982. Israeli forces overran or bypassed positions controlled by the UN Interim Force in Lebanon (UNIFIL), surrounded Beirut, and bombed densely populated areas. Despite assurances to President Ronald Reagan from Begin that Beirut would not be invaded, and despite UN Security Council demands for an immediate end to military activities, the immediate and unconditional withdrawal of Israeli forces from Lebanon, and respect for the rights of Lebanese and Palestinian civilians in accordance with internationally recognized rules of war, the Israeli army destroyed much of West Beirut and killed many civilians.[21] In an area of Beirut controlled by the Israelis, more than 1,400 Palestinian and Lebanese Muslims were killed in the Sabra and Shatila refugee camps by Phalangist troops allied with the Israelis. The United States and the international community condemned the massacres as well as Israel's invasion of Lebanon. The humanitarian aspect of U.S. culture prevented many Americans from ignoring Israel's actions.

In America's view, Israel's actions were detrimental to U.S. interests. The invasion was perceived as damaging U.S. credibility because it occurred despite Israeli assurances that it would not take place. Israel's military activities were seen as contributing to regional instability. Furthermore, there was the political problem of Israel's occupation of an Arab capital. But the United States, although opposing the invasion and taking the unusual step of supporting UN resolutions condemning it, preferred to convey its concerns privately, believing that "an on-going and serious negotiating process" was the most effective approach to the problem.[22] In sharp contrast to America's response to Turkey's invasion of Cyprus eight years earlier, when the U.S. government suspended all military assistance to Turkey, American military aid to Israel was unaffected by the Israeli invasion of Lebanon and occupation of the southern part of that country. Some American leaders even attempted to portray the destruction of Beirut as a humanitarian venture. Charles Wilson, U.S. Representative from Texas, declared after visiting Lebanon that: "As far as the Lebanese communities are concerned, the Israelis are furnishing health services, water, and everything they can to make life more livable for the inhabitants. I do not know of a single case of abuse. The Israelis' biggest problem is keeping the soldiers from smuggling $4 scotch across the line when they go back, because there are no taxes in Lebanon."[23]

In an attempt to consolidate the Arab alliance against Iraq following Hussein's invasion and occupation of Kuwait, the United States adopted a relatively evenhanded approach to the Palestinian-Israeli problem and endorsed UN resolutions that strongly condemned certain Israeli activities. Bush sought to separate the Arab-Israeli dispute from the specific problem in Kuwait by persuading Israel to refrain from involving itself in the Gulf crisis. However, when violence erupted at the Al Aqsa Mosque in the Old City of Jerusalem, the third-holiest shrine in the Islamic world, during which twenty-one Palestinians were killed and more than 150 wounded by Israeli police, Saudi officials expressed concern about the implications of the violence for the cohesiveness of the international coalition against Iraq, and called Israel's action "a grave offense for millions of Muslims."[24] Cultural considerations and military objectives became inseparable.

Having mobilized international opposition against Iraq, and having obtained more than twelve UN Security Council

resolutions to legitimize using force to compel Hussein to withdraw immediately and unconditionally from Kuwait, the United
States condemned Israel's actions, to demonstrate its sensitivity
to Arab culture and religion, and, partly, to avoid being accused
of applying double standards, which seem to accompany the
clash of distant cultures. But Washington also sought to diminish the negative consequences to Israel of the Jerusalem violence. To accomplish its objectives, the United States took the
unusual step of drafting a resolution that condemned Israel, a
development that caused concern even among liberal Jewish
groups such as Americans for Peace Now. Yet the general view
within the Bush administration was that the United States had
had to act, to prevent Hussein from rallying Arab public opinion
behind him and diverting attention from his own aggression.
Cultural ties had clashed with U.S. military objectives.
However, as one U.S. official stated, "sure, it may cause the
Israelis some grief, but they have as much interest as us in seeing this thing put back in the bottle as quickly as possible."[25] In
this case, U.S. national interests took precedence over cultural
links with Israel.

UN Resolution 672, which was passed unanimously by the
Security Council, expressed alarm at the violence, condemned
the acts of violence committed by the Israeli security forces,
"called upon Israel, as the Occupying Power, to abide scrupu-
lously by its legal obligations and responsibilities under the
Fourth Geneva Convention, which is applicable to all the territories occupied by Israel since 1967," and requested the UN
Secretary General to submit a report to the Security Council on
the violence in Jerusalem.[26] But the United States' Permanent
Representative to the UN, Thomas R. Pickering, emphasized
that the Secretary General's mission was confined to investigating the circumstances that led to the specific incident addressed
by the resolution and that the Secretary General was not em-
powered to deal with any other issues. As Pickering put it,
"most obviously and certainly, this resolution makes clear it
does not address in any way the status of the Middle East peace
process, nor does it change in any way the role of the United
Nations in that regard."[27] Even as it championed UN involvement in the Persian Gulf crisis, the United States downplayed
the role of the UN in the Occupied Territories. This strong sup-

port of Israel could not be explained by Cold War politics, because the Cold War was over. Cultural bonds between the United States and Israel help to explain America's policy.

Asserting that the UN Security Council's resolution was unjustified, the Israeli government refused to receive the delegation of the UN Secretary General or to cooperate with the UN. Many Israeli officials perceived the UN mission to Israel as a UN attempt to demonstrate that Jerusalem was part of the Occupied Territories and to involve itself in the Arab-Israeli conflict.[28] Instead of accepting the UN mission, the Israeli government appointed its own commission to investigate the violence at Al Aqsa Mosque. The commission concluded that "the Temple Mount police, who were attacked by wild masses, were in danger of losing their lives. The police feared for their lives and the lives of the many worshipers at the Western Wall during the holiday prayers."[29] Although these findings may have been valid, the United States and other Security Council members believed that the UN should have been allowed to conduct its own investigation. Consequently, they passed a resolution that expressed alarm at Israel's rejection of Resolution 672 and its refusal to accept the UN mission. Israel was urged to reconsider its decision and to comply with the resolution.[30]

Israel's Violations of Human Rights in the Occupied Territories

Cyclical cruelty on both sides in the West Bank and Gaza, Israel's general disregard for international public opinion and its emphasis on military aspects of security, and Palestinian violence against both Israelis and other Palestinians helped to perpetuate human rights abuses in the Occupied Territories. While some pro-Israel analysts perceive any criticism of Israel's actions as an attempt to demonize that country, U.S. State Department reports, and other objective sources, indicate that the Israeli government and armed forces were responsible for a wide range of human rights abuses against Palestinian civilians.

America's reluctance to pressure Israel to observe human rights was attributable in part to its awareness of the violent nature of Middle East societies and of Arab hostility toward Israel. American policy is shaped partly by the perception of Israel as a democratic state forced to do unpleasant things to ensure its survival. Furthermore, the American public's favorable image of Israeli society, and its general view of Palestinians as terrorists and troublemakers, buttressed the argument that the Palestinians themselves were largely responsible for their treatment by the Israeli armed forces.

Believing that democratic societies are inherently peaceful, just, and fair, Americans are inclined to view Israel's behavior as self-correcting. However, Tom Farer emphasizes that "democracies can be as cruel as other forms of government in their treatment of those who stand beyond the racial, cultural, religious, or geographical boundaries defined by dominant groups. Where the alien is also seen as a material threat, the likelihood of atrocity expands."[31] In other words, cultural distance was a major factor in motivating the Israeli government to adopt harsh policies against the Palestinians. Cultural similarities between the United States and Israel influenced the former to overlook many of the latter's violations of human rights.

It appears that those Americans who are most concerned about the exclusion of groups domestically and human rights violations abroad are most empathetic toward the Palestinians. This points to the inconsistencies inherent in the complexity of American culture. President Carter symbolized that aspect of the culture that stresses fairness and equality. He stated: "Since I had made our nation's commitment to human rights a central tenet of our foreign policy, it was impossible for me to ignore the very serious problems on the West Bank. The continued deprivation of Palestinian rights was...contrary to the basic moral and ethical principles of both our countries."[32] Drawing upon the humanitarian component of American society, Carter was able to pursue foreign policies that were sensitive to the Palestinians' plight.

In the State Department's *Country Reports on Human Rights Practices*, prepared for Congress, Israel's violations of fundamental human rights have been carefully documented. For example, in the report published in 1991, the U.S. government stated that "Israel is not recognized internationally to have sovereignty over any of the occupied lands, but has asserted sovereignty over and annexed East Jerusalem." It also pointed out that "the United States considers Israel's occupation to be governed by the Hague Regulations of 1907 and the 1949 Fourth Geneva Convention on the Protection of Civilian Persons in Time of War. Israel does not consider the Convention applicable, but states that it observes its humanitarian provisions."[33] The U.S. government documented human rights abuses by the Israeli Civil Administration (CIVAD), which reports to the Minister of Defense. Abuses included measures imposed by CIVAD, such as restraints on nonviolent political activity and expression, the closure of schools and universities, travel bans and restrictions, deportations, administrative detentions, restrictions on family reunification, and discriminatory policies or practices affecting land, resource use, and trade and commerce.

Israel's Defense Forces (IDF) responded to the Palestinian uprising with what was widely viewed as excessive and unnecessary force. The Israeli government adopted a policy that allowed soldiers to shoot fleeing persons if there were "reasonable" grounds to suspect them of being involved in terrorism or a serious felony, or if they failed to stop when ordered to do so, or when shots were fired in the air. As the violence intensified on both sides, security forces were given greater discretionary power. According to the U.S. State Department, many Palestinians were killed because they behaved "suspiciously." Others were shot by undercover soldiers without warning. The increased use of weapons by Palestinians and growing violence among them also exacerbated the problems in the Occupied Territories. Many Palestinians were shot in the head and upper body by soldiers. Tear gas was used in houses and enclosed spaces, with deadly consequences. In some cases, several family members were killed on the same day.[34]

Amnesty International, the U.S. State Department, and various human rights groups documented reports of torture by the IDF. Although torture is forbidden by Israeli law, there were numerous reports of harsh and demeaning treatment of prisoners, which included sleep deprivation, electric shock, hooding, cold showers, incarceration in unclean and physically confining spaces, enforced standing in one position for prolonged periods, and slaps and severe beatings.[35] In early 1992, human rights groups alleged that Mustafa Akawi, a Palestinian detainee, had been tortured to death during interrogation. Two American physicians who participated in the autopsy concluded that the prisoner's death had been induced by conditions of incarceration, including being forced to stand handcuffed with a hood over his head in the cold and the lack of adequate medical care. Robert Kirchner, Chicago's chief medical examiner, asserted that "if we had a similar case in this country, this kind of death would be classified as a homicide."[36] Obtaining confessions from detainees by applying "moderate pressure" during interrogation was approved by the Israeli government in 1987.

Having placed the West Bank and Gaza under military rule, the Israeli government imposed a legal system on a people who had their own laws, customs, and civilization. To force Palestinians to comply, the Israelis issued approximately two hundred military orders between 1967 and 1971. The military was allowed to regulate all transactions of immovable property and the use of water and natural resources, and to confiscate Palestinian property, grant travel permits and licenses to practice various professions, and to control the movement of the population by issuing identity cards.[37] Military judges and district military commanders had virtually unlimited power to arrest and detain Palestinians who had committed or were suspected of committing an offense under the security regulations. The evidence used to detain a person was not presented in open court, and detainees and their attorneys did not have access to it. Rulings by military judges could be reviewed by the High Court, which was permitted to see the secret evidence. Military authorities were allowed to enter private Palestinian homes and institutions without a warrant. Forced entries were regularly used in IDF operations, and were sometimes accompanied by beatings and destruction of property. The U.S. State Department also asserted that Israeli authorities had transferred detainees and prisoners out of the Occupied Territories to detention facilities in Israel. In the view of the United States, such transfers "contravene Article 76 of the Fourth Geneva Convention."[38] But Washington did not take any meaningful action to persuade Israel to observe the law.

Unlike any other democratic society, Israel demolished the homes of individuals suspected of committing crimes prior to trying the suspects. Security forces had the right under Israeli law to demolish or seal a suspect's home, whether he or she was the owner or only a tenant. Any house the Israeli forces determined to be connected in any way to violations of security regulations could be sealed or destroyed. Owners of such properties were not permitted to rebuild. Between 1988 and early 1991, at least 336 houses were demolished and more than 200 sealed shut. In one case, Munzer Abdallah, a Palestinian, hit a soldier with his car and another soldier shot him eight times, killing him. Abdallah had never been arrested, and it was widely believed that the collision had been an accident. Nevertheless, Israeli authorities punished the dead man by demolishing his house, thereby depriving his wife and six children of their home.[39] Demolitions and sealings, which were enforced only against Arab residents of the Occupied Territories, were viewed by the United States as a violation of the Fourth Geneva Convention, and Washington "urged the Israeli government to end the practice."[40] Given the centrality of the rule of law in American culture, some U.S. policymakers, although sympathetic to Israel, could not ignore obvious violations of international law.

Even before the Gulf crisis, the United States had considered supporting a proposal to send UN observers to the Occupied Territories to monitor the treatment of Palestinians by Israeli security forces. The escalating violence seemed to have engendered a shift in Washington's position. That component of American culture that favors the victim was ascending. After blocking for a month a UN resolution designed to protect Palestinians from Israel's violations of the Geneva Convention, the United States voted with other UN Security Council members to pass Resolution 681 in December 1990. Israel rejected the resolution, and the United States made no serious effort to enforce it, thus reinforcing the view that cultural similarities between Israel and America were responsible for the application of "double standards."[41]

Ignoring UN Resolution 194 of 1948, which gave Palestinian refugees the right to return to their homes, Israel implemented laws that effectively denied Palestinians residency in the Occupied Territories. According to the U.S. State Department, Palestinians who obtained foreign citizenship were generally not allowed to return, and those who had resided outside the Territories for more than three years were seldom permitted to remain in the West Bank and Gaza. They were treated as tourists, and were sometimes denied entry entirely.[42] Israel's policy was based in part on the fear that a large-scale return of Palestinian refugees, estimated to number 2.6 million, would jeopardize the Jewish state's existence. But since 1948, the United States had supported the UN resolution, a position restated in 1992 by Margaret Tutwiler, spokesperson for the State Department.

Israel also engaged in the collective punishment of Palestinians by deporting them, a practice no other democratic state has adopted. Under Israel's deportation policy, Palestinians suspected of terrorist activities and other crimes under Israeli law were rounded up by security forces, blindfolded, and dumped into a neighboring state to be taken care of by their "Arab brethren." In addition to asserting that Israel's behavior was detrimental to the peace process, the United States viewed deportations as "a violation of Article 49 of the Fourth Geneva Convention which prohibits individual or mass forcible transfers regardless of their motive."[43] But Washington, prior to the Gulf War, remained largely passive. In early 1992, the United States supported a UN resolution condemning Israel's deportation of Palestinian civilians from the Occupied Territories. Security Council Resolution 726, passed unanimously, also reaffirmed the applicability of the Fourth Geneva Convention to all Palestinian territories occupied by Israel since 1967, including Jerusalem. It called on Israel to refrain from deporting Palestinians and to insure the safe and immediate return to the Occupied Territories of all those deported.[44] Israel not only failed to comply with the UN resolution but actually increased the number of deportations.

Following the murder of five Israeli servicemen in the Occupied Territories in late 1992, allegedly by members of fundamentalist Muslim groups known as Hamas and Islamic Jihad, the Israeli government, headed by Yitzhak Rabin—a former defense minister and the architect of the "iron fist policy" in the Occupied Territories—rounded up 415 Palestinians for deportation. They were arrested, bound, blindfolded, placed on buses, transported to Lebanon, and left in the freezing weather. Denied entry by Beirut into the area of Lebanon beyond Israel's self-declared security zone in the southern part of the country, the Palestinians attempted to return to Israeli-controlled territory. Military forces in the Israeli-controlled security zone fired mortars and machine-guns, wounding two Palestinians. Israeli civil-rights lawyers' appeals to Israel's High Court for the

Palestinians to be returned were denied. The United States believed that Prime Minister Rabin's decision to deport the Palestinians, the largest number since the 1967 war, endangered Middle East negotiations. To some extent, America's closer ties to the Gulf countries during Operation Desert Storm increased Washington's sensitivity to Arab concerns. Furthermore, the end of the Cold War diminished the perceived importance of Israel as an essential ally. Despite its failure to persuade the UN Security Council to also condemn the Palestinian terrorists who killed the Israelis, the United States voted for a resolution, which passed unanimously, that denounced the deportations and demanded that Israel return the Palestinians to their homes.[45] But the UN vote was not followed by concrete actions to persuade Israel to comply with the resolution.

Israeli Settlements in the Occupied Territories

Since 1971, the Israeli government had encouraged Jews to settle in the Occupied Territories, a policy that was viewed by many as a direct violation of international law. To accommodate the influx of Israeli citizens into the West Bank and Gaza, the Israeli government confiscated large amounts of Palestinian land. President Carter and other American officials were aware of the methods employed by Israel to acquire Palestinian property. In some cases the land was purchased. However, the Israelis seized most of the land for what they called "security purposes." The government also claimed state control of areas formerly held by Jordan, used carefully selected ancient laws to establish ownership of Palestinian land, and seized land that was not cultivated or specifically registered as owned by Palestinians. Carter pointed out that to ensure that no land was farmed, the government implemented a policy in 1983 that prohibited, under penalty of imprisonment, any agricultural activities in those areas by Palestinians.[46] The fundamental right to own private property, which is embedded in America's culture and enshrined in its constitutional framework, was routinely disregarded by the Israeli government in the Occupied Territories. Carter represented American cultural values when he publicly disagreed with Israel's seizure of Palestinian property. Many Palestinians have been evicted from their homes in the Old City of Jerusalem and the buildings, owned in many cases by Palestinians living in the United States and other countries, have been confiscated by Israeli authorities.[47]

New Zionists and officials in the Likud government, among others, embraced the view that the Israeli settlements were part of the process of Jewish redemption of their biblical homeland, and that Palestinians had no claim to any of the land. As economic conditions deteriorated in Israel, and as the Soviet Union allowed Jews to emigrate, the Israeli government faced housing shortages in Israel, a development that strengthened the security and religious arguments for expanding Jewish settlements in the Occupied Territories. By 1992, more than 230,000 Jews had moved to the West Bank and Gaza, induced to leave Israel by generous government subsidies.[48] Settlers who constructed their own homes received free land, and half the amount of their mortgages was given to them, interest-free. According to a British Broadcasting Corporation (BBC) report, Israelis were granted building permits immediately. Palestinians, by contrast, had to wait approximately ten years to obtain building permits, and Palestinian contractors were required to install roads, street lights, water, and the rest of the infrastructure for the housing development.

A comparatively more confrontational approach, influenced in part by the end of the Cold War and the growing perception of Israel's diminished importance as an ally, was adopted by the Bush administration. Addressing AIPAC in May 1989, Secretary of State James Baker told a surprised audience: "For Israel, now is the time to lay aside, once and for all, the unrealistic vision of a greater Israel. Forswear annexation. Stop settlement activity. Reach out to the Palestinians as neighbors who deserve political rights."[49] But the Israeli government continued to build settlements in the Occupied Territories, even as Baker was attempting to take advantage of the opportunity created by the Gulf crisis for a negotiated end to the Arab-Israeli conflict. Baker was visibly disturbed when the Israeli government approved the establishment of a new settlement on the West Bank during one of his visits to Israel.

Operating in a radically altered strategic international environment, symbolized by the end of the Cold War, the demise of the Soviet Union, and new partnerships with several Arab States, the United States increased its opposition to Israeli settlements. Israel's request for $10 billion in loan guarantees from the United States to help settle Soviet Jewish immigrants was delayed by Congress in accordance with the Bush administration's recommendation. While regarding the immigration of Soviet Jews as an important humanitarian issue, Bush linked granting the loan guarantees to a freeze of Israeli settlements. For the first time since Eisenhower's administration, the United States had decided to withhold economic assistance to pressure Israel to change its policies. Israel would be allowed to complete only those housing units in the Occupied Territories already under construction. New housing starts would not be allowed, and the United States would deduct from the loan guarantees one dollar for every dollar Israel spent to complete the housing units already under construction.[50] Washington's new approach was motivated in part by growing American Jewish concerns about the hardline policies of the conservative Likud government. As discussed, many American Jews favored exchanging land for peace, a view that was at odds with Israel's settlements policy.

Given the general agreement among Americans that more attention should be paid to domestic issues, there was little public support for granting Israel $10 billion in loan guarantees without attaching certain conditions. Furthermore, many American Jews saw settlements as obstacles to peace. Few members of Congress favored assisting Israel's efforts to undermine American interests by expanding settlements in the Occupied Territories. Between 1967 and 1992, Israel received roughly $77 billion from America, approximately $16,500 for every man, woman, and child in Israel per year. During that time, America was willing to allow Israel to work at cross-purposes with some U.S. objectives in the Middle East. Now Israel's policies were seen by Baker and others as the greatest obstacle to peace.[51] The influence of cultural ties had been modified by changing American perceptions of U.S. national interests.

Negotiating With Friends

Although American-Israeli relations have been characterized by periodic rhetorical turbulence, Washington has consistently emphasized its support for a negotiated settlement of the broader Arab-Israeli conflict. Referring to the Arab-Israeli conflict, President Gerald Ford said: "There will be no imposed solutions, but agreements whose terms are hammered out between the parties. There will be no one-sided concessions, but a balanced quid pro quo in exchange for everything given up. We will proceed as we have in the closest, constant consultation with Israel before, during, and after any negotiations."[52] U.S. policy toward Israel reflects the American cultural tendency to reason with, show respect for, and be patient with those who are perceived to be within the same cultural circle.

Instead of adopting a confrontational approach and dismissing negotiations as ineffective, the United States emphasized that negotiation was the only workable method. American presidents, whether they saw Israel as a Cold War ally or viewed it through the prism of culture and religion, endorsed this position. However, despite its constant support for Israel, America also considered itself to be an honest broker for Palestinians, partly because of security and economic ties between the United States and several Arab countries. President Reagan, like many other policymakers, stated that "no other nation is more qualified than America to support the Palestinian people's right to self-determination. This is a stand that is consistent with the American heritage and values. This country was founded on the principle that all men are equal and were created by God Almighty to live in freedom and dignity."[53] These cultural beliefs undoubtedly contributed to some of the ambiguities and contradictions in America's policy toward the Palestinian-Israeli conflict.

In addition to the cultural affinity between the United States and Israel, other considerations played a role in America's decision to pursue a negotiated settlement. The West European allies, particularly after the 1967 war, developed closer economic and political links with the Arab States, and were more critical of Israel's refusal to make the compromises necessary for a peaceful resolution of its dispute with the Palestinians. The Europeans also positioned themselves to be able to moderate PLO demands. Concerned about maintaining a cohesive Western alliance against Soviet expansionism, Washington was pressured to assume greater responsibility for lessening tensions in the Middle East.

Inter-Arab conflicts, rivalries, and tensions enabled America to patiently encourage a negotiated settlement, and to avoid seriously pressuring Israel to make concessions to solve the problem. Moreover, after the 1973 war, President Anwar Sadat of Egypt realized that cooperation with the United States and negotiations with Israel provided the best opportunity for him to relieve Egyptians' suffering by addressing domestic social and economic problems in an environment free from war or the threat of war with Israel. Despite divergent views within the Arab world on how to deal with the Palestinian-Israeli conflict, most Arab leaders and the PLO realized that a negotiated solution was the only viable option.

During the Cold War, one of America's principal objectives was to prevent the Arab-Israeli conflict from involving the superpowers in a direct confrontation in the Middle East. The Soviet Union's alliance with Egypt, Syria, and Iraq posed a threat to Israel's security specifically and world peace in general. Arab dependence on Soviet support was perceived as a step toward excessive Soviet influence in the region. Communist expansionism also exacerbated problems many of America's Arab friends had with radical groups. The general view in Washington, articulated by President Nixon, was that "if the Arab-Israeli conflict cannot be finally resolved, at least its scope must be contained and the direct engagement of the major powers limited."[54] The demise of communism, increased cooperation between Russia and the United States, and developments during the Gulf War in 1991 helped to revitalize the search for a negotiated end to the Palestinian-Israeli conflict, and facilitated the signing of a peace agreement between Israel and the PLO in September 1993.

Religious factors also contributed to America's embrace of negotiations. Commitment to religious freedom, deeply embedded in American culture and enshrined in the U.S. Constitution, necessitated the view that there must be adequate recognition of the special interests of the three great religions in the Holy Places of Jerusalem. Judaism and Christianity, fountainheads of America's values, institutions, and self-definition, compete with Islam for access to and preservation of Jerusalem. Shortly after the Israelis captured East Jerusalem in 1967, President Johnson reiterated its importance to the three religions:

"Before any unilateral action is taken on the status of Jerusalem there will be appropriate consultation with religious leaders and others who are deeply concerned."[55] The United States believed that it had a moral imperative to secure a negotiated settlement to a religious dispute that unleashed such violent passions. But this belief was not shared by all Americans. For the religious right, a negotiated resolution of the broader Arab-Israeli conflict in general, and of the status of Jerusalem in particular, would only postpone the "triumph of good over evil" in the inevitable battle of Armageddon.

Yet America's commitment to Israel's military superiority in the region became a serious impediment to a negotiated solution. The American assumption, consistent with dominant U.S. cultural beliefs, was that military might guaranteed real security and peace. Threats to Israel from surrounding Arab states and terrorist organizations would decline, in the view of many American policymakers, only when Israel and the United States demonstrated their determination to "stand together as solid as a rock."[56] Israel's military might would convince the Arabs that the only way to obtain peace and justice was through direct negotiations with Israel. But America's role in militarizing the Middle East by selling sophisticated weapons to its Arab allies undermined its own objective of achieving peace in the region.

In his major policy statement on the Middle East shortly after Israel invaded Lebanon, President Reagan proclaimed that "in the words of the Scripture, the time has come to follow after the things which make for peace."[57] Reagan believed that the war in Lebanon had shown that the PLO's military defeat had not diminished the Palestinians' yearning for a solution to their claims, and that "while Israel's military successes in Lebanon have demonstrated that its armed forces are second to none in the region, they alone cannot bring just and lasting peace to Israel and her neighbors."[58] Reagan called upon Israel, the Palestinians, and the Arab countries to compromise and to recognize the interdependence of their objectives. The Palestinians' aspirations were seen as inextricably bound to their recognition of Israel's right to a secure future.

Both Nixon and Carter had demonstrated that progress toward peace could occur only when American presidents or their secretaries of state were directly involved in negotiation efforts. Arabs and Israelis viewed the personal involvement of

America's leaders as an indication of America's commitment to resolve the conflict. Henry Kissinger, Nixon's secretary of state, conducted "shuttle diplomacy" between Israel and the Arab countries to end the 1973 war and establish the foundation upon which Carter constructed the Camp David Peace Accords. Although Carter realized that his direct participation carried high political risks in the United States, he became personally involved because, as he put it: "In conscience there is really no choice for me. We simply must continue to move away from war and stalemate to peace and to progress for the people of Israel and for the people of Egypt."[59] Carter's own personal commitment to negotiation as a method of resolving conflicts enabled him to draw on that component of American culture which supports nonviolent solutions to problems.

In sharp contrast to the American approach that had failed to bring peace to the Middle East, Carter exemplified how to make negotiations effective. Instead of reiterating the wrongs of the past, he focused on the future. Carter understood that small, symbolic gestures could be extremely important in helping Israel and Egypt reach an agreement. Toward the end of the Camp David meeting between Sadat and Begin, there appeared to be little hope for a negotiated settlement. As they prepared to leave Camp David, Begin sent Carter some photographs of the three leaders and asked him to sign them for his grandchildren. Carter asked his secretary to find out the names of Begin's grandchildren, and wrote each name on a photograph and signed it. Instead of sending the photographs to Begin, he delivered them himself. Later, Carter recalled how focusing on the future made the Camp David meetings successful: "And we stood there on the porch of one of those little cabins at Camp David, and he began to go through the photographs and told me about each one of his grandchildren. And I told him about my grandchildren, too. And we began to talk about the future and the fact that what we did at Camp David was not just to be looked upon as a political achievement that might bring accolades or congratulations on us. It was not just an investment in peace for our own generation; it was an investment in the future."[60]

Instead of stressing differences between Israelis and Egyptians, Carter emphasized similarities and common interests, and challenged both sides to face the problems together and avoid confronting each other. By so doing, Carter was embracing an important American cultural attitude. While Carter recognized that Jews, Muslims, and Christians held different beliefs, he noted that they worshiped the same God and that the message of Providence has always been the same. Emphasizing common beliefs, Carter quoted the Holy Koran, the Old Testament, and the New Testament to show how cultural and religious values supported peace. Quoting the Koran, Carter said: "If thine adversary incline towards peace, do thou also incline towards peace and trust in God." He quoted the Old Testament passage that admonished Jews to "depart from evil and do good; seek peace, and pursue it." He ended with the New Testament's Sermon on the Mount: "Blessed are the peacemakers, for they shall be called the children of God."[61] While not ignoring the security concerns of Israelis and Egyptians, Carter focused on those fundamental values and beliefs upon which many Americans believe that concepts such as security and national interests are ultimately based. The fact that Carter also represented American cultural values highlights the diversity and inconsistency within U.S. culture.

Carter's close relationships with African-Americans, and his involvement in efforts to end desegregation in Georgia and elsewhere in the American South, arguably contributed to his willingness to try to understand people who were perceived to be different and beyond America's dominant cultural circle. Even as Carter appeared to be challenging American culture, he actually embodied important aspects of it. Before meeting Sadat, Carter made a concerted effort to learn as much as possible about him and about Egypt. Carter tried to understand Sadat's fears and perceived choices, as well as Egypt's relations with other Arab countries, its economic problems, its perceptions of threats from Israel, Libya, and Soviet-influenced Ethiopia, and its hopes for the future. He also realized that many Arab leaders, despite their public statements against negotiations with Israel, were privately supportive of a peaceful resolution of the conflict.[62]

Carter also reached out to the American Jewish community, to deal with its criticisms of his peace initiatives and his highly publicized and friendly meetings with Arab leaders. In other words, he understood the importance of cultural links in the formulation and implementation of U.S. foreign policy. He turned to Senator Hubert Humphrey, who was a trusted friend of Israel and knowledgeable about the Arab-Israeli problem, for advice and support. He patiently explained his policies to congressional as well as Jewish leaders, thereby gaining their understanding, if not support, for his diplomatic efforts.[63] And Carter demonstrated his empathy for the Jewish people by acknowledging their suffering, both historically and from more recent wars with the Arabs. But instead of becoming a prisoner of the past, Carter focused on creating a future free of war between Jews and Arabs.

However, America's failure to seriously address Palestinian concerns became a major obstacle to a negotiated settlement. Washington's rhetorical empathy for Palestinians was not accompanied by significant actions that improved their situation, partly because of Kissinger's pledge to Israel that the United States would not communicate directly with the PLO— regarded by many Palestinians as their representative—until it recognized Israel's right to exist and renounced terrorism. The Palestinians' plight, especially in the aftermath of the 1967 war, aroused America's humanitarian instincts. All U.S. presidents expressed their concern for the Palestinian refugees displaced by war and exposed to the cold weather in camps in neighboring countries. Johnson saw their problem as "a symbol of a wrong that must be made right before 20 years of war can end."[64] In the same vein, Nixon contended that no lasting settlement could be achieved without addressing "the legitimate" aspirations of the Palestinian people. Asserting that they have been the victims of conditions that command sympathy, Nixon believed that fruitful lives for Palestinians and their children, and a just settlement of their claims, were essential prerequisites for peace in the Middle East.[65]

But without active Palestinian participation in the peace process, it was virtually impossible to achieve a negotiated settlement of the Palestinian-Israeli dispute. Fearing that direct contact with Palestinians would imply an acknowledgement of their existence as an independent people with legitimate claims to their own homeland, Israel pressured the United States to deal with the Palestinians only as part of the Jordanian delegation. Nevertheless, covert contacts between the PLO and the

United States occurred even after UN Ambassador Andrew Young had resigned in 1979 due to controversy concerning his discussions with a PLO official. Having chosen negotiation as the best way to resolve the dispute, the United States had essentially allowed Israel to sabotage the peace process, by pledging not to communicate with a major participant in the conflict.

Due largely to European diplomacy and the willingness of many Jewish-Americans to reach out to Yasir Arafat, the PLO's chairman, the PLO issued a statement in late 1988 in which it accepted UN Security Council Resolutions 242 and 338, recognized Israel's right to exist, and renounced terrorism. Without the support of American Jews for the peace process, negotiations between the PLO and Israel would undoubtedly have been more difficult to achieve. The Reagan administration responded by authorizing the State Department to enter into substantive dialogue with PLO representatives.[66] Despite setbacks in communications between the PLO and the United States in early 1990, stemming from an attempted terrorist attack on Israel by the Palestine Liberation Front, the Palestinians were now recognized by Washington as legitimate participants in the peace process. Greater American understanding of the Palestinians' plight, as well as the PLO's willingness to renounce terrorism, recognize Israel's right to exist, and negotiate, increased American empathy for Palestinians. Israel, however, refused to acknowledge the Palestinians' right to choose their own representatives, and would not negotiate directly with the PLO.

War Brings Peace

After launching the most intensive bombing campaign in history against Iraq, the Bush administration seemed convinced that out of devastation a new world order would emerge, one in which nations might settle their disagreements peacefully. Although it was obvious that the United States itself had failed to negotiate a nonviolent end to Iraq's occupation of Kuwait, the dominant view in Washington was that the Gulf War would facilitate the negotiated settlement of the Palestinian-Israeli conflict. Whether violence on that scale was necessary to regenerate the Middle East peace process is debatable. Could the Bush administration have accomplished both Iraq's with-drawal from Kuwait and Israel's withdrawal from the Occupied Territories simultaneously? Perhaps not. But Bush never seri-ously tried to achieve that objective. Bush believed that a new opportunity had been created for negotiations to succeed. America's strengthened credibility in the Middle East would en-able Baker to bring the Arabs and Israelis to the table to re-solve their differences.[67]

Many Arab and European countries, especially those which were members of the coalition against Hussein, believed that the United States should have pressured Israel to observe various UN resolutions. Leaders such as King Hassan of Morocco, François Mitterrand of France, Hafez al-Assad of Syria, and Britain's Foreign Secretary Douglas Hurd asserted that there was a moral linkage between Hussein's occupation of Kuwait and Israel's occupation of Arab territories. While dis-agreeing with Iraq's view that ending the crisis in the Gulf should be directly linked to resolving the Arab-Israeli dispute, these leaders felt that one should lead to the other. Hurd stat-ed, following a meeting in Cairo with Egyptian President Hosni Mubarak, that: "Once the aggressor is out of Kuwait, we will have to turn our minds—and vigorously—to finding a just solu-tion of the Palestinian-Israeli conflict."[68] Though the specific circumstances behind the two occupations were radically differ-ent, it became extremely difficult for the United States to mobi-lize international support to force Hussein to fully comply with all UN resolutions, and, simultaneously, to ignore Israel's viola-tions of numerous UN resolutions. Many Arabs and others had pointed out the double standards in American foreign policy, at-tributable in part to cultural factors.

The Bush administration appeared to be sensitive to accu-sations that it applied two different sets of rules to Iraq and Israel by using military force against the former and tolerating the latter's occupation of the West Bank, Gaza, and the Golan Heights. Further, given the radically altered international strategic environment, the argument that Israel was essential to America's security interests was challenged. With several Arab states working with the United States, conditions were ripe, as it were, for Bush to seize the moment and persuade Israel to pursue what it had always wanted, namely, negotiations with the Arab states. Baker initiated a new round of diplomacy, which eventually brought Israel and its neighbors together in Madrid in October 1991.

Washington had achieved a significant breakthrough. But Bush and Baker stressed that the United States could not impose peace. Only the parties themselves could achieve peace by doing the "hard, nitty-gritty work" required. However, the United States was "willing to do the hard, repetitive work that will clearly be involved if we're going to make progress on this very, very difficult problem."[69] Progress toward a negotiated settlement depended to a large extent on Baker's personal involvement and the United States' willingness to urge Israel to embrace the peace process. But Bush's determination to be re-elected influenced him to put Baker in charge of his presidential campaign, thereby contributing to a loss of momentum in the negotiations. Consequently, the United States played only a marginal role in the historic breakthrough in Norway that culminated in the signing of a peace agreement between Israel and the PLO. Although the United States had made a negotiated settlement on the Palestinian-Israeli conflict a centerpiece of its foreign policy, and had regarded itself as the only country that could bring Israelis and Palestinians together, the accord was facilitated by Norwegians.[70] America's policy of not talking directly to the PLO had undoubtedly undermined the United States' ability to be a peace broker. However, actual signing of the Israeli-PLO peace agreement occurred in Washington, thereby underscoring not only America's power in the post-Cold War world but also the confidence exhibited by both Israel and the PLO in the United States' commitment to a negotiated settlement fashioned primarily by Israel.[71] It also demonstrated America's ability to expand its cultural circle and to compromise. While dominant American cultural values had induced Washington to adopt a pro-Israel policy, other American values influenced Carter and others to try to understand Arab concerns, and to work with them to secure peace.

Chapter Six

Bosnia: Cultural Distance and U.S. Military Inaction

Whereas President Bush aggressively mobilized international and domestic support for military action to end Saddam Hussein's occupation of Kuwait, ethnic cleansing in Bosnia-Hercegovina was met with what has been widely regarded as a timid response, the result of indifference by the United States in particular and the West in general. While it might be argued that President Bush's action in the Gulf stands in sharp contrast to President Clinton's initial indecisiveness in world affairs, a closer analysis of America's policy toward Bosnia under both Bush and Clinton shows a significant degree of consistency between the two presidents' actions. It was Clinton, the presidential candidate, who urged Bush to take stronger action in Bosnia, advice which Clinton himself largely disregarded when he became President. U.S. policy consistently rejected any American military involvement in the Bosnian conflict. Having ruled out either placing American troops in Bosnia or conducting surgical air strikes, the United States seemed unwilling to negotiate or accept compromises that might have led to a relatively early diplomatic settlement but would have rewarded Serbian brutality. Principles that the United States had ardently proclaimed and forcefully implemented in the Gulf were essentially ignored in Bosnia only a few months later. Instead of mobilizing public support for greater U.S. involvement in Bosnia, American policymakers appealed to those American cultural values that favor nonintervention.

The Collision of Distant Cultures

Bosnia's lack of oil, Clinton's concentration on domestic problems, the resurgence of isolationist tendencies in America, bureaucratic infighting among the agencies responsible for national security policy, and the complex nature of the Bosnia conflict helped to explain U.S. reluctance to use military power. American cultural values, beliefs, and attitudes also played a significant role in determining U.S. perceptions of and response to the war. The cultural distance between Bosnia, especially its Muslim population, and the United States was a major determinant of American foreign policy.

For the majority of Americans, Bosnia in particular, and the Balkans generally, are geographically as well as culturally distant, a remote part of the world where few Americans have meaningful ties, or, about which they know much.[1] Despite their physical connection to Europe, the Balkans are culturally distant from the rest of the continent. George F. Kennan, a leading American diplomat and scholar who served as U.S. ambassador to Yugoslavia from 1961 to 1963, contends that Turkish conquests of the Balkans resulted in a leveling of all the nationalities there and preserved them all alike "in a condition of torpor, in a manner comparable to the action of a vast refrigerator," a situation he believes was perpetuated by communism.[2] Kennan states: "What we are up against is the sad fact that developments of those earlier ages . . . had the effect of thrusting into the southeastern reaches of the European continent a salient, non-European civilization that has continued to the present day to preserve many of it non-European characteristics."[3]

Prominent among these "non-European" qualities is a predilection for conflict, which makes the Balkans a perpetual

quagmire. To many Americans and Europeans, the Bosnian sit-
uation is typical of the culturally distant Third World. Yet the
Balkans undoubtedly remind some Americans of Europe's old
and bloody conflicts, from which their ancestors fled, and from
which the United States has long endeavored to isolate itself.
The tendency to perceive Bosnians as violent is reinforced by
the fact that a Bosnian Serb contributed to the outbreak of
World War I by assassinating Archduke Francis Ferdinand of
Austria-Hungary, in Sarajevo in 1914. Because many
Americans expect violent behavior from people whose cultures
are distant from their own, they are likely to regard the outbreak of widespread hostilities among those distant people as
unfortunate but essentially unavoidable, and beyond America's
ability to alleviate. William Pfaff argues that "the assumption
that atrocity is natural to the Balkans has rationalized the
United States' and the West's acquiescence in aggressive war
and their indirect collaboration in Yugoslavia's ethnic
cleansing."[4]

Relative cultural distance between the United States and
the principal factions in the Bosnian conflict has resulted in noticeable inconsistencies in U.S. policy. On the cultural scale,
Croatia has been closest to Western Europe and the United
States, Serbia in the middle, and Muslim-controlled Bosnia the
most distant. The Croats have been historically the most thor-
oughly integrated into European civilization, a consequence of
their domination by Austria-Hungary and Venice. Serbs have
been identified with Eastern Orthodox countries such as Greece
and Russia, and the Muslims, though European and Slavic,
have been regarded as remnants of the Ottoman civilization.
The cultural differences between Croatia and Bosnia are articulated by Robert D. Kaplan. The latter country is viewed as always "light years removed" from the former. Zagreb is
portrayed as "an urbane, ethnically uniform community on the
plain," whereas Bosnia is viewed as "a morass of ethnically
mixed villages in the mountains. Bosnia is rural, isolated, and
full of suspicions and hatreds."[5]

An analysis of news stories about the Bosnian conflict in
particular, and developments throughout the former Yugoslavia
generally, discloses that great emphasis was placed on the cultural proximity between the Croats and the West. Croats were
described as Catholic, Westernized, technologically advanced

and sophisticated, and practicing Western-style democracy. The Serbs, by contrast, were labeled as Eastern Orthodox, Byzantine, and "primitive remnants of the Ottoman Empire."[6] If the Serbs have been perceived as removed from European civilization, the Muslims have been depicted as existing outside the West's cultural circle.

Yugoslavia's leader, Marshal Josip Tito, helped reinforce the perception of his country as distant from the United States, not only through his communist ideology and practice but also because of his prominent role as founder of the Nonaligned Movement, composed of many former European colonies. Tito's association with Jawaharlal Nehru of India, Kwame Nkrumah of Ghana, and Gamal Abdel Nasser of Egypt strengthened the view that Yugoslavia was more closely connected to the Third World than to Europe, despite its significant ties to Germany, Greece, and the Soviet Union. Yugoslavia's need for hard currency and its desire to limit its dependence on Soviet oil supplies contributed to the development of close relations with countries like Iran, Iraq, Libya, Angola, and Algeria.[7] However, during the Cold War, Yugoslavia's independence from the Soviet bloc, and its adherence to nonalignment in international affairs, fostered a limited degree of interdependence between Washington and Belgrade.

Several of the principal architects of America's policy toward Bosnia had closer professional and personal connections with Serbia-Montenegro (Serbia) than with the rest of Yugoslavia. Secretary of State Lawrence Eagleburger, who was also the U.S. ambassador to Yugoslavia in the late 1970s, often emphasized that he represented a government that "historically has enjoyed a special relationship with the people of Serbia."[8] Belgrade was not only the site of diplomatic activity but also hosted many international conferences. Consequently, some prominent Americans developed closer relationships with the Serbians than with the Muslims. Eagleburger and Slobodan Milosevic, who later became the president of Serbia and the architect of ethnic cleansing, were social friends. According to Roy Gutman, both Eagleburger and Brent Scowcroft, Bush's National Security adviser, were on the board of Yugo America, the U.S. branch of the Serbian-based automobile manufacturer. Eagleburger and Scowcroft served as president and vice president, respectively, of Henry Kissinger Associates, a consulting

firm which received several Serbian State contracts.[9] Both men
spoke Serbo-Croatian. Cultural bonds between the United
States and Serbia were further consolidated by the limited emi-
gration of Serbs to America. For example, Milan Panic, a natu-
ralized United States citizen from California, who was born in
Serbia, was granted special permission by the Bush administration to serve as prime minister of Serbia-Montenegro.

In addition to political and ethnic considerations, religion,
a central component of American culture, is at the heart of the
Bosnian conflict and is widely believed to have a direct influence on U.S. policy. Croats, Serbs, and Muslims have all attempted to mobilize religious sentiment to achieve their
political and military objectives, and the lines of conflict basically coincide with religious boundaries. Despite their common
Slavic origins, the Croats are predominantly Roman Catholic,
the Serbs Eastern Orthodox Christians, and the Muslims belong primarily to the Sunni branch of Islam. From the Croats'
perspective, the Serbs and Muslims belong outside of Western
civilization.[10] Alliances with foreign countries, which helped to
exacerbate the Bosnian conflict and have created serious barriers to a negotiated settlement, reflect religion's power to shape
international relations. Whereas Eastern Orthodox Russians
and Greeks supported the Serbs, the Christian West was seen
as pro-Croat, and the Islamic world rallied around the Muslims.

Given the United States' unchallenged military power and
its military victory in Operation Desert Storm, many Muslims,
as well as leading American scholars and foreign policy experts
such as Samuel P. Huntington of Harvard University and
Richard Holbrooke, an assistant secretary of state in the Carter
administration and adviser to Democratic Presidential
Candidate Bill Clinton, have concluded that religious differences have helped to explain the largely passive Western policies toward Bosnia. Huntington observes that "relatively little
Western concern was expressed over Croatian attacks on
Muslims and participation in the dismemberment of Bosnia-
Hercegovina."[11] Similarly, Holbrooke asserted that "if the situation were reversed and the Christians and Jews were being
attacked in Bosnia, there would be a lot more (Western) concern."[12]

Serbian efforts to portray the conflict as an attempt by the
Bosnian Muslims to create an Islamic State in the heart of

Europe were relatively successful, partly because the dominant American culture predisposed many U.S. foreign policymakers and a large part of the general public to be apprehensive about Muslims. The emerging perception of Islam as a major threat to the United States in the post-Cold War period, and the widely held assumption that Islam is essentially inconsistent with democracy and other Western values, helped to shape America's Bosnian policy. Despite Assistant Secretary of State Edward P. Djerejian's statement that the United States government does not view Islam as the next 'ism' confronting the West or threatening world peace,[13] developments such as the bombing of the World Trade Center in New York in 1993 by Muslim extremists, and increased terrorist attacks against Israel and other pro-Western states by Islamic groups opposed to the peace process in the Middle East have rekindled American concerns about radical Islamic fundamentalism and given additional credibility to the Islamic conspiracy theory.[14]

Furthermore, Islamic support for the Bosnian Muslims seemed to confirm American suspicions. This assistance was in part a response to what many Islamists believed to be the West's lack of resolve and the application of a double standard in Bosnia. They had concluded from America's actions in the Persian Gulf that the West in general, and the United States in particular, was willing to intervene forcefully when Muslims were killing other Muslims in an area where the West had major interests, but were dismayed to find the West willing to remain militarily passive when Muslim Bosnians were being killed by Christian Serbs.[15] Iranian officials, as well as ordinary citizens, offered military assistance to Bosnia's Muslims, in violation of the UN arms embargo. The Doctors Syndicate and other Islamic organizations in Egypt sent medical supplies and health care practitioners to Bosnia, reflecting Egypt's religious ties with Yugoslavia's Muslims.[16] However, because the Islamic groups in Iran and Egypt which assisted Bosnian Muslims tended to be radical, and intolerant of Christians, their involvement in Bosnia seemed to confirm the view that Bosnia was part of the larger confrontation between Islam and the West. The cultural distance between the Bosnian Muslims and the United States, as well as specific aspects of the conflict in the former Yugoslavia, undoubtedly influenced America's perceptions of the threat emanating from the Balkans.

Perception of the Threat

Composed of six republics—Bosnia-Hercegovina, Croatia, Macedonia, Montenegro, Serbia, and Slovenia—and the two provinces of Kosovo and Vojvodina, Yugoslavia was, essentially, an artificial nation-state held together by Tito's domineering personality and the power of the League of Communists of Yugoslavia (LCY), until Tito's death in 1980 and the fall of communism in Eastern Europe and the Soviet Union in the late 1980s. Believing that "a power-sharing government by consensus" offered the only realistic hope of preserving Yugoslavia's unity, Tito initiated major constitutional reforms that included giving the constituent republics greater political autonomy by reducing the central government's control, and allowing the republics to veto federal legislation. This strategy prevented Tito's potential rivals from emerging as national political figures; it also facilitated the disintegration of Yugoslavia along ethnic and religious lines.[17]

Of the six republics, Bosnia-Hercegovina was the most severely affected by clashing cultures precisely because of its ethnic complexity. Elections held in late 1990 gave Muslims, led by Alija Izetbegovic, a plurality (ninety-nine) of the 240 seats in the assembly. Serbs and Croats won eighty-three and fifty seats respectively. Despite the Bosnians' efforts to consolidate their multicultural state, they were soon caught in the vortex of political change in the former Yugoslavia. The Republic of Serbia escalated its attempts to arrest Yugoslavia's fragmentation and to continue its dominance of the Balkans. Bosnia's Serbs, led by Radovan Karadzic, began to favor increased centralism. The Muslims and Croats, however, opted for a loose confederation. Fearing each other's appetite for territorial acquisition, Croats and Serbs began to dismember Bosnia. The Muslims, aware that Bosnia had been divided between Croatia and Serbia prior to World War II, resisted reabsorption into those states.[18] It was obvious that Serbia intended to use its superior military might to fashion Greater Serbia out of Croatia and Bosnia. American policymakers, like their European counterparts, avoided dealing with Yugoslavia's disintegration, partly because they feared that to abet in the formation of independent countries in the former Yugoslavia would encourage the growth of a similar process in the Soviet Union and elsewhere. Internal stability was of paramount importance. Yugoslavia, unlike the Gulf, had neither valuable resources nor nuclear weapons potential. Furthermore, compared to Hungary, Czechoslovakia, and Poland, Yugoslavia was not only culturally distant but also less promising in terms of being integrated into the market structure of Western Europe and the United States.[19]

Instead of dealing realistically with what many experts in the State Department believed would be the inevitable disintegration of Yugoslavia, the Bush administration stressed dialogue, to settle disputes among the republics and ethnic groups and to preserve national unity. Margaret Tutwiler, spokesperson for the State Department, reiterated that the United States believed that the ethnic heterogeneity of most of the republics meant that any dissolution of Yugoslavia would be likely to exacerbate rather than resolve ethnic tensions. She also stated that: "The United States will not encourage or reward secession; it will respect any framework, federal, confederal, or other, on which the people of Yugoslavia peacefully and democratically decide. We firmly believe that Yugoslavia's external or internal borders should not be changed unless by peaceful consensual means."[20] Secretary of State James Baker, restating U.S. policy in Belgrade on the eve of Yugoslavia's demise, warned both Solvenia and Croatia, the first two republics to declare their independence, that Washington would not grant them recognition.

Based on America's opposition to Yugoslavia's dissolution, Michael Lind, among others, concludes that "the Bush administration's statements in favor of Yugoslav unity may have convinced Serb nationalist that they would not be penalized seriously for attacking Slovenia and Croatia."[21] When the United States and the European Community (EC) recognized Bosnia in early 1992, after earlier being pushed by Germany to recognize Croatia and Slovenia, it was, in Josef Joffe's view, "a formal act bereft of the practical consequences that would ensure independence and territorial integrity."[22] Bosnia's right to defend itself against superior Serbian forces was effectively denied when the United States supported the UN arms embargo on all of the former Yugoslavia. America's perception of Bosnia as not being a major national interest helped to shape its response to the Balkan wars.

Addressing the annual meeting of the Harvard Alumni Association in 1994, Vice President Al Gore alluded to the broader implications of the Bosnian tragedy for the United States. He said: "Make no mistake: Just as repeated injuries to our national esteem can seriously jeopardize our ability to solve the problems which confront us, so too can the convergence of too much chaos and horror in the world of too many Bosnias and Rwandas seriously damage the ability of our global civilizations to get a grip on the essential task of righting itself and regaining a measure of control over our destiny as a species."[23] Jeane Kirkpatrick, America's ambassador to the United Nations during the Reagan administration, emphasized the cultural as well as security ramifications of the Bosnian conflict. The United States, she stressed, is grounded in European civilization. Consequently, threats to a shared civilization would have direct and indirect consequences for its members. She stated: "I do not believe that countries either thrive or survive without the survival of the civilizations of which they are a part."[24] But neither the Europeans nor the Americans considered the Bosnian Muslims full members of Western civilization. George Kenny, who left his position in the State Department in protest over U.S. policy in Bosnia, asserted that for Bush and Baker, "Yugoslavia is far away, something for which if the administration were to take a leading role, the administration risks getting blamed by Congress and the public for not scoring a success."[25] America's cultural emphasis on winning constrained U.S. policymakers' options in Bosnia.

In light of the nature of ethnic cleansing in Bosnia and Slobodan Milosevic's implementation of his Greater Serbia policy so soon after Iraqi troops had been forcefully removed from Kuwait, it was almost inevitable that Bosnia and Kuwait would be connected in many political observers' minds. Bush had convinced the majority of Americans, and much of the international community, that aggression and the acquisition of territory by military means "would not stand," and that dictators only understood their own language: force. In the new world order, proclaimed by Bush, the rule of law would be enforced. Consequently, America's failure to take strong action against aggression in Bosnia made the concept of a new world order meaningless and threatened America's credibility. More specifically, the double standards, which have often characterized U.S. relations with distant cultures, also posed a dilemma for American policymakers. While it maintained a relatively passive policy toward Bosnia, the Bush administration was aware of the need to "demonstrate to the world, especially the world's one billion Muslims, that the Western democracies will oppose aggression under all circumstances, not oppose it in one region and appease it in another."[26] But unlike the Gulf, where developments directly impinged on Americans' way of life and jobs, the argument that the Bosnian crisis would eventually result in a loss of jobs and income in this country seemed farfetched.[27]

A more credible threat arising out of the Bosnian war is that the resurgence of nationalism based on ethnicity will create a major source of instability in the post-Cold War era. In many countries around the world, ethnic groups that claim to have distinctive cultural traditions and practices find themselves sharing political systems with others they perceive as hostile and competitive. As Stephen R. Bowers notes, policies affecting cultural expression of ethnicity produce a disruptive and often violent brand of ethnic politics.[28] Such confrontations are common in Africa, much of Asia, parts of Latin America, and throughout the former Soviet Union (as events in Chechnya in 1995 showed); they are increasingly becoming a reality in Western Europe and, to a lesser extent, the United States. The continuing conflict in Rwanda is the product of an extreme clash of perceived cultural differences, in which ethnic identity has literally become a matter of life and death.

Clashing cultures in Bosnia have resonated throughout the region and beyond, thereby creating significant threats to American geopolitical interests. Margaret Thatcher, the former British prime minister who had urged Bush to use force to end Iraq's occupation of Kuwait, and Warren Zimmerman, America's ambassador to Yugoslavia between 1989 and 1992, who resigned to protest what he believed to be U.S. inaction in Bosnia, strongly stated the potential risk of the war in Bosnia spreading to other countries.[29] Zimmerman in particular underlined how cultural conflict—the volatile mixture of religion, ethnicity, and nationalism—might influence America's friends and allies to confront each other militarily. From his viewpoint, "Bosnia lies across a traditional fault line of instability stretching from Poland to Albania. The Catholic world of the Austrian Hapsburgs, the Muslim world of the Turks, and the Orthodox world of Serbia all jostle each other in Bosnia. Shock waves from Bosnia have already stunned its neighbors—Catholic Italy,

Croatia, and Hungary; Orthodox Greece and Macedonia; Muslim Turkey and Albania."[30] Equally important, cultural conflict in Bosnia rejuvenated Russian interest in the Slavic Serbs, and thus directly affected American-Russian cooperation in the post-Cold War world.

Turkey and Greece, both members of the North Atlantic Treaty Organization (NATO) and close American allies, have attempted to prevent the Bosnian war from exacerbating relations between them, already tense because of their dispute over Cyprus. Although a primary objective of Turkey's foreign policy has been to exercise influence over Balkan developments (and protect its erstwhile possessions), Turkey's policymakers have had to balance their country's regional interests against its desire to obtain EC membership and to maintain its strong alliance with the United States. Because Turkey needs American assistance, to enhance its chances of integration into the EC and manage its problems with Greece, the Turkish impulse to militarily assist the Bosnian Muslims has been restrained.[31]

The United States perceived the Bosnian conflict as a threat to Europe's stability, which has been a major American preoccupation since the end of World War II. Refugees from the turmoil in the former Yugoslavia put a severe strain on neighboring countries. The ability of NATO to maintain peace in Europe was in doubt. While the United States recognized these problems, Washington relied on the Europeans to deal with Bosnia.[32] The cultural tendency of most Americans to focus on the present enabled the United States to ignore potentially long-term dangers. Having initially asserted their responsibility for controlling events in the Balkans, the Europeans soon found themselves mired in national competition. When Germany sought to return Slovenia and Croatia to its sphere of influence, Britain and France (Serbian allies during the First and Second World Wars), endeavored to restrain Germany by strengthening Serbia.[33] The Bosnian Muslims were peripheral to intra-European rivalries and ambitions. European confidence, once buttressed by optimism about European unity, soon faded, partly because ordinary Europeans were more cautious about integration than their leaders, and rejected many provisions of the 1991 Maastricht Treaty, designed to hasten European union. Furthermore, most leaders in Europe, unpopular in their own countries and concerned with their own political survival, were unable or unwilling to conduct effective foreign policies. Simultaneously, Bush, worried about his election to a second term as president, perceived significant American involvement in the Bosnian quagmire as an almost insurmountable electoral liability.[34]

Ethnic Cleansing: Downplaying the World War II Analogy

Kristallnacht, Mein Kampf, Munich, the final solution, and Auschwitz remind many Americans that perceived cultural and religious differences were responsible for the Holocaust. International relations and American foreign policy since World War II have been profoundly affected by the lessons of the Holocaust. Consequently, Serbia's policy of ethnic cleansing in Bosnia and elsewhere has challenged the foundations of the postwar order that was largely shaped by the United States. While Serbia clearly does not pose the same threat that Nazi Germany did, and although the Munich analogy has been overused in relation to what is regarded as Western appeasement in the face of Serbian aggression, there are similarities between Nazi Germany's genocidal practices and Serbian ethnic cleansing in Bosnia.

Like Czechoslovakia in 1938, Bosnia is generally regarded by the United States as a small, distant country where no significant American interests are at stake. Reflecting a cultural tendency toward isolationism, the United States is turning inward and is reluctant to shoulder its responsibilities as a global power, especially in situations where there is a possibility that American lives might be lost in the process. Instead of standing up to Adolf Hitler and attempting to force him to relinquish his conquest of Sudetenland, Britain and France sacrificed Czechoslovakia in an agreement with Hitler in Munich. The Munich deal, a symbol of appeasement, gave rise to a central lesson that has guided America's foreign policy since World War II, namely, that negotiating with dictators who seize territory by force only encourages them to conquer more. But this analogy has been largely ignored by American foreign policymakers as the Serbs have seized Muslim land, mainly because Washington did not want to emphasize those cultural values that support military intervention.

Like Hitler, who articulated his program for exterminating Jews in *Mein Kampf*, Milosevic adopted a blueprint for a Greater Serbia that had been drawn up in 1986, in a "memorandum" of the Serbian Academy of Arts and Science.[35] Indeed, Milosevic boasted that the Serbs were on the threshold of the "final solution" and that "the remaining question was the question of maps."[36] An essential ingredient of Serbia's policy was to convince Bosnians, who had lived together relatively peacefully, that they could no longer coexist, because of religious and ethnic differences. Historical experiences were recalled, to fuel the Serbs' hatred of "the other." Just as Hitler had portrayed Jews as dangerous not only to Germany but also to Europe as a whole, the Serbs described the Muslims as part of the Islamic threat to the West.

Despite the fact that Muslims and Croats engaged in their own campaigns of ethnic cleansing, the Serbs were perceived as being primarily responsible for genocide, and the Muslims were its main victims. After depriving Muslims of their jobs and property, the Serbs began to destroy the Muslims' villages and cities, and forced them to leave, thereby helping to create the greatest refugee crisis in Europe since World War II. Many refugees were shipped out of northern Bosnia in sealed freight trains, a practice reminiscent of Nazi Germany's. Inhabitants of Muslims villages paid Serb businessmen to arrange their escape.[37] Those who could not leave faced a cruel fate. As early as September 1992, the State Department reported that atrocities included the massacre of villagers, the torture, rape, and killing of prisoners, the use of human shields, and the taking of hostages. Kenneth Blackwell, America's representative to the UN Human Rights Commission, observed thousands of men being held in cattle sheds under conditions of terror and severe hardship.[38] Many civilians, imprisoned in approximately forty-five concentration camps, were executed. Serbian gunmen systematically and brutally raped more than fifty thousand Muslim women and children as part of their program of ethnic cleansing.

Echoing Nazi Germany's campaign to eliminate all traces of Jewish existence, Serb nationalists attempted to destroy the Muslims' culture. In this (perceived) struggle between Serbian Orthodox Christianity and Islam, mosques, central to Muslims' identity and society, were principal targets. Many of these holy places, as well as historical monuments and libraries that were depositories of more than five centuries of Muslim culture and tradition, were reduced to rubble. Other mosques were used as slaughterhouses, prisons, and morgues. Many Muslim clergymen were tortured, sent to concentration camps, and killed in the most gruesome manner.[39]

But in the context of the Balkan history, such atrocities were easily rationalized. While the Serbs are the primary aggressors today, in 1941, Croatian nationalists and their Nazi allies massacred approximately 340,000 Serbs. Croatian nationalists, known as the *Ustashi*, engaged in ethnic cleansing, on the pretext that the Serbs were a threat to their national integrity.[40] Like Jews in Nazi Germany, many Serbs refused to believe that they were indeed the objects of genocide. While the Croats carried out most of the massacres, the Germans formed a Muslim S.S. division, called *Handzar*, which cleansed Serbian areas.[41] Muslim participation in genocide recalled Serbia's defeat by the Turks in the Battle of the Blackbird Fields, in Kosovo in 1389. Five centuries of Ottoman domination, along with the challenges Islam posed for Christianity, helped to define Serbian identity. Partly because of these historical experiences, Serbs thought of themselves as victims who would never allow history to be repeated. Although Serbia's ethnic cleansing today evokes memories of Nazi Germany, many Serbs compare themselves to the Jews of Hitler's Reich, and regard themselves as victims, especially in relation to the Croatians.[42]

Confronted with ethnic cleansing so soon after having mobilized domestic and international support for war against Saddam Hussein (who was depicted as a new Hitler), the United States appeared indecisive in relation to developments in Bosnia. During a news conference in early August 1992, Bush seemed to be adopting a forceful position. He stated: "The pictures of prisoners rounded up by Serbian forces and being held in these detention camps are stark evidence of the need to deal with this problem effectively. The world cannot shed its horror at the prospects of concentration camps. The shocking brutality of genocide in World War II in those concentration camps are burning memories for us all. That can't happen again, and we will not rest until the international community has gained access to any and all concentration camps."[43]

The United States avoided demonizing any particular leader, and deemphasized the Munich analogy. The conflict was not presented in terms of good versus evil, but was increasingly called an ethnically and historically based war in which all sides were culpable and ruthless. By characterizing the Bosnian crisis this way, U.S. policymakers appealed to American cultural values that favor nonintervention. Despite mounting evidence of Serbian atrocities, the Bush administration seemed to endorse the view, heard around the State Department, that "the conflict will die down," and that "the Serbs don't really want to kill all non-Serbian Bosnians, just drive them out."[44] The United States' unwillingness to act influenced several U.S. foreign service officers to resign. A central lesson of the Holocaust, that when people are being systematically killed the world cannot be indifferent, seemed to have been ignored by the United States in Bosnia. For some Americans, the plight of the Muslims evoked the story about the Jewish prisoner in Auschwitz, who asked, "Where is God?" Another prisoner replied, "Where is man?"[45]

Ignoring the Rule of Law

Two cornerstones of the new world order were that aggression would not stand and that the UN would be instrumental in enforcing international law. Dictators who seized territory by force would be punished. When Yugoslavia's constituent republics declared their independence, they were recognized by the United States as sovereign states on April 7 1992. America accepted the pre-crisis Republic borders as the legitimate international boundaries of Bosnia-Hercegovina, Croatia, and Slovenia.[46] As early as October 1991, the Bush administration had indicated that it strongly opposed the use of violence and intimidation to resolve political problems, would not tolerate violations of human rights, and would not accept changes in internal or external borders achieved by force.[47] Similarly, the United Nations Security Council adopted numerous resolutions which demanded an end to Serbia's interference in Bosnia's affairs. It authorized UN Secretary-General Boutros Boutros-Ghali to deploy military observers to supervise the withdrawal of heavy weapons and ensure an effective cease-fire, and demanded that unimpeded and continued access to all camps, prisons, and detention centers be granted to the International Red Cross and other humanitarian organizations. To provide humanitarian assistance to Bosnians through Sarajevo's airport, the UN authorized its Secretary-General to deploy additional troops as part of the United Nations Protection Force (UNPROFOR), and demanded that the belligerents cooperate fully with UNPROFOR and various international humanitarian organizations.[48]

Although there are significant and obvious differences between the Gulf crisis and the Bosnian conflict, given America's forceful and inflexible implementation of UN resolutions against Iraq shortly before and during the conflagration in Bosnia, it was almost inevitable that comparisons be made between the two situations in relation to enforcing the rule of law. Jeane Kirkpatrick observed that both Saddam Hussein and Slobodan Milosevic carried out military operations marked by gratuitous brutality, disregarded the laws of civilization, and had an unbounded appetite for conquest and violence. She was "very struck with the difference in the response of the United States and of our allies and all of us through the UN to these two problems."[49]

Whereas Hussein was clearly identified as the ruthless aggressor, the outlaw, who had to be brought to justice, Milosevic was not. While the Security Council, under U.S. leadership, issued an ultimatum to Iraq with a deadline, and authorized member-states to use force to secure Iraq's compliance, the United States, its allies, and the UN appeared to embrace a nonjudgmental, value-free, neutral policy on Bosnia. Instead of ultimatums, the Bush administration "urged the Serbian government to take clear and concrete steps to demonstrate that it will respect the territorial integrity of Croatia, Bosnia-Hercegovina, and Macedonia." The Serbian leadership was entreated to "spare the Serbian people and the other Yugoslav peoples the terrible costs of warfare, and to demonstrate their readiness to offer non-Serbs in Serbia the same rights and protection they claim to seek for Serbs outside Serbia."[50]

Unlike the Gulf crisis, in which adherence to the rule of law was stressed, there seemed to be a deliberate effort by both Bush and Clinton to downplay the importance of upholding the rule of law in Bosnia, in order to avoid tapping into American cultural values that might have prompted more Americans to support using force in Bosnia. Whereas UN resolutions were broadly construed to allow the United States to act in the Gulf, Bush and Clinton narrowly interpreted and often ignored UN resolutions on Bosnia, to justify inaction. Instead of stressing justice and compensation for victims, the United States and the United Nations were primarily interested in a cessation of hostilities. Few arguments were advanced for waging a just war to stop genocide.

Concerned about the possibility of widespread starvation and death as winter approached, and undoubtedly aware of parallels between the Kurds of northern Iraq and the Muslims of Bosnia, President Bush increased American humanitarian assistance to Bosnia and supported the deployment of UN forces to protect relief convoys. It was estimated that 400,000 Croats and Muslims would die from the combined effects of Serb shelling and the Serb policy of freezing and starving their enemies. Roger P. Winter, the director of the U.S. Committee for Refugees, believed that all necessary measures were not taken to get humanitarian relief deliveries to needy populations, despite the explicit language of UN Security resolutions.[51] This was partly due to the view, articulated by Eagleburger, that providing humanitarian assistance "could, if we're not careful, help consolidate the land-grab in Bosnia and the political cantonization which the United States categorically opposes."[52] But without credible threats and forceful actions to stop Serbian aggression, the United States, arguably, contributed to the realization of Serbian objectives.

Serb nationals repeatedly defied UN Security Council demands to permit relief supplies to reach besieged Muslims. The aggressors were expected to authorize safe passage for UN convoys. It was quite common for unarmed UN drivers to be stopped at gunpoint and have relief supplies and personal possessions stolen.[53] The Serbs expected the UN to be neutral, despite pervasive evidence of gross violations of human rights. Essentially, Serbs pledged not to attack UN troops, provided that the troops did not assist the victims of ethnic cleansing. The U.S. State Department and other sources documented several instances of international cease-fire monitors being attacked. For example, in January 1992, despite a United Nations-imposed "no-fly zone," two fighter planes under Serbian control shot down an unarmed, clearly marked helicopter carrying EC monitors. All five monitors were killed.[54]

When the Serbs launched a three-week offensive against the Muslim town of Gorazde, designated by the UN as a safe area, as part of a concerted effort to uproot the entire population from the Drina River valley which formed the border between Bosnia and Serbia, United Nations troops watched helplessly. Serbian assurances to the UN that attacks on Gorazde would be terminated proved to be empty. In fact, UN officers in Gorazde were used by the Serbs to gain leverage. This prompted Sir Michael Rose, the UN commander in Bosnia, to comment: "It is a very sad week for the world when the UN peacekeeping operation has been so blatantly used to cover the prosecution of war by the Serbs."[55] Perhaps one of the greatest ironies was the United Nations' decision to escort Serbian tanks away from Gorazde, only to have the same tanks attack other "safe zones" later. When Serb forces attacked Bihac, another safe haven, and took more than four hundred UN peacekeepers hostage in December 1994, the United States continued to favor a negotiated settlement and avoided taking actions that might anger the Serbs. This selective implementation of the rule of law might have been due to America's cultural tendency to avoid using force on behalf of victims from a distant culture when no clear U.S. interests are at stake.

Reluctance to Use Force: Stressing the Vietnam Analogy

Although President Bush often referred to the diplomatic and military campaign that liberated Kuwait from Iraqi occupation as evidence of his strong leadership in a perilous post-Cold War world, when a reporter asked him if he was planning to take similar actions to rescue the people of Bosnia from being slaughtered, Bush replied that America would not use the military, especially ground forces, to help end the Bosnian conflict. Instead, the President pointed out that there was a lot of consultation going on that he hoped "would encourage the people in that area to find peaceful means of solving these questions."[56] Bosnia's military complexities convinced the United States that applying force in that specific situation would be dangerous and perhaps counterproductive. But military decisions were intertwined with cultural factors that help to shape American foreign policy in general and the use of force in particular. America's failure to reconcile its readiness to resort to military solutions in Iraq with what appeared to be studied neutrality in Bosnia cannot be isolated from cultural influences on U.S. foreign policy.

Intervention in Bosnia would inevitably lead to a nebulous outcome, the achievement of which would be relatively expensive in terms of lives and money. Sports metaphors, so closely tied to U.S. military action in the Gulf and elsewhere, seemed inapplicable to Bosnia. Unlike a sporting contest, the Bosnian conflict was complex, multi-sided, unpredictable, and America's team was not guaranteed to win. It would be a long, drawn-out game replete with uncertainty. Heavy American casualties would undoubtedly dampen whatever public support initially existed for military action. Unlike the Persian Gulf region, with its mostly clear skies and flat desert terrain, Bosnia was cloudy, mountainous, and heavily forested. The battle lines were not neatly drawn. The conflict was murky.

Michael Mandelbaum, Clinton's foreign policy adviser during the presidential campaign, observes that: "In the wake of Vietnam, the American public has come to expect military engagement in other countries to correspond to surgery: The United States diagnoses the problem, performs the appropriate operation—the shorter, cheaper, and cleaner the better—and then moves on."[57]

Whereas the complexities of post-Cold War developments call for patience, long-term thinking, and a nuanced approach to foreign policy that balances force with diplomacy, most U.S. policymakers have been influenced by America's cultural tendency to engage in zero-sum thinking. By taking an all-or-nothing approach to Bosnia, the United States effectively reduced its ability to help manage that conflict.

Having decided not to intervene in what was perceived as the Bosnian morass, Bush reached into America's dominant culture to justify his policy. The Vietnam analogy predominated. Zimmerman, who was intimately involved in the implementation and, to some extent, the formulation of U.S. policy in Bosnia, claimed that "the Bush administration was paralyzed by a conviction that even the smallest U.S. military presence in Bosnia would end up in a Vietnam-sized army."[58] The concept of mission creep, the view that before the United States engage militarily Washington must know that clearly defined objectives can be achieved, and the idea that massive force must be employed and casualties kept at a minimum, operated to endorse Bush's relative inaction in Bosnia. The President stressed that he would not commit American troops to Bosnia until he had been assured by the military of our mission, what needed to be done, and how the United States would get its troops out. Concluding that Bosnia was more reminiscent of Vietnam than the Gulf, Bush said the answer to Bosnia "is to continue to push emergency relief."[59]

Despite earlier disagreements with Bush's approach to the Balkan conflict, once he assumed office Clinton pursued a policy that was remarkably similar to his predecessor's. Clinton's opposition to the Vietnam War and his unwillingness at that time to risk shedding his own blood undermined his credibility with the military and, consequently, diminished his ability to argue convincingly for using force in Bosnia. Within the context of American culture, he had failed one of the major tests of commitment and patriotism. Furthermore, approximately twenty members of Clinton's generation who had served in Vietnam are now leaders in Congress. Their positions on Bosnia are clearly influenced by a conflict that helped to shape their lives. But they were divided on the issue of using force in the former Yugoslavia. For example, Senator John McCain, a former naval aviator who had spent six years as a prisoner of war in Vietnam and was now a member of the Senate Armed Services Committee, and Representative John P. Murtha, a former Marine and chairman of the Defense Appropriation Subcommittee, opposed U.S. military involvement in Bosnia. On the other side were Senator John Kerry, a naval officer on gunboats in the Mekong Delta and now a senior member of the Foreign Relations Committee, and Senator Charles S. Robb, a Marine infantry officer in Vietnam and currently a member of the Armed Services Committee.[60]

Divisions in Congress were reflected in the general public. Most polls showed that approximately 47 percent of the American public opposed U.S. military action, with only 43 percent favoring it. When asked if the United States should unilaterally use military force, opposition increased to 68 percent. On the other hand, when the question was changed to whether

Americans favored their country's participation in a multilateral force, more than 60 percent answered affirmatively.[61] Contrary to the view, articulated by both Bush and Clinton, that Bosnia resembled Vietnam more than the Gulf, 49 percent of the public believed that if U.S. troops were sent to Bosnia, the outcome would be similar to that of the Persian Gulf War. Only 43 percent believed it would be more like Vietnam.[62] However, polls also showed that an overwhelming majority (82 percent) of Americans wanted their leaders to reduce the country's international involvement and to focus instead on domestic problems.[63] Public opinion on Bosnia was sufficiently ambiguous to enable President Bush to assert that: "I have had no pressure from the United States Congress or any citizens here to say why aren't we putting more troops into Sarajevo right now. I haven't had any feeling that there is great demand for that."[64]

Ethnic group influence on America's Bosnian policy was insignificant, due to the relatively small size of the American Serbian and Bosnian Muslim communities. Bosnian Muslims, most of whom arrived in the United States around 1900, are concentrated in Chicago and Gary, Indiana. Their interests have been supported principally by Senator Robert Dole and Representative Thomas Lantos. Dole, advised by Mira Baratta, who is of Croatian background, has been a strong critic of Milosevic's expansionist policies, partly because of sustained political pressure from Americans with ties to Kosovo. On the other side is the better organized Serbian-American community, supported by Representative Helen Delick Bently, who is of Serbian ancestry, and Representative Jim Moody, who spent four years in Yugoslavia in the 1950s as a volunteer for CARE.[65] SerbNet, the Serbian-American lobby, attempted to persuade policymakers that Serb fighters were not primarily responsible for Bosnia's bloodshed. They also tried to portray Serbia as a close American ally. On the fiftieth anniversary of D-Day, Serbian festivities in Chicago emphasized the Serbs' role in Operation Halyard, in which eight hundred Allied airmen— mostly Americans—were rescued by Serbian Chetnik forces under the command of a resistance leader, General Draza Milhailovich.[66]

Reluctant to mobilize public support for U.S. intervention in Bosnia by portraying the conflict in terms of good versus evil, Bush and Clinton declined to focus on Milosevic as one of the persons most responsible for ethnic cleansing in the former Yugoslavia. During the early stages of the conflict, Secretary of State James Baker, in an address to the United Nations, asserted that the Serbian government and its leaders bore a special responsibility for the bloodshed in the former Yugoslavia.[67] However, unlike the Gulf crisis, in which a central character was easily identified and demonized, the evil characters in the former Yugoslavia and their victims were physically indistinguishable from the overwhelming majority of Europeans, a fact which carries some weight in cultures where race matters. The aggressors did not conform to television's portrayal of "the evil other" in the cartoons. Furthermore, it may be argued that diversity of opinions and the veneer of democracy in Serbia militated against efforts to demonize Milosevic. Demonstrations by peace organizations, comprised of students, professors, and leaders of the Serbian Orthodox Church in Belgrade, strengthened the view that Milosevic was not a dictator who totally controlled events in Serbia and beyond.[68] Partly because of this perceived absence of a monolithic decision-making structure, Serbs who engaged in genocidal activities were often perceived as autonomous actors whose behavior was divorced from the policies and practices of Serbia and Milosevic.

By interpreting the Bosnian conflict as a civil war, the "intractable problem from hell," Bush and Clinton further decreased the likelihood that Americans might perceive the fighting in moral terms.[69] Casting the problem as a moral tragedy would have made American inaction amoral at best, which is usually tantamount to being immoral in the context of America's dominant culture. If the war were essentially a clash of ethnic groups that was centuries old and extremely complex, then there was little the United States could do, except provide humanitarian assistance.[70] Ancient tribal feuds, conducted by people who are regarded as uncivilized and beyond the United States' cultural circle, are not the kinds of conflicts in which Americans are culturally predisposed to participate, despite their terrifying and emotional nature. Even though the conflict was in some significant ways a civil war, it was widely regarded as principally an act of aggression by Serbs against Muslims.

In contrast to America's providing leadership of the international community in the Gulf Crisis, the United States deferred to the UN and the EC in Bosnia. There are several explanations for this. With a dominant cultural tendency to re-solve conflicts of ends by force, and a tradition of political stabil-ity, the United States found it difficult to devise the complicated and painstaking political settlements that a resolution of the Bosnian conflict demanded. Unlike many Europeans, who have had extensive experience creating governments in areas with complex and distant cultures, the United States is not cultural-ly inclined to expend the effort and resources required for peacebuilding. The frustration, confusion, and uncertainty that characterized the Bosnian problem was clearly inconsistent with the cultural preference of most Americans for dealing with crises that are relatively uncomplicated and which can be easily portrayed in terms of good versus evil. Compared to the Gulf, Bosnia was both extremely complex and peripheral to specific American interests. Consequently, most Americans did not sup-port U.S. involvement beyond participating in multilateral ef-forts to provide humanitarian assistance to the Bosnians. The United States' deference to the EC and the UN was due in part to Americans' proclivity for isolationism in the absence of a clearly defined threat. But the United States was also avoiding responsibility for dealing with a problem that was widely per-ceived as protracted and not easily managed.

Within the context of American culture and foreign policy, this reliance on others usually occurs when the United States believes that it has no significant interests at stake. When America cares about a problem it tends to act unilaterally and, more often than not, forcefully and quickly. During the Cold War and in the Gulf the United States expected its NATO allies to follow, often without much consultation or involvement in the policymaking process. Although it may be argued that the Europeans favored EC leadership because Yugoslavia was re-garded as an opportunity for the "new Europe" to demonstrate its independence and cohesiveness,[71] evidence also shows that America was not anxious to compete with Europe for leadership on the Bosnian issue. Washington, fearing mission creep, con-sistently ignored requests from its European allies for American troops to join British, French, Canadian, Spanish, Nigerian, and other troops on the ground in Bosnia. The United States did not encourage stronger European or UN action. Instead, it seemed satisfied to follow in Europe's shadow. As Warren Christopher, Clinton's secretary of state, put it: "The first principle (that guides our participation in Bosnia) is that we will not act alone in taking actions in the former Yugoslavia. This is a multilateral problem, and it must have a multilateral response. Furthermore, at heart, this is a European problem."[72] But without decisive American leadership, it was unlikely that multilateralism would be successful.

While the effectiveness of American air strikes in the Persian Gulf testified to the United States' ability to cause significant damage to enemy targets without endangering American troops, the general public and Presidents Bush and Clinton were reluctant to call upon these capabilities in Bosnia. Despite Clinton's support of air strikes during the presidential campaign, he did not strongly support them once he had assumed the presidency.[73] Advocates of air strikes included Margaret Thatcher, Senators Richard Lugar and Alfonse D'Amato, and General Michael J. Dugan, the Chief of Staff of the U.S. Air Force in the Persian Gulf who had been later dismissed by Bush for inadvertently revealing that the President had secretly approved a timetable for launching an air war against Iraq. David Owen, a principal EC negotiator in Bosnia and co-author of the Vance-Owen peace plan, stated that he had argued publicly that selective air strikes should be used to tip the balance against the Bosnian Serbs, while candidate Clinton had been making the same case.[74] Suggested targets had included power plants, bridges, gas fields, ammunition dumps, communication centers, and Serbian troops.

Polls showed that between 55 and 60 percent of the American public opposed unilateral U.S. air strikes. But approximately 51 percent supported air strikes if they were part of a NATO operation.[75] NATO, however, was disinclined to advocate massive air strikes. Britain and France feared that bombing the Serbs would almost certainly jeopardize the safety of their own troops in Bosnia and negatively affect diplomatic initiatives. Yet British and French refusal to sanction air strikes assured the Serbs that they would not be punished for implementing their policy of ethnic cleansing. European opposition to air strikes made it easier for a reluctant America to remain neutral.

Following the heavy shelling of Sarajevo by Serb forces and the deaths of 68 civilians in a marketplace in early 1994, the UN Secretary-General requested NATO to conduct air strikes against artillery or mortar positions determined by UN-PROFOR to have been involved in attacks on civilian targets, pending UN approval. This change in policy was endorsed by Clinton.[76] Although the Serbs had complied to an extent with NATO's demands that they withdraw their artillery from Sarajevo, six Serbian planes bombed a munitions plant controlled by the Bosnian government, despite the UN-imposed "no-fly" zone. Radically departing from previous practices, NATO commanders authorized a military response, which resulted in the downing of four Serbian planes.[77] This use of force to gain Serbian compliance with the rule of law temporarily strengthened the credibility of NATO threats to bomb Serb positions around Sarajevo.

The Clinton administration's apparent incohesion and confusion on Bosnia undermined the effectiveness of the limited NATO military response, however. Defense Secretary William J. Perry publicly announced that the United States would refrain from intervening militarily to prevent Gorazde from being occupied by the Serbs. General John M. Shalikashvilli, Chairman of the Joint Chiefs of Staff, had stated earlier that he did not see a need to broaden the threat of air strikes to protect other "safe areas." Perry, when asked if the Clinton administration was prepared to allow the Serbs to conquer Gorazde, replied: "We will not enter the war to stop that from happening."[78] Shortly thereafter, the Serbs attacked Gorazde. But, contrary to Perry's statements, two American warplanes under NATO command attacked Serbian positions outside besieged Gorazde. When the Serbs retaliated by forcefully taking weapons they had earlier surrendered to the UN and by shooting at and abducting UN peacekeepers, the Clinton administration seemed preoccupied with trying to convince the Serbs of NATO's neutrality in order to dissuade them from taking more aggressive actions against UNPROFOR.[79]

Arming the Bosnian Muslims

Based on the assumption that all the various belligerents in the former Yugoslavia were responsible for the horrific developments there, the UN Security Council unanimously adopted Resolution 713 in September 1991, which called on all countries to immediately implement a "general and complete embargo on all deliveries of weapons and military equipment to Yugoslavia" until the Security Council decided otherwise.[80] In May 1992, the Security Council imposed comprehensive economic sanctions against Serbia, which included an oil embargo, a freeze on Serbia's foreign assets, the cessation of trade, and the suspension of regular traffic between Serbia and other countries. President Bush simultaneously issued Executive Orders 12808 and 12810, which made the UN sanctions part of American law.[81] When the United States and other countries recognized Bosnia's independence and established full diplomatic relations with Sarajevo, the pre-crisis borders were accepted as the legitimate international boundaries of Bosnia and the comprehensive sanctions imposed by the UN Security Council were lifted against Bosnia. Sanctions against Serbia would be terminated when that country ended its own economic blockade of Bosnia and Macedonia. But the arms embargo would remain in effect on all of the former Yugoslavia.[82]

An integral component of sovereignty and, consequently, a cardinal principle of international law, is the right of self-defense, a right implicitly acknowledged by the United States when it recognized Bosnia-Hercegovina as an independent state. Furthermore, denying the Bosnian Muslims the right to protect their lives, property, and political system against a clear policy of aggression contradicted a fundamental American cultural value, namely, the right of people to keep and bear arms. Both domestically and internationally, the United States has supported the view that guns are instrumental in obtaining and preserving freedom. American denial of weapons to the Bosnian Muslims prompted Albert Wohlstetter, a former adviser to both Democratic and Republican administrations on military strategy, to assert that "the West invited Serbia's genocidal war."[83]

Serbia had a great advantage in weaponry over Bosnia. To gain greater military self-sufficiency, Yugoslavia had embarked on a strategy in the mid-1970s to replace imported weapons with less expensive, domestically manufactured arms. It had transformed itself from an importer to an exporter of military equipment, to obtain hard currency. By 1990, Yugoslavia produced approximately 80 percent of its own military equipment, including infantry weapons, anti-tank systems, and armored vehicles.[84] The Yugoslav People's Army had stockpiled large quantities of arms, which remained under Serbian control when Yugoslavia disintegrated. Classified American intelligence reports, according to Michael R. Gordon, indicated that Serbian forces in Bosnian had about three hundred tanks, while the Bosnian Muslims had two. The Serbs had more than two hundred armored personnel carriers, compared to one or two under Muslim control. Whereas the Serbs had six to eight hundred artillery pieces, the Muslims had roughly twenty-four.[85] The military disparity between the belligerents was generally believed to be the principal determinant of the war's outcome.

During the 1992 presidential campaign, Clinton castigated the Bush administration for not doing more to help Bosnia. Clearly aware of the central American cultural belief that guns are essential to obtaining freedom, Clinton advocated lifting the arms embargo because the Bosnians "are in no way in a fair fight with a heavily armed opponent bent on ethnic cleansing." Bush, on the other hand, believed that the Balkans harbored too many weapons, a situation which would only be exacerbated by lifting the arms embargo against Bosnia.[86] Yet the freshness of the images of World War II which Bush had evoked to help mobilize support for war against Iraq almost inevitably led to comparisons between current conditions in Bosnia and conditions fifty years earlier in Warsaw, where poorly equipped Polish Jews had confronted a fully supplied German Wehrmacht. Despite the public's opposition to airstrikes or involving U.S. troops in the Bosnian conflict, approximately 57 percent of Americans surveyed supported ending the arms embargo, and only 22 percent favored maintaining it.[87] Public opinion on arming the Bosnians was consistent with values inherited from the American Revolution and frontier experiences.

But the public's ambivalence toward the Bosnian conflict helped reinforce the ambiguity that had characterized American policy from the inception of the crisis in Yugoslavia. On one hand, President Clinton argued that the best way to increase pressure on the Bosnian Serbs and to contain the fighting was to lift the arms embargo against Bosnia. On the other hand, he opposed ending the embargo unilaterally, contending that there were substantial questions about whether under international law the United States could do it. Furthermore, he was concerned about the broader implications of American unilateral action in Bosnia for maintaining widespread international support for sanctions against countries such as Iraq, Libya, and Haiti. And, like Bush, Clinton believed that allowing the Bosnian government to obtain weapons would result in a "lot of other people fighting and killing. In the end there would not be a decisive victory for either side in the war."[88]

Similarly, the Senate was divided on whether the United States should lift the arms embargo unilaterally or in cooperation with other countries. In mid-1994, the Senate approved two conflicting resolutions on terminating the sanctions. The Senate voted 50 to 49 to lift the embargo unilaterally. It also voted 50 to 49 in favor of ending it in cooperation with the NATO allies and other states.[89] Senators who supported ending the embargo unilaterally believed that that American action would indicate the United States' willingness, as the sole superpower, to influence its allies to allow the Muslims to defend themselves. Senators favoring multilateral action on the embargo argued that unilateral American action would end the country's neutrality, make the United States responsible for Bosnia's fate, encourage others to violate international sanctions against countries elsewhere, and strain relations between the United States and its allies. Britain, France, Canada, and other countries with troops in the UN Protection Force in Bosnia would be pressured by their citizens to withdraw because of Serbian attacks, which, in turn, would endanger U.S. humanitarian mission. Furthermore, arming the Bosnians unilaterally was likely to derail negotiations and force the Serbs to take preemptive action against the Muslims.[90]

Despite their differing approaches, those in favor of and those opposed to unilaterally ending the embargo saw arming the Muslims as not only being consistent with cultural values, but also as a low-cost foreign policy that would appear to be moral without risking American lives. But Europeans, concerned about their troops' safety and annoyed at the United States for refusing to join peacekeeping operations in Bosnia, strongly disagreed with both resolutions passed by the Senate. Russia, facing nationalistic pressures at home and concerned about the implications of arming the Muslims to fight against its Serbian allies, also rejected attempts to remove the arms embargo. However, Russia supplied weapons to the Serbs, and several hundred Russians served with Serbian forces.[91] Washington's cooperation with Moscow helped to modify the influence of American cultural values that supported arming the Bosnians. Nevertheless, in late 1994, the Clinton administration directed the U.S. Navy to cease enforcing the arms embargo against Bosnia.

Perceiving the Bosnian conflict primarily in terms of Christianity versus Islam, many Muslim countries, such as Saudi Arabia and Iran, not only advocated lifting the arms embargo but also sent both weapons and men to help the Bosnian Muslims. King Fahd Bin Abdul Aziz of Saudi Arabia, as the custodian of two of Islam's Holy Mosques, was under increasing pressure from Islamic fundamentalists to provide military assistance to Bosnia.[92] Iran was the clearest violator of the sanctions. In late 1992, Croatian officials who intercepted an Iranian plane on its way to Bosnia, ostensibly to deliver humanitarian aid, found more than four thousand guns, a million rounds of ammunition, and approximately forty Iranians in the back of the Iranian Boeing 747.[93] Cultural links partly explain the positions of the United States, Russia, and the Islamic world on arming the Bosnians. They also influenced the West's decision to focus on a negotiated settlement of the conflict.

Ineffective Negotiations: Rewarding Aggression?

The United States eschewed a military solution but did not vigorously pursue a diplomatic settlement. Although President Bush had stated that the Serbs' flagrant disregard for human life required a response from the international community,[94] Ralph Johnson, Bush's Principal Deputy Assistant Secretary for European and Canadian Affairs, summarized America's actual, as opposed to stated, policy. Responding to many Americans who asked why the United States was not doing more to resolve the conflict, Johnson said: "The bottom line in the crisis is that the world community cannot stop Yugoslavs from killing one another so long as they are determined to do so."[95] Similarly, President Clinton stressed that his administration was committed to stopping the bloodshed and implementing a fair and enforceable peace agreement, "if the parties in the conflict can reach one. The conflict in Bosnia ultimately is a matter for the parties to resolve."[96]

America's cultural ambivalence toward relying on diploma-cy to achieve its security objectives was clear from the begin-ning of the Yugoslav crisis. Instead of asserting its usual claim to leadership, the United States decided to follow the Europeans and the UN. At the London Economic Summit in July 1991, Bush stated: "I salute them (the EC) for some diffi-cult diplomacy. And I'm hoping that this matter can be resolved through conversation, through dialogue. But it wouldn't be the part of the United States to stand up if the parties agreed on one direction and say, hey, that is unsatisfactory to us. It is es-sentially a European matter, and they're coping, I think, in a difficult situation quite well right now."[97]

Consistent with U.S. dominant cultural values, many Americans believed that negotiating with ethnic cleansers was morally wrong. Whereas the Europeans were willing to accept the facts on the ground, and to push through a compromise set-tlement, Americans found it difficult to do so. To some extent, U.S. moralism in foreign policy clashed with Europe's tradition-al emphasis on diplomacy and power politics. As Representative Robert McCloskey put it: "Genocidal Serb ag-gression cannot be stopped by diplomacy. It is fueled by viru-lent nationalism that has much in common with Nazism, and that responds to diplomacy much as Nazism did."[98] Prior to mid-1994, when the United States, as a member of the Contact Group (which included Russia, France, Britain, and Germany), agreed to a division of Bosnia that was perceived as rewarding Serbian aggression, American officials had rejected peace pro-posals that would have forced the Bosnian Muslims to accept the loss of their territory. Despite the United States' rhetorical embrace of diplomacy, R.W. Apple observes that "almost from the start, the mediation efforts of the UN and EC met with re-sistance and public skepticism in Washington."[99] But David Owen contended that it was extremely difficult to achieve a diplomatic solution to the Bosnian conflict as long as the United States remained a bystander.[100]

America's hesitancy to seriously negotiate was reinforced by conditions in Bosnia and the attitudes and strategies of the belligerents. The situation in Bosnia was more complex than in the Gulf, which made drawing lines in the sand, as it were, ex-tremely difficult. Bosnia required a nuanced combination of pa-tience, credible threats, incentives and disincentives, and a sense of urgency on the part of the United States. Without a strong commitment to a negotiated outcome, American policy in Bosnia was vulnerable to European and Russian influence.

Given the Serbs' military superiority and the West's reluctance to use force against them, they had little incentive to seriously negotiate. They violated the vast majority of the agreements they made with the EC and the UN, and were as content to maintain the status quo as the Bosnian Muslims were determined to change it. Consequently, the Muslims also disregarded cease-fires, and provoked the Serbs into taking military actions. As Bosnia's Muslim Prime Minister Haris Silajdzic stated: "We will try to negotiate, but who knows when we will stop. We do not have to justify our intention to liberate that territory if they (the Bosnian Serbs) don't give it up, because it is our natural right .... One day, we are entitled to do that. One day when we feel strong enough."[101] Both sides believed they could gain by refusing to settle.

This reluctance of the parties to negotiate influenced Washington's policies. When told by a reporter at a news conference that the situation in Bosnia had deteriorated since his election, Clinton replied that "none of the parties now, including the government, are of the mind to make peace on any terms that others will accept, because there are different military results being achieved on the ground."[102] Under these circumstances, the Clinton administration decided to limit its diplomatic efforts principally to securing the delivery of humanitarian assistance to victims on both sides of the war. These negotiations were reasonably successful, and large numbers of lives were saved from starvation.

Even though the United States found it difficult to ignore the Bosnian Muslims' plight, Washington adopted a relatively even-handed approach, which involved treating victims and aggressors similarly. Despite the fact that Radovan Karadzic was vilified as a war criminal by former Secretary of State Eagleburger, and was to face prosecution at the Balkan war-crimes tribunal in Hague headed by Judge Richard J. Goldstone of South Africa, Karadzic was granted permission to enter the United States to participate in peace talks.[103] The United States seemed to have unlimited patience with the Serbs and was inclined to believe them. Instead of dismissing Serbian gestures of goodwill as hoaxes in light of an incontrovertible record of broken promises, the United States chose to view them positively. Bush in particular was anxious to show that diplomacy was working. At the height of the Serbs' ethnic cleansing campaign, Bush told the nation that Yugoslavia's Prime Minister Panic gave Bosnian Serb leaders an ultimatum: they had to close all detention camps or resign. Bush stated that it was a move in the right direction and that "the diplomacy that is going on behind the scenes will push that kind of resolution of the question."[104]

Washington's minimal involvement in diplomatic efforts was due partly to its realization that a negotiated settlement would inevitably have to include territorial concessions to the Serbs, a development that would be inconsistent with American cultural values that reject compromise with leaders and groups designated as evil. The Vance-Owen plan, worked out by Cyrus Vance and David Owen as co-chairmen of the Conference on the Former Yugoslavia, was not enthusiastically embraced by the United States, chiefly because it was perceived as legitimizing Serbian control of land from which Muslims had been driven. The Vance-Owen plan would have maintained Bosnia as an independent state within its current borders but would have significantly weakened the central government's power, while giving provincial governments a high degree of autonomy. It proposed dividing Bosnia into ten provinces: three majority Serb, three majority Croat, three majority Muslim, and one mixed.[104]

Because the Europeans and Russians were primarily responsible for diplomacy in Bosnia, America was confronted with the choice of accepting their proposals, taking unilateral action, or doing nothing in the face of mounting criticism at home. The Clinton administration decided to accept a compromise that would give the Muslim-Croat federation, formed in mid-1994 and supported by the United States, approximately 51 percent of Bosnia. The Serbs, who controlled 70 percent of Bosnia, would be left with 49 percent of the territory. This shift in U.S. policy was acknowledged by Charles E. Redman, America's special envoy to Bosnia, who said: "We had to jump over the moral bridges in the interests of wider peace and of keeping Bosnia together."[106] Within the context of the dominant American culture, such compromises with aggressors are difficult to justify to the public. Further complicating U.S. policy was the Serbs' rejection of the territorial arrangements that had gained the unanimous approval of the Contact Group.[107]

Adopting an all-or-nothing approach to using force in Bosnia, and relying on the Europeans and the UN to find diplomatic solutions to the conflict in the former Yugoslavia, the United States seemed to flounder in an uncertain and uncharted post-Cold War world. Instead of assuming the role of the superpower that would exercise leadership to assist the creation of a new world order, America found itself facing a proliferation of tragedies in areas that were culturally distant. Problems in Bosnia underscored the nature of post-Cold War foreign policy challenges for the United States.

Chapter Seven

Resolving Conflicts Peacefully

Although complex and often inconsistent cultural factors influence foreign affairs, it is difficult to measure their impact on particular policies. Consequently, the role of culture in international relations is regarded by most political scientists as too nebulous to be scientifically analyzed. But the failure of political realism and other approaches to international politics to predict revolutionary changes that culminated in the end of the Cold War, the reunification of Germany, and the disintegration of the Soviet Union has created serious doubts about the reliability of the dominant theories of and approaches to international relations and foreign policy. The proliferation of ethnic conflicts, and increased attention to the role of culture in relations among countries, undermine many assumptions of realism. The Bosnian conflict demonstrates how perceived cultural differences, as well as cultural links, directly affect international relations.

Realism's emphasis on external influences on a country's foreign policies, its preoccupation with military and economic factors, and its virtual exclusion of ideational considerations from the formulation and implementation of foreign policy, are at odds with the growing reality of the connection between a state's internal cultural values and its external behavior. Foreign policies are increasingly viewed as extensions of domestic policies and vice versa, as international boundaries erode and interdependence among nations, as well as nonstate actors, is consolidated.

Despite the unprecedented interaction of people from different countries, the exchange of ideas, and the globalization of business, cultural distances still matter. A central thesis of this book is that the United States is inclined to resolve disputes peacefully with countries that have cultures similar to its own, and to rely primarily on force or the threat of force to settle conflicts with countries that have significantly different cultures. Although the case studies focused on the Palestinian-Israeli problem, Operations Desert Shield and Desert Storm, and the Bosnian conflict, there are many other examples of the United States' reliance on force or negotiations to terminate a dispute being motivated by cultural values. The growing body of scholarly literature explaining why democracies refrain from fighting each other, and the outbreak of conflicts between distant cultures after the Cold War ended, seem to support this general thesis.

However, it may be argued that countries with similar cultures, such as the United States and Britain, have fought each other and that states with very different values, such as the United States and Russia, have been strong allies at various times in history. Such an argument overlooks the temporary nature of alliances between the United States and Russia, on the one hand, and the durability of the culturally based special relationship between the United States and Britain on the other. Despite their membership in a common European civilization, the Germans, French, and British have engaged in some of the bloodiest wars in history. These wars would have to be examined in detail to determine the specific causes of conflict or cooperation in order to ascertain the role of culture in each situation. However, it seems reasonable to conclude, based on historical evidence as well as current developments, that, faced with similar challenges from Britain and Russia, the United States is likely to negotiate with the former and adopt a more confrontational approach to the latter. As discussed in Chapter One, even though Britain and the United States fought each other in the American Revolution and the War of 1812, strong kinship ties and a widespread sense of a shared culture have militated against an ongoing hostile relationship. The Anglo-American special relationship was effectively used in World War II, the Falklands War, the Persian Gulf, and other conflicts. Despite cooperation between France and Britain, the French have been suspicious of the enduring Anglo-American alliance, a relationship based to a large extent on cultural similarities. The values and attitudes undergirding this partnership are deeply rooted. Furthermore, it may be argued that the term "European civilization" obscures significant cultural differences between the Germans and the British, for example. As discussed earlier, Britain defined itself largely through wars with France. Cultural distances, which are relative, have played a decisive role in many European conflicts.

While other considerations help to determine a state's international behavior in general and its use of force or negotiations in particular, cultural beliefs, values, and attitudes often provide the foundation of many foreign policies. In Bosnia, for example, the cultural distance between the Muslims and the Christian West was generally perceived to be an important cause of the West's decision not to intervene more decisively against the Serbs. A Muslim state in Europe, especially in light of rising Islamic fundamentalism in Algeria and elsewhere during the Bosnian crisis, produced what Roger Cohen termed "thinly veiled anxiety in Western Europe."[1] But many Islamic countries supported the Muslims and called on the United Nations to take stronger measures to protect them. However, the cultural proximity between the Serbs and the Russians essentially prevented both a reluctant West and the UN from restraining what many observers viewed as Serbian aggression. Only when Russia decided to play a more decisive role on behalf of the Serbs was there meaningful progress toward resolving the conflict. Lacking major interests in Bosnia and attempting to focus its attention on domestic problems, the United States stressed the need for a negotiated settlement. Unlike Operation Desert Storm, where force was used with minimum American casualties, it was believed that U.S. military action in Bosnia would be extremely costly in terms of lives, money, and prestige.

America's reluctance to use force was also influenced by generational change, symbolized by President Clinton, and the antiwar subculture that grew from his generation's opposition to the Vietnam War. Vietnam undermined the national consensus on using force in situations in which the threat to American interests were indirect and not immediate. Bush's use of massive force against Iraq, partly to "kick the Vietnam syndrome," did not end Bill Clinton's generation's ambivalence toward war.

Negotiations were also the preferred method of conflict resolution in relation to the dispute with North Korea over its alleged development of nuclear missiles. When North Korea refused to allow International Atomic Energy Agency inspectors to examine its nuclear facilities, and decided to withdraw from the Nuclear Non-Proliferation Treaty in mid-1994, it appeared as though Washington and Pyongyang would be involved in another crisis on the Korean peninsula. President Clinton, seemingly sensitive to cultural pressure to appear tough, decided to send Patriot missiles to South Korea, where approximately 36,000 American troops are stationed, to help protect it against an attack by North Korea. At the same time, however, Clinton clearly did not want to precipitate another crisis, especially in light of the fact that the threat from North Korea was not immediate. The President also took into consideration South Korea's, Japan's, China's, and Russia's concerns about the implications of a military confrontation between the United States and North Korea. Based on America's experiences in the Korean War, it was almost certain that there would be unacceptably high casualties on both sides if war erupted. Although the United States and North Korea are culturally distant, both the interests at stake and the growing American support for negotiations combined to help defuse the crisis.

Instead of humiliating and demonizing North Korea's leader, Kim Il Sung, Clinton refused to personalize the conflict, and focused on the underlying problem. The Clinton administration was also sensitive to cultural and military links between China and North Korea. While arguing for sanctions against the latter, Clinton favored gradually imposing modest measures, such as curbs on cultural exchanges and UN technical assistance, and implementing a possible arms embargo. Harsher sanctions, including an oil embargo and restrictions on the flow of hard currency from Japan to North Korea, would be implemented at a later stage.[2] Clinton, realizing that former President Carter could negotiate with the North Koreans without having to appear tough—as a current president is generally expected by most Americans to be—endorsed Carter's private visit to North Korea while simultaneously distancing himself from it. Carter's negotiating skills and his reputation throughout the world and at home as someone who is genuinely concerned about people from distant cultures undoubtedly contributed to the breakthrough in talks with North Korea that enabled Clinton to pursue a negotiated settlement without threatening Pyongyang.

When Kim Il Sung died shortly after tensions between North Korea and Washington had diminished, Clinton seized the opportunity to act inconsistently with North Korea's expectations by extending "sincere condolences to the people of North Korea," and expressing appreciation for Kim's leadership in resuming talks with the United States. By so doing, Clinton, in the tradition of Nixon and Carter, recognized the importance of small gestures to facilitate diplomacy, and created an opening for more constructive negotiations with Kim's son and successor, Kim Jong Il. Roger Fisher and William Ury point out that "the best way to change other people's perceptions is to send them a message different from what they expect."[3] By considering the North Koreans' choices, putting himself in their shoes, and regarding negotiations as a cooperative effort to solve problems, Clinton managed to defuse the crisis. In August 1994, the United States and North Korea agreed to a complex series of tradeoffs. These included a promise by the United States to help North Korea to acquire safer nuclear technology that would not facilitate the production of plutonium for bombs. In exchange, North Korea would observe a freeze on nuclear activities, would not produce plutonium, and would continue to be a signatory to the Nuclear Non-Proliferation Treaty. Furthermore, diplomatic relations would be established between Washington and Pyongyang, and barriers to trade and investments would be eliminated, as part of the process of normalizing political and economic relations between the two countries.[4] The crisis with North Korea was resolved peacefully largely because American policymakers, Jimmy Carter, and Robert L. Gallucci, who was the U.S. chief negotiator in North Korea, embodied those aspects of U.S. culture that are conducive to peacefully solving problems with distant cultures.

The United States, in the late 1970s, successfully negotiated with culturally distant groups in Zimbabwe to end the civil war there and move that country toward independence. Few tangible American interests were involved, parties to the conflict were divided into various ideological camps, and African-Americans—the interest group primarily concerned with U.S. policy in southern Africa—favored a negotiated agreement. Furthermore, the leaders of the various factions had decided to negotiate and President Carter strongly supported nonviolent solutions.[5] Leaders of the opposition to white minority rule included bishops, priests, and school teachers who were neither strongly anti-American nor pro-Soviet. A key determinant of U.S. policy toward Zimbabwe was America's cultural proximity to Britain. Britain was the colonial power in Zimbabwe when the white minority under Ian Smith's leadership unilaterally declared independence. The kith and kin factor undoubtedly influenced the United States to support Britain's reliance on negotiations to persuade Smith to relinquish control over the black majority. Given the significance of race in the United States, it was unlikely that America would have used force against the white minority regime. Therefore, the cultural distance between Zimbabwe and the United States was not as great as it might have appeared.

Cultural factors also played a prominent role in America's efforts to help abolish apartheid in South Africa by peaceful means. Contrary to the realists' assumptions, domestic forces and ideational considerations strongly influenced American policymakers to pressure the white minority government to respect human rights and to negotiate a transition to majority rule. Whereas President Reagan, viewing conflicts in southern Africa as part of the broader East-West struggle, emphasized the communist threat and the need for "constructive engagement" with the white minority government, antiapartheid groups stressed that South Africa's apartheid policy was the problem. They did not perceive developments in South Africa as a major threat to U.S. interests. For many Americans, especially those of African descent, South Africa's problems were reminiscent of their own civil rights struggles.

Despite the cultural distance between America and South Africa, the racial issue helped to engender empathy and familiarity. The antiapartheid movement, composed of African-Americans, religious organizations, shareholders in American companies in South Africa, students, members of Congress, and various civil rights groups, directly challenged Reagan's policies by appealing to those American cultural values that support human rights, racial equality, equality of opportunity, the peaceful resolution of conflicts, and the rule of law. When Reagan vetoed the Comprehensive Antiapartheid Act that would have imposed a wide range of sanctions against South Africa, Congress overrode the President's veto.[6] U.S. policy toward South Africa clearly demonstrates the crucial role that cultural factors play in foreign policy. It also shows that ordinary Americans as well as prominent policymakers may appeal to cultural values to persuade the government to pursue a negotiated settlement. The abolition of apartheid and the transition to majority rule in South Africa undoubtedly would have been more protracted and violent without grassroots support in the United States for a peaceful resolution of the conflict.

Similarly, the component of American culture that favors negotiation was dominant in U.S. policy toward Central America, despite Reagan's preference for military solutions. Embodying many of America's cultural values, Reagan attempted to mobilize public support for his policies by drawing upon particular beliefs and values. These efforts failed, largely because many ordinary Americans who visited Nicaragua and El Salvador could ascertain for themselves the underlying causes of the conflicts. The Society of Friends, Jesuit organizations, various other Catholic groups, members of Congress, and others developed strong ties in Central America, thereby augmenting the cultural similarities which already existed between that region and the United States. American interest groups, many with cultural ties to Central America, mobilized support for negotiations. Political diversity within Nicaragua, and efforts by various Central American countries, especially Costa Rica, to find a negotiated settlement, encouraged attempts by Americans to find a peaceful solution. Furthermore, violence, including murder, against American citizens in El Salvador by groups funded by the United States ultimately helped undermine Reagan's arguments in favor of greater U.S. military involvement. Divisions within the Reagan administration, and strong Congressional opposition to American involvement in what many Americans regarded as "another Vietnam" quagmire, eroded public support for military solutions.[7] Direct U.S. military action was not perceived to be a low-cost policy. Refugees from Central America were already migrating to the United States, a problem that would only be exacerbated by a regional military conflict. An active Sanctuary movement had emerged in the United States to assist refugees. These developments underscored that war in Central America would have significant repercussions for the United States. Due to concerted domestic pressure by groups that represented that component of American culture that favors nonviolence and negotiations, Reagan's efforts failed, and hostilities between opposing factions in El Salvador and Nicaragua were terminated.

America's preference for using force instead of negotiations to resolve conflicts with distant cultures is demonstrated by the invasions of Grenada and Panama. Although both crises were complex, there is evidence to support the conclusion that cultural values played an important role in shaping America's decision to resort to military force. In both cases, the outcome was never in doubt. Victory was quick and decisive. In both Grenada and Panama, the specter of Americans being held hostage in the Third World was effectively used by Presidents Reagan and Bush to mobilize public support for their respective invasions.

The assassination of Grenada's leader, Maurice Bishop, other Cabinet members, and a number of Grenadian civilians served as a catalyst for Reagan to act. Whether the invasion, labeled as a "rescue operation" to prevent a reoccurrence of the Iranian hostage crisis by the Reagan administration, was the most appropriate action is still debatable. On October 22 1983, three days before the invasion, American and British representatives in St. George's, Grenada, had spoken with Hudson Austin and the newly established provisional military government members and had been assured that there was no threat to American students attending St. George's medical school. Furthermore, they were informed that the students could be evacuated. A day before the invasion, Canada had successfully transported its nationals off the island without any interference from the new leaders.[8] It took the U.S. rescue forces, many of whom relied on tourist maps to find their way around, approximately thirty-six hours after landing to reach a sizable number of Americans. Using the analogy of the Iran hostage crises had been an exaggeration of the threat. The Grenadians had time and opportunity to hold Americans hostage; they did not.[9] U.S. perception of the students' vulnerability had influenced Washington to resort to the quick use of military force. Britain, with political and cultural ties to Grenada, had favored negotiations.

Similar to Grenada, developments in Panama under Manuel Noriega partly influenced Bush to invade that country. Noriega's view of America as an impotent giant and his self-perception as invincible—combined with Bush's efforts to demonize him by portraying him as the devil incarnate, who was poisoning Americans with drugs, threatening the security of the Panama Canal, and constantly defying the United States— made negotiations almost impossible.[10] Noriega's control of Panamanian society and his use of the *Machos del Monte*—the macho men of the mountains—to intimidate his opposition helped reduce diversity within Panama, thereby diminishing the possibility of successful negotiations. Noriega's own violent behavior and his declaration of a "state of war" with the United States facilitated America's use of force against him.

Noriega's threats against Americans, the murder of a U.S. marine who ran a roadblock erected by the Machos, and the brutal treatment of another serviceman and his wife prompted America to act. President Bush stated: "General Noriega's reckless threats and attacks upon Americans in Panama created an imminent danger to the 35,000 American citizens in Panama. As President, I have no higher obligation than to safeguard the lives of American citizens."[11] The prospect of Americans being held hostage by a Third World dictator was effectively utilized by the Bush administration to arouse culturally-based fears and to gain support for a massive U.S. military operation that was designed to capture Noriega and bring him to the United States to be tried on drug trafficking charges.

A central argument advanced by the Bush administration for invading Panama was that Noriega's arrest would help to significantly reduce the flow of illegal drugs into the United States. To some extent, Bush's action indicated an attempt to avoid some of the responsibility for America's own consumption of almost half of the illegal drugs sold on the world market. The war was portrayed as a solution to a problem that continues to plague American society. Operation Just Cause, as the invasion of Panama was called, was a guaranteed success in terms of its brief duration and the low number of American casualties. The cases of Grenada and Panama demonstrate the United States' impatience with, and its willingness to use force against, distant cultures, when the costs to Americans are relatively low and victory is certain. The popularity ratings of Presidents Reagan and Bush increased dramatically following their military actions in Grenada and Panama.

On the other hand, Carter's decision to negotiate with Panama concerning the management and status of the Panama Canal reflected that component of American culture which strongly supports nonviolence and preventive diplomacy. Whereas Reagan and others who favored a military solution to the dispute with Panama (over largely symbolic issues concerning Panamanian sovereignty and control over the Canal) managed to mobilize significant opposition to negotiations, Carter appealed to Americans' sense of fairness, and their tolerance of distant cultures. Carter considered the Panama Canal treaties symbolic of America's new approach to U.S.-Latin American relations, one that would demonstrate greater respect for and sensitivity to Latin American concerns. By focusing on the underlying interests of the United States and Panama, the Carter administration and the Panamanian government worked out a formula that provided for America's continued use and defense of the Canal in exchange for U.S. recognition of Panama's sovereignty over it.[12] By respecting distant cultures, Carter secured U.S. foreign policy objectives without using force. However, David Skidmore concludes that "the experience did little to advance Carter's overall foreign policy agenda. Instead, Carter found his efforts mired in controversy, and the high price the administration paid for its final triumph provided a measure of its domestic weakness."[13] While Reagan and Bush increased their popularity ratings by using force, Carter's diplomatic efforts were generally ignored or perceived as evidence of weakness by most Americans.

In light of the United States' emergence as the world's dominant power, only self-restraint will prevent it from plunging into post-Cold War conflicts. Whereas the East-West rivalry engendered a degree of certainty in international affairs, the growing complexity of economic and political relations in the post-Cold War world directly challenges many American cultural values and assumptions. Ironically, the superpower rivalry, with all its inherent dangers and costs, was more consistent with U.S. worldviews, primarily because the contrast between good and evil was apparent to the vast majority of Americans. American financial resources seemed unlimited, and the nation was willing to take unilateral military actions. But new international as well as domestic realities demand an unusual degree of diplomatic and political patience. As William G. Hyland, editor of *Foreign Affairs*, notes, the post-Cold War world requires greater subtlety and sensitivity than the United States displayed during the East-West rivalry.[14]

Altering America's foreign policy, especially in relation to using force to settle problems, is a formidable task. Major changes in the underlying assumptions and operating principles of international affairs can occur only when a nation is willing and able to confront itself and reconsider its self-definition, self-perceptions, and perceptions of others. The cultural values that have influenced U.S. behavior toward other countries, especially those that are culturally distant, must be reexamined. Yet the strong tendency toward political conformity in America, a cultural trait that was reinforced by the military and psychological threats of the Cold War, will impede America's attempts to understand itself. American insecurities will remain a barrier to comprehending others. J. William Fulbright observed that "only a nation at peace with itself, with its transgressions as well as its achievements, is capable of a generous understanding of others."[15]

As the first among increasingly equal groups of nations, America will be challenged to lead by example. While force will remain an important instrument of foreign policy, its frequent use not only reduces its effectiveness but also raises questions about Washington's competence in managing foreign affairs. Moreover, reliance on military power to resolve problems that might be worked out through negotiations inadvertently strengthens arguments for using violence advanced by those regimes whose behavior threatens international peace and security. The massive bombardment of Iraq during Operation Desert Storm failed to deter Saddam Hussein from brutally suppressing Kurdish and Shiite rebellions shortly after the war, from continuing to rely on force to maintain control over Iraq, or from amassing Iraqi troops near Kuwait in late 1994.

Had the Gulf crisis been resolved relatively peacefully, with Iraq coerced into withdrawing from Kuwait through a combination of international sanctions and skillful diplomacy, a major step would have been taken toward diminishing the role of force in accomplishing foreign policy objectives. The rule of law would have been asserted through a collective but essentially nonviolent response to Hussein's aggression. Perhaps such efforts might have failed; but they were never given an opportunity to succeed. As Senator Joseph Biden asked, "What model—of any possible future utility—would be established by a process whereby the UN imposes sanctions briefly, after which the United States undertakes massive and unilateral military action with a veil of UN approval?"[16] America's hesitant and belated responses to ethnic cleansing in Bosnia have confirmed the limited usefulness of the lessons to be learned from Operation Desert Storm.

Complex international political and economic realities of the 21st century will make it increasingly difficult for policymakers to rely on analogies and operating principles that guided American foreign policy for much of the Cold War period. The costs of resolving conflicts violently are likely to become more burdensome as economic competitors seek to take advantage of the opportunities created by U.S. preoccupation with demonstrating resolve and leadership through the application of force. Contrary to the view, advanced by Charles Krauthammer, that the best hope for safety in the post-Cold War world is in America's "strength and will to lead a unipolar world, unashamedly laying down the rules of world order and being prepared to enforce them,"[17] significant threats to American and international security interests will be far more amenable to diplomacy than to military solutions.

The United States will need the cooperation of other countries, as well as nonstate actors, to achieve its objectives. This growing interdependence will inevitably engender the expansion of diplomatic activities. If isolationism is more conducive to unilateralism in international affairs, complex interdependence encourages dialogue, cooperation, compromise, and less confrontation among states.[18] Strong cultural links between

Israel and the United States foreclosed any consideration of military options to end the Palestinian-Israeli conflict.

To enhance the success of diplomatic initiatives, Americans will need to be better informed about national priorities and the role negotiations play in securing them. However, given the cultural ambivalence toward diplomacy and general distrust of diplomats, this will be a difficult undertaking. Instead of straightforward, black-white, good-evil thinking, society will have to grasp the complexities of international problems and accept the subtle diplomacy needed to address them. Because cultural factors that complicate U.S. foreign policy are deeply ingrained, Zbigniew Brzezinski believes that "only through sustained public education will America acquire the capacity to shape and sustain a policy that does justice to the complexities of our age."[19]

While it may be virtually impossible to modify those aspects of the dominant American culture that encourage using violence to solve international conflicts with distant cultures, the United States sustains many other values that, when emphasized, might contribute to the maintenance of American power and influence in the post-Cold War period. The American political system's remarkable stability, despite the country's racial, ethnic, and religious diversity, demonstrates an ability to compromise and to negotiate to settle differences internally. Furthermore, there is a strong aspect of U.S. culture that has always favored nonviolence and embraces humanitarianism. President Jimmy Carter's decision to tap into this component of American culture contributed to a breakthrough in the Middle East peace process that culminated in the Camp David agreement between Israel and Egypt. Those cultural values that are conducive to international negotiations should be strengthened. The proliferation of peace studies programs in American universities and colleges, the increased emphasis in elementary and high schools on strategies for peacefully resolving disputes, a growing willingness by policymakers and ordinary citizens alike to face up to the crime epidemic in the United States, a greater reluctance to sanction the gun culture and violence on television, and increased efforts to improve communication within families and various organizations may ultimately strengthen attempts to peacefully settle disputes with distant cultures.

As America expands its cultural circle domestically, to include groups that have been traditionally excluded, perceptions of "others" will be modified. While there is no guarantee that greater equality for women, racial minorities, and other groups that have historically suffered from society's adherence to values that perpetuate dominance, confrontation, and violence will directly affect American foreign policy, it seems reasonable to assume that these groups' growing influence on the policymaking process is likely to contribute to the ascendancy of negotiations. Women and minorities, especially African-Americans, tend to be relatively reluctant to support U.S. clashes with distant cultures. For example, their opposition to the use of force was pronounced in the Gulf War.

Given the importance of leaders' personalities, beliefs, and perceptions in their selection of instruments for conflict resolution, a new generation of leadership, symbolized by Bill Clinton's election as the first president who was not directly affected by World War II, is likely to emphasize different cultural values. Shaped by many of the negative consequences of the Cold War, particularly Vietnam, younger Americans have demonstrated a greater reluctance than their elders to support military intervention abroad. Their experiences as travelers and exchange students may have broadened their worldviews and modified their perceptions of distant cultures. They are likely to be more inclined than their predecessors to promote values that support negotiations with societies that are culturally distant. Nevertheless, the tenacity of those cultural values that support the use of force might make it difficult for this new generation of leaders to resist using military power to demonstrate American resolve and global leadership. President Clinton's use of force against Iraq shortly after his inauguration, his approval of UN military operations in Somalia, his initial response to North Korea, and his decision to militarily intervene in Haiti to restore democracy underscore the durability of cultural values and their influence on foreign affairs.

If negotiations are to succeed, communication with distant cultures must be improved. Cultural barriers often become impediments to negotiated settlements because of one side's inability or unwillingness to listen to the other, and vice versa. Effective communication can occur only when both sides attempt to understand each other's culturally influenced perceptions of reality. Too often, Americans assume that the other side is simply refusing to compromise. In many cases, the other side's hands may be tied by problems within their own society. To make their decisions easier for them, they must be helped to communicate what they perceive to be barriers to a negotiated settlement. Sometimes third parties might be more suitable interlocutors.

Presidents Richard Nixon and Jimmy Carter realized the importance of focusing on the future to secure a negotiated agreement. They resisted the dominant culture's preoccupation with immediate gratification, short-term thinking, and quick results. They patiently worked with the other side and made significant efforts to understand the other party's concerns, as well as the kind of world both sides wanted for future generations. Carter stated that "we would never have been successful in Camp David had it not been for our attention to the future."[20] Similarly, President Nixon, almost two decades before the Cold War ended, focused on the kind of future he wanted. At a dinner at San Clemente, Nixon told Leonid Brezhnev, the Soviet leader, that "I only hope that Russians and Americans in future generations may meet as we are meeting, in our homes as friends because of our personal affection for each other, not just as officials because of the necessity of settling differences."[21] The complex challenges of the 21st century will undoubtedly require policymakers to think about the long-term consequences of their actions and to give greater consideration to cultural influences on foreign policy.

NOTES

Introduction

1. Samuel P. Huntington, "The Clash of Civilizations?" *Foreign Affairs* 72, no. 3 (Summer 1993): 22. See also John J. Mearsheimer, "Back to the Future: Instability in Europe After the Cold War," *International Security* 15, no. 1 (Summer 1990): 6.

2. James N. Rosenau, "Introduction," in *The Domestic Sources of Foreign Policy*, ed. James N. Rosenau (New York: Free Press, 1967), 2.

3. William J. Clinton, "Address to the Nation on the Strike on Iraqi Intelligence Headquarters, June 26 1993," *Weekly Compilation of Presidential Documents* 29, no. 26 (July 5 1993): 1181.

4. Charles Ostrom and Brian Job, "The President and the Political Use of Force," *American Political Science Review* 80, no. 2 (June 1986): 559. See also Daniel C. Hallin and Todd Gitlin, "The Gulf War as Popular Culture and Television Drama," in *Taken By Storm: The Media, Public Opinion and U.S. Foreign Policy in the Gulf War*, eds. W. Lance Bennett and David L. Paletz (Chicago: University of Chicago Press, 1994), 149; John E. Mueller, *War, Presidents, and Public Opinion* (New York: John Wiley and Sons, 1973), 115–118.

5. James Meernik, "Presidential Decision Making and the Political Use of Military Force," *International Studies Quarterly* 38, no. 1 (March 1994): 127.

Chapter 1

1. Michael Vlahos, "Culture and Foreign Policy," *Foreign Policy*, no. 82 (Spring 1991): 59.

2. Eugene V. Rostow, *Toward Managed Peace: The National Security Interests of the United States, 1759 to the Present* (New Haven: Yale University Press, 1993), 384.

3. Christopher Coker, *Reflections on American Foreign Policy Since 1945* (New York: St. Martin's Press, 1989), 1; James N. Rosenau, "Introduction," in *The Domestic Sources of Foreign Policy*, ed. James N. Rosenau (New York: Free Press, 1967), 2; I.M. Destler, Leslie H. Gelb, and Anthony Lake, *Our Own Worst Enemy: The Unmaking of American Foreign Policy* (New York: Simon and Schuster, 1984), 14; Michael Vlahos, "The End of America's Postwar Ethos," *Foreign Affairs* 66, no. 5 (Summer 1988): 1091.

4. Vlahos, "Culture and Foreign Policy," 63.

5. Bruce J. Bueno de Mesquita, et al. "Introduction," *Journal of Conflict Resolution* 35, no. 2 (June 1991): 182. See Kenneth N. Waltz, *Theory of International Politics* (Reading, Mass.: Addison-Wesley, 1979), 173.

6. Kenneth N. Waltz, *Man, the State, and War* (New York: Columbia University Press, 1959), 238.

7. George F. Kennan, "Morality and Foreign Policy," *Foreign Affairs* 64, no. 2 (Winter 1985/86): 206.

8. Hans J. Morgenthau, *Politics Among Nations* (New York: Alfred A. Knopf, 1960), 9.

9. Bruce M. Russett, *Controlling the Sword: The Democratic Governance of National Security* (Cambridge, Mass.: Harvard University Press, 1990), 8–9. Kiron Skinner argues that strategies of security linking (tying progress in nuclear arms control and détente to Soviet international behavior) was as much about the domestic politics of national defense as it was about Soviet malfeasance. See Kiron Skinner, *Executive and Congressional Use of Security Linkage* (Santa Monica, California: Rand, 1994), 6.

10. Jack Citrim, et al., "Is American Nationalism Changing? Implications for Foreign Policy," *International Studies Quarterly* 38, no. 1 (March 1994): 2.

11. Mark M. Nelson, "Transatlantic Travails," *Foreign Policy*, no. 92 (Fall 1993): 76.

12. William S. Lind, "Defending Western Culture," *Foreign Policy*, no. 84 (Fall 1991): 40.

13. John A. Kroll, "The Complexity of Interdependence," *International Studies Quarterly* 37, no.3 (September 1993): 322.

14. Quincy Wright, *A Study of War* (Chicago: University of Chicago Press, 1964), 334.

15. Samuel P. Huntington, "The Clash of Civilizations?" *Foreign Affairs* 72, no. 3 (Summer 1993): 36.

16. Bruce M. Russett, *Controlling the Sword*, 121–124; D. Marc Kilgour, "Domestic Structure and War Behavior," *Journal of Conflict Resolution* 35, no. 2 (June 1991): 266–284; T. Clifton Morgan and Sally Howard Campbell, "Domestic Structure, Decisional Constraints, and War," *Journal of Conflict Resolution* 35, no. 2 (June 1991): 187–211; and William J. Dixon, "Democracy and the Management of International Conflict," *Journal of Conflict Resolution* 37, no. 1 (March 1993): 42–68.

17. Rostow, *Toward Managed Peace*, 104.

18. Ibid., 140.

19. Chris Jenks, *Culture* (New York: Routledge, 1993), 8; Raymond Scupin, *Cultural Anthropology* (Englewood Cliffs, N.J.: Prentice Hall, 1992), 53.

20. Norbert Elias, *The History of Manners* (New York: Pantheon, 1987), 4.

21. Clifford Geertz, *The Interpretation of Cultures* (New York: Basic Books, 1973), 89.

22. William A. Haviland, *Cultural Anthropology* (Forth Worth, Texas: Holt, Rinehart and Winston, 1990), 38.

23. Geertz, *Interpretation*, 407.

24. Ibid., 408.

25. Jenks, *Culture*, 10.

26. Anthony Giddens, ed. *Emile Durkheim: Selected Writings* (Cambridge: Cambridge University Press, 1972), 5.

27. Peter L. Berger and Thomas Luckman, *The Social Construction of Reality* (New York: Doubleday, 1966), 115.

28. Melford E. Spiro, *Culture and Human Nature* (New Brunswick, N.J.: Transaction Books, 1994), 209.

29. Berger and Luckman, *The Social Construction of Reality*, 118; Robert Wuthnow, et al. *Cultural Analyis* (London: Routledge and Kegan Paul, 1986), 25.

30. Edward T. Hall and Mildred Reed Hall, *Hidden Differences* (Garden City, N.Y.: Anchor Press/Doubleday, 1987), XVII.

31. K.J. Holsti, *International Politics* (Englewood Cliffs, N.J.: Prentice Hall, 1992), 293.

32. Ibid., 292.

33. Jack S. Levy, "Misperceptions and the Causes of War," *World Politics* 36, no. 1 (October 1983): 88.

34. Ole R. Holsti, "The Belief System and National Images," in *Analyzing International Relations*, eds. William D. Coplin and Charles W. Kegley (New York: Praeger Publishers, 1975), 23. See also Lucian W. Pye, *Asian Power and Politics: The Cultural Dimensions of Authority* (Cambridge, Mass.: Harvard University Press, 1985), 20; Grace Ganter and Margaret Yeakel, *Human Behavior and the Social Work Environment* (New York: Columbia University Press, 1980), 9; Elliot P. Skinner, "Development in Africa: A Cultural Perspective," *The Fletcher Forum* 13, no. 2 (1989): 206; Donald J. Devine, *The Political Culture of the United States* (Boston: Little, Brown and Company, 1972), 6.

35. Douglas W. Blum, "The Soviet Foreign Policy Belief System: Beliefs, Politics, and Foreign Policy Outcomes," *International Studies Quarterly* 37, no. 4 (December 1993): 376.

36. Ibid., 377.

37. Michael Vlahos, "Culture and Foreign Policy, *Foreign Policy* no. 82 (Spring 1991): 72. See also Aaron Wildavsky, "Frames of Reference Come From Cultures: A Predictive Theory," in *The Relevance of Culture*, ed. Morris Freilich (New York: Bergin and Garvey, 1989), 61; and Seymour Martin Lipset, *The First New Nation: The United States in Historical Perspective* (New York: W.W. Norton, 1979), 103.

38. Scupin, *Cultural Anthropology*, 63.

39. Richard W. Cottam, *Foreign Policy Motivation* (Pittsburgh: University of Pittsburgh Press, 1977), 325.

40. Max Weber, *The Protestant Ethic and the Spirit of Capitalism* (New York: Charles Scribner's Sons, 1958).

41. James Davison Hunter, *Culture Wars: The Struggle to Define America* (New York: Basic Books, 1991), 58.

42. Will Herberg, *Protestant, Catholic and Jew: An Essay in American Religious Sociology* (Chicago: The University of Chicago Press, 1983), 3.

43. Haynes Johnson, *Sleepwalking Through History: America and the Reagan Years* (New York: W.W. Norton, 1991), 141.

44. Morton H. Halperin and Jeanne M. Woods, "Ending the Cold War at Home," *Foreign Policy*, no. 81 (Winter 1990–91): 129.

45. Stephen J. Whitfield, *The Culture of the Cold War* (Baltimore: The Johns Hopkins University Press, 1990), 54. See also Richard Bernstein, "Long Conflict Deeply Marked the Self-Image of Americans," *The New York Times*, February 2 1992, A9.

46. Louis Hartz, *The Liberal Tradition in America* (New York: Harcourt, Brace, and Company, 1955), 287. See also J. William Fulbright, *The Arrogance of Power* (New York: Random House, 1966), 245–250; and John P. Lovell, "The United States as Ally and Adversary in East Asia: Reflection on Culture and Foreign Policy," in *Culture and International Relations* (New York: Praeger, 1990), 92.

47. John Spanier, *American Foreign Policy Since World War II* (Washington, D.C.: Congressional Quarterly Press, 1991), 9.

48. Alexis de Tocqueville, *Democracy in America, Vol. 1*, ed. J.P. Mayer (New York: Doubleday, 1969), 254–55.

49. Max Lerner, *America as a Civilization: Life and Thought in the United States Today* (New York: Henry Holt and Company, 1987), 981; Daniel C. Hallin and Todd Gitlin, "The Gulf War as a Popular Culture and Television Drama," in *Taken by Storm: The Media, Public Opinion, and U.S. Foreign Policy in the Gulf War*, eds. W. Lance Bennett and David L. Paletz (Chicago: University of Chicago Press, 1994), 150; John E. Mueller, *War, Presidents, and Public Opinion* (New York: John Wiley and Sons, 1973), 116; John E. Mueller, *Policy and Opinion in the Gulf War* (Chicago: University of Chicago Press, 1994).

50. Michael H. Hunt, *Ideology and U.S. Foreign Policy* (New Haven: Yale University Press, 1987), 16; Christopher Coker, *Reflections*, 2–4; Stanley Hoffmann, "On the Political Psychology of Peace and War: A Critique and an Agenda," *Political Psychology* 7, no. 1 (March 1986): 14; Stanley Hoffmann, *Gulliver's Troubles, or the Setting of American Foreign Policy* (New York: McGraw-Hill, 1968), xv.

51. Ronald Reagan, "Remarks at the Annual Convention of the American Legion in Salt Lake City, Utah, September 4 1984," *Public Papers of the Presidents of the United States: Ronald Reagan, Book II* (Washington, D.C.: U.S. Government Printing Office, 1987), 1230.

52. Ronald Reagan, "Final Radio Address to the Nation, January 14 1989," *Public Papers of the Presidents of the United States: Ronald Reagan, Book II* (Washington, D.C.: U.S. Government Printing Office, 1991), 1736.

53. Fritz Gaenslen, "Culture and Decision Making in China, Japan, Russia, and the United States," *World Politics* 39, no. 1 (October 1986): 81.

54. Robert Jervis, "Domino Beliefs and Strategic Behavior," in *Dominoes and Bandwagons*, eds. Robert Jervis and Jack Snyder (New York: Columbia University Press, 1991), 40.

55. Gaenslen, 101.

56. Ken Booth, *Strategy and Ethnocentrism* (New York: Holmes and Meier Publishers, 1979), 13; Marshall H. Segall, et al. *Human Behavior in Global Perspective* (New York: Pergamon Press, 1990), 343.

57. Noel Kaplowitz, "National Self-Images, Perception of Enemies, and Conflict Strategies," *Political Psychology* 11, no. 1 (March 1990): 47.

58. Mahmoud G. El Warfally, *Imagery and Ideology in U.S. Policy Toward Libya* (Pittsburgh: University of Pittsburgh Press, 1988), 7; and Martha L. Cottam, "The Carter Administration Toward Nicaragua," *Political Science Quarterly* 107, no. 1 (Spring 1992): 126.

59. H. Mark Carlsnaes, *Ideology and Myth in American Politics* (Boston: Little, Brown, and Company, 1976), 4.

60. Walter Carlsnaes, *Ideology and Foreign Policy* (Oxford: Basil Blackwell, 1986), 159.

61. John B. Thompson, *Ideology and Modern Culture* (Stanford: Stanford University Press, 1990), 7; Mona Harrington, *The Dream of Deliverance in American Politics* (New York: Alfred A. Knopf, 1976), 15.

62. Geertz, *The Interdependence of Cultures*, 218.

63. Ibid., 219.

64. Ibid., 220.

65. Holsti, *International Politics*, 296.

66. Ibid., 296.

67. Roelofs, *Ideology and Myth*, 4.

68. Richard Slotkin, *Regeneration Through Violence: The Mythology of the American Frontier* (Middletown, CT.: Wesleyan University Press, 1973), 7.

69. Richard Slotkin, *Gunfighter Nation: The Myth of the Frontier in Twentieth Century America* (New York: Atheneum, 1992), 10.

70. Carl N. Degler, *Out of Our Past: The Forces That Shaped Modern America* (New York: Harper and Row, 1984), 5.

71. See Arthur Schlesinger, "Foreign Policy and the American Character," *Foreign Affairs* 62, no. 1 (Fall 1983): 1.

72. Hunt, *Ideology*, 14.

73. Loren Baritz, *City On A Hill: A History of Ideas and Myths in America* (New York: John Wiley and Sons, 1964), 17.

74. Ronald Reagan, "Remarks at the Annual Convention of the National Religious Broadcasters, January 31 1983," *Public Papers of the Presidents of the United States: Ronald Reagan, Book I* (Washington, D.C.: U.S. Government Printing Office, 1984), 152.

75. Linda Colley, *Britons: Forging the Nation 1707–1837* (New Haven: Yale University Press, 1992), 54.

76. James Schlesinger, *America At Century's End* (New York: Columbia University Press, 1989), 7. Tami R. Davis and Jean M. Lynn-Jones, "City Upon a Hill," *Foreign Policy*, no. 66 (Spring 1987): 21; Seymour Martin Lipset, "American Exceptionalism Reaffirmed," in *Is America Different? A New Look At American Exceptionalism*, ed. Byron E. Shafer (Oxford: Clarendon Press, 1991), 6.

77. Baritz, *City On A Hill*, 98.

78. Loren Baritz, *Backfire: A History of How American Culture Led Us Into Vietnam and Made Us Fight the Way We Did* (New York: William Morrow and Company, 1985), 37; Richard J. Kerry, *The Star-Spangled Mirror: America's Image of Itself and the World* (Savage, Maryland: Rowman and Littlefield, 1990), 115.

79. Thomas Paine, *Common Sense and Other Political Writings*, ed. Nelson F. Adkins (Indianapolis: The Bobbs-Merrill Company, 1953), 51.

80. Coral Bell, *The Reagan Paradox: American Foreign Policy in the 1980s* (New Brunswick, New Jersey: Rutgers University Press, 1989), 139–140.

81. Garry Wills, *Reagan's America: Innocents at Home* (New York: Doubleday and Co., 1987), 4.

82. Lipset, *The First New Nation*, 166–169.

83. See various public opinion polls on religion in *The Christian Science Monitor*, December 21 1990, p. 19; and "Political Attitudes, Social Values, and Religious Beliefs," *The Christian Science Monitor*, November 22 1991, p. 19.

84. George Gallup, Jr. and Jim Castelli, *The People's Religion: American Faith in the 90s* (New York: Macmillan Publishing Company, 1989), 21.

85. Samuel P. Huntington, *American Politics: The Promise of Disharmony* (Cambridge, Mass.: Harvard University Press, 1981), 158–159.

86. Baritz, *City On A Hill*, 96.

87. Tocqueville, *Democracy in America*, 294.

88. Nathan O. Hatch, *The Democratization of American Christianity* (New Haven: Yale University Press, 1989), 9.

89. Tocqueville, *Democracy in America*, 293.

90. Cynthia Toolin, "American Civil Religion From 1789 to 1981: A Content Analysis of Presidential Inaugural Addresses," *Review of Religious Research* 25, no. 1 (September 1983): 45. See also Robert N. Bellah, "Civil Religion in America," *Daedalus* 96, no. 1 (Winter 1967): 3–4.

91. Bellah, "Civil Religion in America," 13.

92. Lloyd E. Ambrosius, *Wilsonian Statecraft: Theory and Practice of Liberal Internationalism During World War I* (Wilmington, Delaware: Scholarly Resources, 1991), 13.

93. Richard Marius, "Musings on the Mysteries of the American South," *Daedalus* 113, no. 3 (Summer 1984): 155–162; Flo Conway and Jim Siegelman, *Holy Terror: The Fundamentalist War on America's Freedoms* (New York: Doubleday, 1982), 4; Robert Dallek, *Ronald Reagan: The Politics of Symbolism* (Cambridge, Mass.: Harvard University Press, 1984), 133.

94. Ronald Reagan, "Message to the Congress Transmitting the Proposed Constitutional Amendment on Prayer in Schools, March 8 1983," *Public Papers of the Presidents of the United States: Ronald Reagan, Book I* (Washington, D.C.: U.S. Government Printing Office, 1984), 365.

95. George Bush, "Remarks at the National Prayer Breakfast, January 31 1991," *Weekly Compilation of Presidential Documents* 27, no. 5 (February 1991): 101.

96. Andrew Rosenthal, "President Strikes a Religious Note," *The New York Times*, January 28 1992, A11; George Bush, "Address Before a Joint Session of the Congress on the State of the Union, January 28 1992," *Weekly Compilation of Presidential Documents* 28, no. 5 (February 3 1992): 170–176; and George Bush, "Remarks at the National Prayer Breakfast, January 30 1992," *Weekly Compilation of Presidential Documents* 28, no. 5 (February 3 1992): 178–179.

97. Hunt, *Ideology*, 90.

98. Michael Adas, *Machines as the Measure of Men: Science, Technology, and Ideologies of Western Dominance* (Ithaca: Cornell University Press, 1989), 216.

99. Baritz, *City On A Hill*, 100; see also Michael Paul Rogin, *Ronald Reagan, The Movie* (Berkeley: University of California Press, 1987), 45–47; Richard Drinnon, *Facing West: The Metaphysics of Indian-Hating and Empire Building* (Minneapolis: University of Minnesota Press, 1980), XVII.

100. Richard Hofstadter, *Social Darwinism in American Thought* (Boston: Beacon Press, 1955), 171; Reginald Horsman, *Race and Manifest Destiny* (Cambridge, Mass.: Harvard University Press, 1981), 207; George M. Fredrickson, *White Supremacy: A Comparative Study in American and South African History* (New York: Oxford University Press, 1981), XI.

101. Tamar Lewin, "Study Points to Increase in Tolerance of Ethnicity," *The New York Times*, January 8 1992, A10.

102. Alvin Z. Rubinstein and Donald E. Smith, *Anti-Americanism in the Third Word: Implications for U.S. Foreign Policy* (New York: Praeger, 1985), 4; Charles William Maynes, "America's Third World Hang-Ups," *Foreign Policy*, no. 71 (Summer 1988), 121.

103. Maynes, "America's Third World Hang-Ups," 120.

104. Howard J. Wiarda, *Ethnocentrism in Foreign Policy: Can We Understand the Third World?* (Washington, D.C.: American Enterprise Institute, 1985), 1. For an analysis of racial influences on U.S. policies toward Japan, see John W. Dower, *War Without Mercy: Race and Power in the Pacific War* (New York: Pantheon Books, 1986).

Chapter 2

1. Jonathan Stevenson, "Hope Restored In Somalia?" *Foreign Policy*, no. 91 (Summer 1993): 140.

2. Quincy Wright, *A Study of War* (Chicago: University of Chicago Press, 1964), 325.

3. Ibid., 220.

4. Charles W. Ostrom and Brian L. Job, "The President and the Political Use of Force," *American Political Science Review* 80, no. 2 (June 1986): 559. See also John A. Vasquez, "Foreign Policy, Learning, and War," in *New Directions in the Study of Foreign Policy*, eds. Charles F. Herman, Charles W. Kegley, and James N. Rosenau (Boston: Allen and Unwin, 1987), 367.

5. Rafael Moses, "Empathy and Dis-Empathy in Political Conflict," *Political Psychology* 6, no. 1 (March 1985): 135.

6. Albert Bandura, "Selective Activism and Disengagement of Moral Control," *Journal of Social Issues* 46, no. 1 (1990): 1.

7. Susan Opotow, "Moral Exclusion and Injustice," *Journal of Social Issues* 46, no.1 (1990): 1.

8. J. William Fulbright, *The Arrogance of Power* (New York: Random House, 1966), 5.

9. Reinhold Niebuhr, *The Irony of American History* (New York: Charles Scribner's Sons, 1952), 21.

10. William J. Dixon, "Democracy and the Management of International Conflict," *Journal of Conflict Resolution* 37, no. 1 (March 1993): 45.

11. Bruce M. Russett, "A Post-Thucydides, Post-Cold War World," *The Mediterranean Quarterly* 4, no. 1 (Winter 1993): 55. See also D. Marc Kilgour, "Domestic Structure and War Behavior," *Journal of Conflict Resolution* 35, no. 2 (June 1991): 266.

12. James Meernik, "Presidential Decision Making and the Political Use of Military Force," *International Studies Quarterly* 38, no. 1 (March 1994): 121.

13. Richard Falk, "Reflections on Democracy and the Gulf War," *Alternatives* 16, no. 2 (Spring 1991): 269; and Greg Cashman, *What Causes War?* (New York: Lexington Books, 1993), 151.

14. Dina A. Zinnes and Jonathan Wilkenfeld, "An Analysis of Foreign Conflict Behavior of Nations," in *Comparative Foreign Policy*, ed. Wolfram Hanrieder (New York: David McKay, 1971), 167–213; R.T. Rummel, "The Relationship Between National Attributes and Foreign Conflict Behavior," in *Quantitative International Politics*, ed. J. David Singer (New York: Free Press, 1968), 202–208.

15. Charles W. Kegley, Neil R. Richardson, and Gunther Richter, "Conflict at Home and Abroad: An Empirical Extension," *The Journal of Politics* 40, no. 3 (August 1978): 751.

16. Marc Howard Ross, "Internal and External Conflict: Cross-Cultural Evidence and a New Analysis," *Journal of Conflict Resolution* 29, no. 4 (December 1985), 549.

17. Cashman, 32.

18. Lewis A. Coser, "Conflict With Out-Groups and Group Structure," in *Conflict Behavior and Linkage Politics*, ed. Jonathan Wilkenfeld (New York: David McKay, 1973), 15.

19. Ibid.,17.

20. Ibid., 20. See also Jonathan Wilkenfeld, et al. *Foreign Policy Behavior* (Beverly Hills: Sage Publications, 1980), 62.

21. Jean Bethke Elshtain, "The Problem With Peace," In *Women, Militarization and War*, eds. Jean Bethke Elshtain and Sheila Tobias (Savage, Maryland: Rowman and Littlefield, 1990), 256.

22. Ibid., 259.

23. T.W. Africa, "Urban Violence in Imperial Rome," *Journal of Interdisciplinary History* 2 (Summer 1971): 5.

24. William V. Harris, *War and Imperialism in Republican Rome 327–70 B.C.* (Oxford: Clarendon Press, 1979), 9–10.

25. Ibid., 43.

26. Elias J. Bickerman, "The Roman Republic," in *The Columbia History of the World*, eds. John A. Garranty and Peter Gay (New York: Harper and Row, 1972), 202.

27. Ibid., 247.

28. Linda Colley, *Britons: Forging the Nation 1707–1837* (New Haven: Yale University Press, 1992), 5.

29. Ibid., 168–170.

30. Ted Robert Gurr, "On the History of Violent Crime in Europe and America," in *Violence in America: Historical and Comparative Perspectives*, eds. Hugh Davis Graham and Ted Robert Gurr (Beverly Hills: Sage Publications, 1979), 354.

31. R.K. Webb, "The Napoleonic Era," in *The Columbia History of the World*, 783.

32. Fritz Fischer, *Germany's Aims in the First World War* (New York: W.W. Norton, 1967), 3.

33. Ibid., 118.

34. Ian Buruma, *Behind the Mask* (New York: Penguin, 1984), 10.

35. Paul Varley, Ivan Morris, and Nobuko Morris, *Samurai* (New York: Dell, 1970), 33.

36. Ibid., 43.

37. Buruma, 193.

38. Ibid., 221.

39. See Margaret Mead, "Warfare Is Only An Invention—Not Biological Necessity," in *Peace and War*, eds. Charles Beitz and Theodore Herman (San Francisco: W.H. Freeman, 1973), 112–118.

40. Napoleon A Chagnon, *Yanomamo* (Fort Worth, Texas: Harcourt Brace Johanovich, 1992), 125.

41. Ibid., 183–187.

42. Richard Maxwell Brown, "Historical Patterns of American Violence," in *Violence in America*, 19.

43. Richard Slotkin, *Gunfighter Nation: The Myth of the Frontier in Twentieth Century America* (New York: Atheneum, 1992), 500.

44. Ibid., 13.

45. Stanley Hoffmann, *Gulliver's Troubles, Or the Setting of American Foreign Policy* (New York: McGraw Hill, 1968), 181.

46. Ibid., 183.

47. Louis Hartz, "A Comparative Study of Fragment Cultures," in *Violence in America*, 120.

48. Slotkin, 492.

49. Alexis de Tocqueville, *Democracy in America*, Vol. 1, ed. J.P. Mayer (New York: Doubleday, 1969), 321.

50. Bartholome de Las Casas, " Cruelties of Spaniards," in *The Spanish Tradition in America*, ed. Charles Gibson (New York: Harper and Row, 1968), 106.

51. King Ferdinand and Queen Isabella, "Royal Orders Concerning Indians," in *The Spanish Tradition in America*, 41.

52. Pope Paul II, "Indians Are Men," in *The Spanish Tradition in America*, 105.

53. Lewis Hanke, "Spain and Portugal in America," in *The Columbia History of the World*, 657.

54. Ibid., 656.

55. Charles Gibson, *Spain In America* (New York: Harper Torchbooks, 1967), 79.

56. W.J. Eccles, *France in America* (East Lansing, Michigan: Michigan State University Press, 1990), 40.

57. James Axtell, *The Invasion Within: The Contest of Cultures in Colonial North America* (New York: Oxford University Press, 1985), 247.

58. J.H. Elliot, "The Rediscovery of America," *The New York Review of Books*, June 24 1993, 39.

59. Axtell, 43.

60. Ibid., 71.

61. Brown, 31.

62. Kenneth McNaught, *The Pelican History of Canada* (Middlesex, England: Penguin Books, 1969), 76.

63. Seymour Martin Lipset, *Continental Divide: The Values and Institutions of the United States and Canada* (New York: Routledge, 1990), 94.

64. Gunnar Myrdal, *An American Dilemma: The Negro Problem in Modern Democracy, Vol. II* (New York: Harper Torchbooks, 1962), 560.

65. See John Felton, "Introduction," in *The Iran-Contra Puzzle*, ed. Patricia Ann O'Connor (Washington D.C.: Congressional Quarterly Press, 1987), 3–7; Robert McFarlane, "Reasons for the Arms Sales and Expected Benefits," in *U.S. Policy Toward Iran*, Hearings before the U.S. Senate Committee on Foreign Relations, January 19 1987 (Washington, D.C.: U.S. Government Printing Office, 1987), 36; Ronald Reagan, "U.S. Initiative to Iran," *Department of State Bulletin* (January 1987): 65.

66. Steven R. Weisman, "A Deep Split in Attitudes is Developing," *The New York Times*, December 3 1991, A6.

67. Meernik, "Presidential Decision Making," 130.

68. Brown, 41.

69. Hugh Davis Graham, "The Paradox of American Violence," in *Violence in America*, 481.

70. Fox Butterfield, "Experts Explore Rise in Mass Murders," *The New York Times*, October 19 1991, A6.

71. United Nations Development Program, *Human Development Report 1991* (New York: Oxford University Press, 1991), 176.

72. "Physicians Begin a Program to Combat Family Violence," *The New York Times*, October 17 1991, A16; Richard J. Gelles and Murray Strauss, *Intimate Violence* (New York: Simon and Schuster, 1988).

73. Irwin A. Hyman, *Reading, Writing and the Hickory Stick* (Lexington, Mass.: Lexington Books, 1990), 20; David G. Gil, *Violence Against Children: Physical Child Abuse in the United States* (Cambridge, Mass.: Harvard University Press, 1970), 8.

74. Erik Larson, "The Story of a Gun," *The Atlantic Monthly* 371, no. 1 (January 1993): 65; Josh Sugarmann, "The Gun Market Is Wide Open in America," *The Christian Science Monitor*, April 23 1993, 19.

75. Melanie Kaye Kantrowitz, *The Issue is Power: Essays on Women, Jews, Violence, and Resistance* (San Francisco: Aunt Lute Books, 1992), 20.

76. Douglas Weil and David Hemenway, "Gun Accidents Are Waiting to Happen," *Harvard Gazette*, June 12 1992, 8.

77. Federal Bureau of Investigation, *Uniform Crime Report for the United States* (Washington, D.C.: U.S. Government Printing Office, 1987), 11; Philip J. Hilts, "Gunshots Killing More Teenagers," *The New York Times*, June 10 1992, C18.

78. James Brady, "Straight Talk About Children and Guns," *The New York Times*, March 30 1992, A15; Joseph B. Treaster, "Teen-Age Gunslinging Is On Rise," *The New York Time*, February 17 1992, A1.

79. Lance Murrow, "Childhood's End," *Time*, March 9 1992, 23.

80. A. M. Rosenthal, "If Not Now, When?" *The New York Times*, May 5 1992, A17.

81. James Patterson and Peter Kim, *The Day America Told the Truth* (New York: Prentice Hall, 1991), 123.

82. Deborah Prothow-Stith and Michele Weissman, *Deadly Consequences* (New York: HarperCollins, 1991), 46.

83. Richard Lipsky, *How We Play the Game: Why Sports Dominate American Life* (Boston: Beacon Press, 1981), 109; Wilbert Marcellus Leonard, *A Sociological Perspective of Sport* (New York: Macmillan, 1988), 391.

84. Lipsky, 24.

85. Timothy J. Curry and Robert M. Jiobu, *Sports: A Social Perspective* (Englewood Cliffs, New Jersey: Prentice Hall, 1984), 45.

86. David D. Newsom, "The Gulf War Wasn't A Sports Match That Ended With Victory," *The Christian Science Monitor*, April 10 1991, 19.

87. Myrian Miedzian, *Boys Will Be Boys: Breaking the Link Between Masculinity and Violence* (New York: Doubleday, 1991), 24.

88. Cameron Bar, "U.S.: World's Lock-'Em-Up Leader," *The Christian Science Monitor*, March 7 1991, 12; Fox Butterfield, "U.S. Expands Its Lead in the Rate of Imprisonment," *The New York Times*, February 11 1992, C18.

89. Alec Gallup and Frank Newport, "Death Penalty Support Remains Strong," *The Gallup Poll Monthly*, no. 309 (June 1991): 40.

90. Bruce M. Russett and Alfred Stepan, "The Military in America: New Parameters, New Problems, New Approaches," in *Military Force and American Society*, eds. Bruce M. Russett and Alfred Stepan (New York: Harper and Row, 1973), 5–6.

91. Sam Keen, *Fire in the Belly: On Being a Man* (New York: Bantam Books, 1991), 39.

92. "Arming Dictators," *The Defense Monitor* 21, no. 5 (1992): 1.

93. Chris Hedges, "Many Islamic Militants Trained in Afghan War," *The New York Times*, March 28 1993, A9.

94. David Nyhan, "Another War's Deadly Legacy," *The Boston Globe*, December 6 1990, A5.

95. See Lynne Sharon Schwartz, "This is an Article on Diction?" *The New York Times*, December 15 1991, E15.

96. David C. Hendrickson, "The Renovation of American Foreign Policy," *Foreign Affairs* 71, no. 2 (Spring 1992): 57.

97. James Chace and Caleb Carr, *America Invulnerable: The Quest for Absolute Security From 1812 to Star Wars* (New York: Summit Books, 1988), 13.

98. Hoffmann, 135.

99. Robert Jervis, *Perception and Misperception in International Politics* (Princeton, New Jersey: Princeton University Press, 1976), 230.

100. George Bush, "Interview," *This Week With David Brinkley—ABC News*, December 1 1991.

101. Sidney Blumenthal, *"Our Long National Daydream* (New York: Harper and Row, 1988), 296.

102. Lee E. Dutter, "The Seventy-Five Years' War, 1914–1989: Some Observations on the Psychology of American Foreign Policy Making," *Political Psychology* 12, no. 3 (September 1991): 532.

103. Richard E, Neustadt and Ernest R. May, *Thinking in Time: The Uses of History for Decision-Making* (New York: The Free Press, 1986), 47.

Chapter 3

1. The author is indebted to David D. Newsom for this point. Personal Correspondence, December 20 1992.

2. Glen Fisher, *International Negotiation: A Cross-Cultural Perspective* (Chicago: Intercultural Press, 1980), 11.

3. Ken Booth, *Strategy and Ethnocentrism* (New York: Holmes and Meier Publishers, 1979), 65.

4. Ole Elgstrom, "Norms, Culture, and Cognitive Patterns in Foreign Aid Negotiations," *Negotiation Journal* 6, no. 2 (April 1990): 156.

5. Geert Hofstede, "Cultural Predictors of National Negotiating Styles," in *Processes of International Negotiations*, ed. Frances Mautner-Markhof (Boulder, CO: Westview Press, 1989), 200.

6. See Roger Fisher and William Ury, *Getting to Yes: Negotiating Agreement Without Giving In* (New York: Penguin, 1983), XI; Fred Charles Ikle, *How Nations Negotiate* (New York: Praeger, 1967), 3; R.P. Barston, *Modern Diplomacy* (London: Longman, 1988), 75; Dean G. Pruitt, *Negotiation Behavior* (New York: Academic Press, 1981), 1.

7. Hans J. Morgenthau, *Politics Among Nations: The Struggle for Power and Peace* (New York: Alfred A. Knopf, 1973), 521.

8. Harold H. Saunders, "An Historic Challenge to Rethink How Nations Relate," in *The Psychodynamics of International Relationships, vol. 1: Concepts and Theories*, ed. Vamik D. Volkan et al. (Lexington, Mass.: Lexington Books, 1990), 8.

9. Richard N. Haas, *Conflicts Unending: The United States and Regional Disputes* (New Haven: Yale University Press, 1990), 6; I. William Zartman and Maureen R. Berman, *The Practical Negotiator* (New Haven: Yale University Press, 1982), 45.

10. Roger Fisher, "Four Lessons on Building a Golden Bridge to Peace," *International Herald Tribune*, September 3 1990, 8.

11. Roger Fisher, *International Conflict for Beginners* (New York: Harper and Row, 1969), 11.

12. Saunders, "An Historic Challenge," 15.

13. George A. Lopez and Michael S. Stohl, "Diplomacy, Bargaining, and Coercion," in *International Relations: Contemporary Theory and Practice*, eds. George A. Lopez and Michael S. Stohl (Washington, D.C.: Congressional Quarterly Press, 1989), 216. See also William Ury, *Getting Past No: Negotiating With Difficult People* (New York: Bantam Books, 1991), 7.

14. K.S. Sitaram and Lawrence W. Haapanen, "The Role of Values in Intercultural Communication," in *Handbook of Intercultural Communication*, eds. Molefi Kete Asante, et al. (Beverly Hills: Sage Publications, 1979), 158.

15. "Security Concerns Prompt U.S. to Offer Aid for Foreign Study," *The New York Times*, December 25 1991, A9.

16. Samuel W. Lewis, "Foreword," in Raymond Cohen, *Negotiating Across Cultures: Communication Obstacles in International Diplomacy* (Washington, D.C.: U.S. Institute of Peace Press, 1991), XI.

17. Raymond Cohen, *Negotiating Across Cultures*, 24.

18. Ibid., 25.

19. Fisher and Ury, *Getting to Yes*, 33.

20. Martha L. Cottam, "The Carter Administration's Policy Toward Nicaragua," *Political Science Quarterly* 107, no. 1 (Spring 1992), 126.

21. Fisher and Ury, *Getting to Yes*, 33.

22. Martin Patchen, *Resolving Disputes Between Nations: Coercion or Conciliation?* (Durham: Duke University Press, 1988), 107.

23. Glenn H. Snyder and Paul Diesing, *Conflict Among Nations: Bargaining, Decision Making, and System Structure in International Crises* (Princeton: Princeton University Press, 1977), 298.

24. Martin Patchen, *Resolving Disputes*, 29.

25. David D. Newsom, "The Diplomatic Image," in *The Theory and Practice of International Relations*, ed. William Clinton Olson (Englewood Cliffs, N.J.: Prentice Hall, 1991), 86.

26. Cecil V. Crabb, *American Diplomacy and the Pragmatic Tradition* (Baton Rouge: Louisiana State University Press, 1989), 177.

27. David D. Newsom, *Diplomacy and the American Democracy* (Bloomington: Indiana University Press, 1988), 6.

28. Josef Joffe, "Entangled Forever," in *America's Purpose: New Visions of U.S. Foreign Policy*, ed. Owen Harries (San Francisco: ICS Press, 1991), 146.

29. Seyom Brown, *The Causes and Prevention of War* (New York: St. Martin's Press, 1987), 170.

30. John Spanier, *Games Nations Play* (Washington, D.C.: Congressional Quarterly Press, 1990), 13. See also Clarke E. Cochran, "Normative Dimensions of Religion and Politics," in *Religion in American Politics*, ed. Charles W. Dunn (Washington, D.C.: Congressional Quarterly Press, 1989), 53–57.

31. James Schlesinger, *America at Century's End* (New York: Columbia University Press, 1989), 49.

32. Jean R. Soderlund, *Quakers and Slavery: A Divided Spirit* (Princeton, N.J.: Princeton University Press, 1985), 5; Francis Jennings, "Brother Miguon," in *The World of William Penn*, eds. Richard S. Dunn and Mary Maples Dunn (Philadelphia: University of Pennsylvania Press, 1986), 196.

33. Richard Nixon, "First Annual Report to the Congress on United States Foreign Policy for the 1970s," *Public Papers of the Presidents; Richard Nixon* (Washington, D.C.: U.S. Government Printing Office, 1971), 118.

34. Zbigniew Brzezinski, *Power and Principle* (New York: Farrar, Straus, Giroux, 1983), 515.

35. Louis Kriesberg, *Social Conflicts* (Englewood Cliffs, N.J.: Prentice Hall, 1982), 172.

36. Adam Watson, *Diplomacy: The Dialogue Between States* (New York: McGraw-Hill, 1983), 14.

37. Kriesberg, 189–190.

38. Stanley Hoffmann, *Gulliver's Troubles, Or the Setting of American Foreign Policy* (New York: McGraw-Hill, 1968), 113; and George Ball, *Diplomacy for a Crowded World: An American Foreign Policy* (Boston: Little, Brown and Company, 1976), 9.

39. Alfie Kohn, *No Contest: The Case Against Competition* (Boston: Houghton Mifflin, 1986), 1.

40. Alexis de Tocqueville, *Democracy in America, Vol. 1*, ed. J.P. Mayer (New York: Doubleday, 1969), 536.

41. Henry A. Kissinger, "Domestic Structure and Foreign Policy," *Daedalus* 95, no. 2 (Spring 1966): 515–516.

42. Michael T. Jacobs, *Short-term America: The Causes and Cures of Our Business Myopia* (Boston: Harvard Business School Press, 1991), 7.

43. Watson, 66.

Chapter 4

1. George Bush, "Address to the Nation Announcing the Deployment of U.S. Armed Forces to Saudi Arabia," *Weekly Compilation of Presidential Documents* 26, no. 32 (August 13 1990): 1216.

2. George Bush, "State of the Union Address, January 29 1992," *U.S. Department of State Dispatch* 2, no. 5 (February 4 1991): 65.

3. George Bush, "Kuwait Is Liberated: Address to the Nation From the Oval Office," *U.S. Department of State Dispatch* 2, no. 9 (March 4 1991): 141.

4. *CBS Poll*, January 19 1991.

5. Michael W. Suleiman, *The Arabs in the Mind of America* (Brattleboro, VT.: Amana Books, 1988), 147.

6. "It's Racist, But Hey, It's Disney," *The New York Times*, July 14 1993, A14.

7. "Muslims Don't Fare Well in Poll," *The Pantagraph*, May 13 1993, C1.

8. Youssef M. Ibrahim, "The Arabs Find a World in Which They Count Less," *The New York Times*, April 5 1992, E3.

9. Lucia Mouat, "Arab Resentment Builds Over the UN's Sanctions," *The Christian Science Monitor*, April 23 1992, 3.

10. George Bush, "U.S. Increases Troop Commitment In Operation Desert Shield," *U.S. Department of State Dispatch* 1, no. 11 (November 12 1990): 258.

11. James Baker, "America's Strategy in the Persian Gulf Crisis," *U.S. Department of State Dispatch* 1, no. 15 (December 10 1990): 309.

12. George Bush, "Address Before a Joint Session of the Congress on the Persian Gulf Crisis and the Federal Budget Deficit," *Weekly Compilation of Presidential Documents* 26, no. 37 (September 17 1990): 1360.

13. James Baker, "Statement," U.S. Congress. Senate. *U.S. Policy in the Persian Gulf.* Hearings Before the Committee on Foreign Relations. 101st Cong., 2d Sess., September 5, 20 and October 17 1990 (Washington, D.C.: U.S. Government Printing Office, 1990), 9.

14. George Bush, "The Gulf: A World United Against Aggression," *U.S. Department of State Dispatch* 1, no. 14 (December 3 1990): 295.

15. Matthew L. Wald, "For This Oil War, the Ground Rules Are Different," *The New York Times*, August 3 1990, A5.

16. George Bush, "Remarks at the Annual Conference of the Veterans of Foreign Wars in Baltimore, Maryland," *Weekly Compilation of Presidential Documents* 26, no. 34 (August 27 1990): 1269.

17. Bush, "The Gulf: A World United Against Aggression," 295.

18. George Bush, "The Persian Gulf Crisis: Going the Extra Mile For Peace," *U.S. Department of State Dispatch* 2, no. 1 (January 3 1991): 1.

19. Jerrold Post, "Saddam Hussein's Psychological Makeup," in *The Gulf Crisis: Finding a Peaceful Solution*, ed. U.S. Institute of Peace (Washington, D.C.: U.S. Institute of Peace, 1990), 8; Efraim Karsh and Inari Rautsi, *Saddam Hussein: A Political Biography* (New York: The Free Press, 1991), 272.

20. John G. Healey, "Statement," U.S. Congress. House. *Human Rights Abuses in Kuwait and Iraq.* Hearing Before the Committee on Foreign Affairs, 102d Cong., 1st Sess., January 8 1991 (Washington, D.C.: U.S. Government Printing Office, 1991), 3–5.

21. U.S. Congress. Senate. *Chemical Weapons Use in Kurdistan: Iraq's Final Offensive.* A Staff Report to the Committee on Foreign Relations, October 1988 (Washington, D.C.: U.S. Government Printing Office, 1988), 30–31.

22. Charles Redman, "Iraq's Use of Chemical Weapons," *Department of State Bulletin* 88, no. 2141 (December 1988): 44.

23. U.S. Congress. Senate. Chemical Weapons Use in Kurdistan, 40.

24. U.S. Congress. House. *United States-Iraqi Relations.* Hearings Before the Subcommittee on Europe and the Middle East of the Committee on Foreign Affairs. 101st Cong., 2d Sess., April 26 1990 (Washington, D.C.: U.S. Government Printing Office, 1990), 2.

25. U.S. Congress. Senate. *U.S. Policy in the Persian Gulf.* Hearings Before the Committee on Foreign Relations. 101st Cong., 2d Sess., December 4 and 5 1990, Part I (Washington, D.C.: Government Printing Office, 1991), 2.

26. Karsh and Rautsi, 268

27. See Christopher Layne, "The Munich Myth and American Foreign Policy," in *The Meaning of Munich Fifty Years Later*, eds. Kenneth M. Jensen and David Wurmser (Washington, D.C.: United States Institute of Peace, 1990), 18–19; Gerhard L. Weinberg, "Munich After 50 Years," *Foreign Affairs* 67, no. 1 (Fall 1988): 165.

28. Paul Kennedy, *The Rise and Fall of the Great Powers* (New York: Random House, 1987), 320.

29. Murray Williamson, *The Change in the European Balance of Power, 1938–1939* (Princeton: Princeton University Press, 1984), 127.

30. George Bush, "Address to the Nation Announcing the Deployment of United States Armed Forces to Saudi Arabia," 1217.

31. George Bush, "Remarks at the Annual Conference of the Veterans of Foreign Wars in Baltimore, Maryland," *Weekly Compilation of Presidential Documents* 26, no. 34 (August 27 1990): 1269.

32. George Bush, "Address Before the 45th Session of the UN General Assembly in New York, October 1 1990," *Public Papers of the Presidents of the United States, Book II* (Washington, D.C.: U.S. Government Printing Office, 1991): 1331.

33. George Bush, "Operation Desert Storm is Working," *U.S. Department of State Dispatch* 2, no. 4 (January 28 1991): 54.

34. George Bush, "Operation Desert Storm Launched," *U.S. Department of State Dispatch* 2, no. 3 (January 21 1991): 37.

35. James Baker, "Opportunities to Build a New World Order," *U.S. Department of State Dispatch* 2, no. 6 (February 11 1991): 81.

36. Zbigniew Brzezinski, "Limited War, Maximum Advantage," *The New York Times*, February 4 1991, A13.

37. George Bush, "Address Before the 45th Session of the UN," 1331.

38. Ibid., 1332.

39. George Bush, "The Persian Gulf Crisis: Going the Extra Mile for Peace," 1.

40. George Bush, "Text of the Letter Dated January 5 1991, From President Bush to Iraqi President Saddam Hussein," *U.S. Department of State Dispatch* 2, no. 2 (January 13 1991): 25.

41. Ibid., 25.

42. George Bush, "Address Before a Joint Session of the Congress on the Persian Gulf Crisis and the Federal Budget Deficit," 1361.

43. George Bush, "Interview With Middle Eastern Journalists, March 8 1991," *Weekly Compilation of Presidential Documents* 27, no. 11 (March 10 1991): 280.

44. Jerrold M. Post, "Saddam Hussein of Iraq. A Political Psychological Profile," *Political Psychology* 12, no. 2 (June 1991): 286.

45. "Excerpts From Iraqi Foreign Minister's News Session After Geneva Talks," *The New York Times*, January 10 1991, A5.

46. Thomas L. Friedman, "U.S. Is Seeking to Forestall Any Arab Deal for Kuwait," *The New York Times*, August 5 1990, A8.

47. R.W. Apple, "Bush Says Iraqi Aggression Threatens Our Way of Life," *The New York Times*, August 16 1990, A4.

48. Alan Riding, "French Maneuverings: Taking the Lead for Europe," *The New York Times*, January 6 1991, A4.

49. Peter Stothard, "White House Shows Relief as Diplomatic Complications Fade," *The Times*, January 17 1991, 3. See also Patrick W. Tyler, "Iraq Still Pressuring for Talks Between Baker and Hussein," *The New York Times*, January 6 1991, A4.

50. Clyde Haberman, "Trade Sanctions Against Baghdad Imposed by European Community," *The New York Times*, August 5 1990, A1.

51. Paul Lewis, "Security Council's Rare Unity May Be Threatened Over U.S. Warships in the Gulf," *The New York Times*, August 11 1990, A5.

52. Gary Clyde Hufbauer, "Statement," *U.S. Policy in the Persian Gulf*, December 4 and 5 1990, Part 1, 60.

53. James Baker, "Why America is in the Gulf," *U.S. Department of State Dispatch* 1, no. 10 (November 5 1990): 236; George Bush, "Address Before a Joint Session of the Congress on the Persian Gulf Crises and the Federal Budget Deficit," 1360. See also U.S. Congress. Senate. *U.S. Policy in the Persian Gulf.* Hearing Before the Committee on Foreign Relations, 102d Cong., 1st Sess., January 8 1991 (Washington, D.C.: U.S. Government Printing Office, 1991), 1.

54. Roger Fisher, "For Saddam, Where's the Carrot?" *The Christian Science Monitor*, October 15 1990, 18.

55. *Congressional Record - Senate.* Proceedings and Debates of the 102d Cong., 1st Sess., January 11 1991 (Washington, D.C.: U.S. Government Printing Office, 1991), S238.

56. James Baker, "America's Strategy in the Persian Gulf Crisis," 308.

57. George Bush, "Radio Address to the Nation on the Persian Gulf Crisis, January 5 1991," *Weekly Compilation of Presidential Documents* 27, no. 2 (January 14 1991): 15.

58. U.S. Congress. Senate. *U.S. Policy in the Persian Gulf*, December 4 and 5 1990, Part 1, 5.

59. United Nations, *UN Security Council Resolution 660, August 2 1990* (Washington, D.C.: United Nations Information Center, 1990), 1.

60. U.S. Congress. House. *Update on Costs of Desert Shield / Desert Storm.* Hearing Before the Committee on the Budget. 102d

Cong., 1st Sess., May 15 1991 (Washington, D.C.: U.S. Government Printing Office, 1991).

61. Youssef M. Ibrahim, "Gulf War's Cost to Arabs Estimated at $620 Billion," *The New York Times*, September 8 1992, A4.

62. George Bush, "Address to the Nation Announcing the Deployment of United States Armed Forces to Saudi Arabia," *Weekly Compilation of Presidential Documents* 26, no. 32 (August 13 1990): 1216.

63. George Bush, "Remarks at the All-Star Salute to the Troops at Andrews Air Force Base, Maryland, April 3 1991," *Weekly Compilation of Presidential Documents* 27, no. 14 (April 8 1991): 385.

64. George Bush, "Radio Address to the Nation on the Persian Gulf Crisis, January 5 1991," *Weekly Compilation of Presidential Documents* 27, no. 2 (January 14 1991): 15.

65. Bob Woodward, *The Commanders* (New York: Simon and Schuster, 1991), 41–42.

66. Senator John F. Kerry, "The Gulf Crisis," *Congressional Record: Senate*, Proceedings and Debates of the 101st Cong., 2d Sess., October 24 1990 (Washington, D.C.: U.S. Government Printing Office, 1990), S16560.

67. *Congressional Record: Senate*, Proceedings and Debates of the 102d Cong., 1st Sess., January 10 1991 (Washington, D.C.: U.S. Government Printing Office, 1991), S126.

68. *Congressional Record: Senate*, January 10 1991, S141.

69. *Congressional Record: House*, Proceedings and Debates of the 102d Cong., 1st Sess., January 10 1991 (Washington, D.C.: U.S. Government Printing Office, 1991), H129.

70. George Bush, "Persian Gulf War: Supporting a Noble Cause," *U.S. Department of State Dispatch* 2, no. 5 (February 4 1991): 67.

71. Ibid., 67.

72. "Most Label Gulf War Just," *The Gallup Poll Monthly*, no. 305 (February 1991): 19.

73. Ari L. Goldman, "Council of Churches Condemns U.S. Policy in Gulf," *The New York Times*, November 17 1990, A10.

74. George Bush, "Remarks at the Annual Southern Baptist Convention in Atlanta, Georgia, June 6 1991," *Weekly Compilation of Presidential Documents* 27, no. 23 (June 10 1991): 726.

75. George Bush, "Remarks at the National Prayer Breakfast, January 30 1991," *Weekly Compilation of Presidential Documents* 28, no. 5 (February 3 1992): 178.

76. George Bush, "Message on the Observance of Passover, March 29 1991," *Weekly Compilation of Presidential Documents* 27, no. 13 (April 1 1991): 377.

77. "Excepts From Statements Issued by the President of Iraq," The *New York Times*, September 9 1990, A10.

78. "Address by Saddam Hussein to His Citizens," *The New York Times*, January 21 1991, A8.

79. "Saddam Hussein's Speech on the 'Withdrawal' of His Army From Kuwait," *The New York Times*, February 27 1991, A8.

80. James Baker, "Opportunities to Build a New World Order," *U.S. Department of State Dispatch* 2, no. 6 (February 11 1991): 81.

81. George Bush, "Address to the Nation Announcing Allied Military Action in the Persian Gulf, January 16 1991," *Weekly Compilation of Presidential Documents* 27, no. 3 (January 21 1991): 50–51.

82. Martin Fletcher, "First-Night Assault Dwarfed Any Operation in Vietnam," *The (London) Times*, January 18 1991, 2.

83. George Bush, "Address at the Reserve Officers Association's Annual Dinner, Washington, D.C., January 23 1991," *U.S. Department of State Dispatch* 2, no. 4 (January 28 1991): 53.

84. John Cushman, "U.S. Insists Withdrawal Comes Before Cease-Fire," *The New York Times*, February 16 1991, A8.

85. George Bush, "Comments to the American Association for the Advancement of Science, Washington, D.C., February 15 1991," *U.S. Department of State Dispatch* 2, no. 7 (February 18 1991): 113.

86. Steve Coll and William Branigin, "U.S. Road Raid: Were Iraqis Needlessly Slaughtered?" *The Boston Globe*, March 14 1991, 12.

87. Paul Lewis, "UN Survey Calls Iraq's War Damage Near-Apocalyptic," *The New York Times*, March 22 1991, A1.

88. Harvard Study Team, *Public Health in Iraq After the Gulf War* (Cambridge, Mass.: Harvard Study Team, May 1991), 1–2; "Child Victims of Embargo Put at 500,000," *The Pantagraph*, December 18 1994, A5.

89. "UN Looks Into Gulf War Toxins," *The Christian Science Monitor*, June 14 1993, 20.

90. Al Gore, "Defeating Hussein, Once and For All," *The New York Times*, September 26 1991, A15.

91. Patrick E. Tyler, "U.S. Said to Plan Raids On Baghdad Over Inspections," *The New York Times*, August 16 1992, A1.

92. "Agency Reinstates Tabulator of Iraqi War Deaths," *The New York Times*, April 13 1992, A12.

93. Margaret Tutwiler, "Excepts From the Press Briefing of February 13 1991," *U.S. Department of State Dispatch* 2, no. 7 (February 18 1991): 114.

94. George Bush, "Address Before a Joint Session of Congress, March 6 1991," *U.S. Department of State Dispatch* 2, no. 10 (March 11 1991): 161.

95. David Brown, "Study Says Iraqi Children Dying at Accelerated Rate," *The Washington Post*, October 23 1991, A3.

96. Steve Coll and William Branigin, "Spin Control on the Highway of Death," *The Washington Post National Weekly Edition*, March 18–24 1991, 13.

97. Patrick E. Tyler, "U.S. Juggling Iraq Policy," *The New York Times*, April 13 1991, A5.

98. Kenneth R. Timmerman, *The Death Lobby: How the West Armed Iraq* (Boston: Houghton Mifflin, 1991), 192.

99. Elaine Sciolino, "U.S. Policy On Iraq Is Attacked," *The New York Times*, September 15 1992, C1; Dean Baquet and Elaine Sciolino, "European Suppliers of Iraq Were Known to Pentagon," *The New York Times*, November 2 1992, A6.

100. Bush, "Address Before a Joint Session of Congress on the Persian Gulf Crisis and the Federal Budget Deficit," 1359.

101. Bush, "State of the Union Address," January 29 1991, 65.

102. George Bush, "News Conference," *Weekly Compilation of Presidential Documents* 28, no. 28 (July 13 1992): 1235.

Chapter 5

1. George Bush, "Proclamation 6172—Jewish Heritage Week, April 17 1991," *Weekly Compilation of Presidential Documents* 27, no. 16 (April 24 1991): 454.

2. Peter Grose, *Israel in the Mind of America* (New York: Alfred A. Knopf, 1983), 316.

3. Lyndon Johnson, "Remarks at the 125th Anniversary Meeting of B'nai B'rith," *Weekly Compilation of Presidential Documents* 4, no. 37 (September 1968): 1343.

4. Ibid., 1340.

5. Jimmy Carter, *Keeping Faith: Memoirs of a President* (New York: Bantam Books, 1982), 274.

6. Ibid., 274.

7. George Shultz, "Address Before the Annual Policy Conference of the American Israel Public Affairs Committee, April 21 1985," *Department of State Bulletin* 85 (June 1985): 19.

8. Richard Nixon, "A Conversation About Foreign Policy," *Public Papers of the Presidents of the United States: Richard Nixon* (Washington, D.C.: U.S. Government Printing Office, 1971), 558. See also Gerald Ford, "Remarks at the B'nai B'rith Biennial Convention," *Public Papers of the Presidents of the United States: Gerald Ford* (Washington, D.C.: U.S. Government Printing Office, 1979), 2226; and Carter, *Keeping Faith*, 274.

9. Paul Findley, *They Dare to Speak Out: People and Institutions Confront Israel's Lobby* (Westport, CT.: Lawrence Hill and Company, 1985), 25.

10. Charles R. Babcock, "Israel's Backers Maximize Political Clout," *The Washington Post*, September 26 1991, A21.

11. Thomas L. Friedman, "Pro-Israel Lobbyist Resigns After Boasts Are Made Public," *The New York Times*, November 5 1992, A7; and "Pro-Israel Group Names Leader," *The New York Times*, November 21 1992, A4.

12. Michael W. Suleiman, "The Effect of American Perceptions of Arabs on Middle East Issues," in *Split Vision: The Portrayal of Arabs in the American Media*, ed. Edmund Ghareeb (Washington, D.C.: American-Arab Affairs Council, 1983), 338; Jack G. Shaheen, *The TV Arab* (Bowling Green, Ohio: Bowling Green State University Popular Press, 1984), 4.

13. Mohammed K. Shadid, *The United States and the Palestinians* (New York: St. Martin's Press, 1981), 95.

14. Richard Nixon, "Second Annual Report to the Congress on U.S. Foreign Policy," *Public Papers of the Presidents of the United States: Richard Nixon* (Washington, D.C.: U.S. Government Printing Office, 1972), 287.

15. John E. Reilly, "Public Opinion: The Pulse of the 1990s," *Foreign Policy*, no. 82 (Spring 1991): 93; John Benson, "U.S. Public Supports Continued Strong Ties," *The Christian Science Monitor*, October 25 1991, 19.

16. Gabriel Sheffer, "Shared Values as the Basis For the U.S.-Israeli Special Relationship," in *Dynamics of Dependence: U.S.-Israeli Relations*, ed. Gabriel Sheffer (Boulder, CO: Westview Press, 1987), 2.

17. William Stivers, *America's Confrontation with Revolutionary Change in the Middle East, 1948–83* (New York: St. Martin's Press, 1986), 15.

18. George W. Ball, "Statement," U.S. Congress, Senate. *The Situation in the Middle East.* Hearings Before the Committee on Foreign Relations, 97th Cong., 2nd Sess., July 15 1982 (Washington, D.C.: U.S. Government Printing Office, 1982), 3.

19. Stephen Labaton, "Baker Defends Waiver of Sanctions Against Israel on Missiles," *The New York Times*, October 28 1991, A10.

20. United Nations Security Council Resolution 242, November 22 1967.

21. United Nations, *The Question of Palestine, 1979–1990* (New York: United Nations, 1991), 8; and Ball, 3.

22. Nicholas A. Veliotes, "Statement," U.S. Congress, House. *Developments in the Middle East, July 1982.* Hearing Before the Subcommittee on Europe and the Middle East of the Committee on Foreign Affairs, 97th Cong., 2nd Sess., July 28 1982 (Washington, D.C.: U.S. Government Printing Office, 1982), 30.

23. U.S. Congress, House. *Developments in the Middle East, July 1982*, 14.

24. James LeMoyne, "Saudis Say Jerusalem Killings Could Weaken Alliance Against Iraq," *The New York Times*, October 10 1990, A7.

25. Thomas L. Friedman, "A Parting of Paths?" *The New York Times*, October 11 1990, A6.

26. "Text of Resolution Adopted by UN Council," *The New York Times*, October 14 1990, A6.

27. Thomas R. Pickering, "Statement Before the UN Security Council in New York City, October 12 1990," *U.S. Department of State Dispatch* 1, no. 8 (October 22 1990): 207.

28. Sabra Chartrand, "Israel's Cabinet Denounces Study By UN Inquirers," *The New York Times*, October 15 1990, A1; Joel Brinkley, "Israelis Promise No Help for UN," *The New York Times*, October 14 1990, A6.

29. "Excepts From Report on October 8 Israeli Strife," *The New York Times*, October 27 1990, A5.

30. "Text of UN Resolution on Israel," *The New York Times*, October 26 1990, A7.

31. Tom Farer, "Israel's Unlawful Occupation," *Foreign Policy*, no. 82 (Spring 1991): 40.

32. Carter, *Keeping Faith*, 277.

33. U.S. Department of State, *Country Reports on Human Rights Practices For 1990*. Report Submitted to the Committee on Foreign Relations, U.S. Senate and the Committee on Foreign Affairs, House of Representatives (Washington, D.C.: U.S. Government Printing Office, 1991), 1477.

34. Ibid., 1478.

35. Ibid., 1479.

36. "Israelis Cleared in Death of Arab," *The New York Times*, February 14 1992, A7; Richard Beeston, "Israeli Police Team Torturing Arabs," *The Times*, February 25 1992, 6.

37. Raja Shehadeh, *Occupier's Law: Israel and the West Bank* (Washington, D.C.: Institute for Palestine Studies, 1988), VIII.

38. U.S. Department of State, *Country Reports*, 1481.

39. Sabra Chartrand, "Odd Twist in West Bank Punishment," *The New York Times*, April 25 1991, A3.

40. U.S. Department of State, *Country Reports*, 1485.

41. Paul Lewis, "U.S. Says It Will Consider UN Observers for Israeli-Occupied Territories," *The New York Times*, May 24 1990; Edward W. Said, "Palestinians The Victims of a Sadistic Hypocrisy," *Guardian Weekly*, March 31 1991, 19.

42. U.S. Department of State, *Country Reports*, 1491.

43. Herbert S. Okun, "Statement Before the UN Security Council on Israeli Deportations, January 5 1988," *Department of State Bulletin* 88 (March 1988): 82.

44. "Text of UN Security Council Resolution 726 on Israeli Expulsion Plan," *The New York Times*, January 7 1992, A7.

45. Clyde Haberman, "Lebanese Deploy to Bar Entry of Palestinians," *The New York Times*, December 18 1992, A1; Clyde Haberman, "Gunfire Stops 415 Arab Deportees From Going Back to Israeli Zone," *The New York Times*, December 22 1992, A1; and Ali Jaber, "Ousted Arabs Shiver and Wait in Lebanese Limbo," *The New York Times*, December 24 1992, A3.

46. Jimmy Carter, *The Blood of Abraham* (Boston: Houghton Mifflin, 1985), 122.

47. Sherna Berger Gluck, "Engulfed West Bank," *The Christian Science Monitor*, October 15 1991, 19.

48. Joel Brinkley, "For Israelis, Appeal of Occupied Territories Grows," *The New York Times*, September 23 1990, 6.

49. James Baker, "Address Before the American-Israel Public Affairs Committee on May 22 1989," *Department of State Bulletin* 88 (July 1989): 27.

50. Margaret Tutwiler, "Loan Guarantees to Israel," *U.S. Department of State Dispatch* 2, no. 40 (October 1991): 754; Thomas L. Friedman, "Israeli Loan Deal Linked by Baker to a Building Halt," *The New York Times*, February 25 1992, A1.

51. U.S. Congress. House. *Foreign Operations, Export Financing, and Related Programs Appropriations For 1993*. Hearings Before a Subcommittee on Appropriations, 102d Cong., 2nd Sess. (Washington, D.C.: U.S. Government Printing Office, 1992), 517.

52. Gerald Ford, "Remarks at the B'nai B'rith Biennial Convention," *Public Papers of the Presidents of the United States: Gerald Ford* (Washington, D.C.: U.S. Government Printing Office, 1979), 2226.

53. Ronald Reagan, "Remarks Following Discussions With President Mohammed Hosni Mubarak of Egypt," *Public Papers of the Presidents of the United States: Ronald Reagan, Book I* (Washington, D.C.: U.S. Government Printing Office, 1988), 275.

54. Nixon, "Second Annual Report to the Congress on U.S. Foreign Policy," 154.

55. Lyndon Johnson, "Statement on the Status of Jerusalem, June 28 1967," *Weekly Compilation of Presidential Documents* 3, no. 26 (July 1967): 942.

56. Shultz, "Address Before Annual Policy Conference of AIPAC, April 21 1985," 20.

57. Ronald Reagan, "Address to the Nation on United States Policy For Peace in the Middle East," *Public Papers of the Presidents of the United States: Ronald Reagan, Book II* (Washington, D.C.: U.S. Government Printing Office, 1983), 1093.

58. Reagan, "Address to the Nation on U.S. Policy for Peace in the Middle East," 1094.

59. Jimmy Carter, "Remarks at the Closing Banquet of the Biennial Convention of B'nai B'rith International, September 4 1980," *Public Papers of the Presidents of the United States: Jimmy Carter* (Washington, D.C.: U.S. Government Printing Office, 1982), 1657.

60. Ibid., 1660.

61. Jimmy Carter, "Address Before the People's Assembly, Cairo, Egypt, March 10 1979," *Public Papers of the Presidents of the United States: Jimmy Carter* (Washington, D.C.: U.S. Government Printing Office, 1980), 414.

62. Carter, *Keeping Faith*, 282.

63. Ibid., 289.

64. Johnson, "Remarks at the 125th Anniversary of B'nai B'rith," 1342.

65. Nixon, "Second Annual Report to the Congress," 289.

66. Ronald Reagan, "Statement on Diplomatic Talks With the Palestine Liberation Organization, December 14 1988," *Public Papers of the Presidents of the United States: Ronald Reagan, Book II*, 1627.

67. George Bush, "Remarks on Fast Track Legislation and a Question-and-Answer Session With Reporters, May 23 1991," *Weekly Compilation of Presidential Documents* 27, no. 21 (May 1991): 660.

68. Alan Cowell, "Morocco, a U.S. Ally, Links Gulf Crisis to Israel," *The New York Times*, October 14 1990, A6; Gerald Butt, "Syria Says Any Resolution of Gulf Crisis Should Help Resolve Arab-Israeli Dispute," *The Christian Science Monitor*, September 18 1990, 1.

69. James Baker, "Joint News Conference With Israeli Foreign Minister David Levy, Jerusalem," *U.S. Department of State Dispatch* 2, no. 11 (March 18 1991): 184.

70. Elaine Sciolino, "As History Unfolds, U.S. Takes to Sidelines," *The New York Times*, September 9 1993, A6.

71. "Text of Leaders' Statements at the Signing of the Middle East Pacts," *The New York Times*, September 14 1993, A6.

Chapter 6

1. "A Puzzled People," *The Economist*, May 8 1993, 6.

2. George F. Kennan, *The Other Balkan Wars* (Washington, D.C.: Carnegie Endowment for International Peace, 1993), 13.

3. Ibid.

4. William Pfaff, "Invitation to War," *Foreign Affairs* 72, no.3, (Summer 1993): 99.

5. Robert D. Kaplan, *Balkan Ghosts* (New York: St. Martin's Press, 1993), 22.

6. The author is indebted to Professor Nikolaos Stavrou of Howard University for emphasizing these points.

7. Glenn E. Curtis, ed. *Yugoslavia: A Country Study* (Washington, D.C.: U.S. Government Printing Office, 1992), 160.

8. Lawrence Eagleburger, "Intervention at the London Conference on the Former Yugoslavia," *U.S. Department of State Dispatch* 3, no. 35 (August 31 1992): 673.

9. Roy Gutman, *A Witness to Genocide* (New York: Macmillan, 1993), XXIV.

10. Dusko Doder, "Yugoslavia: New War, Old Hatreds," *Foreign Policy*, no. 91 (Summer 1993): 7.

11. Samuel P. Huntington, "The Clash of Civilizations?" *Foreign Affairs* 72, no. 3 (Summer 1993): 37.

12. Gutman, *A Witness*, 83.

13. Robin Wright, "Security Fears, Political Ties Cloud U.S. View of Islam's Rise," *Los Angeles Times*, March 7 1993, A1.

14. Leon T. Hadar, "What Green Peril?" *Foreign Affairs* 72, no. 2 (Spring 1993): 29. See also John L. Esposito, *The Islamic Threat: Myth or Reality* (New York: Oxford University Press, 1992), 175–176.

15. Ghassan Salame, "Islam and the West," *Foreign Policy*, no. 90 (Spring 1993): 28; and Stanley Reed, "The Battle for Egypt," *Foreign Affairs* 72, no. 4 (September-October 1993): 99.

16. Carol Berger, "Plight of Bosnian Muslims is Deeply Felt in Egypt," *The Christian Science Monitor*, August 26 1992, 3.

17. Curtis, *Yugoslavia*, XXVI.

18. Ibid., XXXVI. See also Josef Joffe, "The New Europe: Yesterday's Ghosts," *Foreign Affairs* 72, no.1 (1993): 31.

19. Misha Glenny, *The Fall of Yugoslavia: The Third Balkan War* (New York: Penguin Books, 1992), 177.

20. Margaret Tutwiler, "U.S. Policy Toward Yugoslavia," *U.S. Department of State Dispatch* 2, no.22 (June 3 1991): 395.

21. Michael Lind, "In Defense of Liberal Nationalism," *Foreign Affairs* 73, no. 3 (May-June 1994): 97. See also Gutman, *A Witness*, XXV.

22. Joffe, "The New Europe," 31.

23. Al Gore, "The Revolutionary Forces of Sympathy and Compassion," *Harvard Gazette*, June 17 1994, 8.

24. Jeane Kirkpatrick, "Statement," in *American Policy in Bosnia*. Hearing Before the Subcommittee on European Affairs of the Committee on Foreign Relations, U.S. Senate, 103rd Cong., 1st Sess., February 18 1993 (Washington, D.C.: U.S. Government Printing Office, 1993): 8.

25. George Kenny, "Does Bosnia Matter to the United States?" *World Policy Journal* 9, no.4 (Fall/Winter 1992): 643.

26. Eagleburger, "Intervention at the London Conference," 673.

27. Christopher Layne and Benjamin Schwartz, "American Hegemony Without an Enemy," *Foreign Policy* no. 92 (Fall 1993): 11.

28. Stephen R. Bowers, "Ethnic Politics in Eastern Europe," *Conflict Studies* 248 (February 1992): 2.

29. Margaret Thatcher, "Stop the Serbs, Now, For Good," *The New York Times*, May 4 1994, 15; and Warren Zimmerman, "Why America Must Save Bosnia," *The Washington Post Weekly Edition*, May 2–8, 1994, 23–24.

30. Zimmerman, "Why America," 23.

31. Morton I. Abramowitz, "Dateline Ankara: Turkey After Ozal," *Foreign Policy*, no. 91 (Sunmmer 1993): 180.

32. Ralph Johnson, "U.S. Efforts to Promote a Peaceful Settlement in Yugoslavia," *U.S. Department of State Dispatch* 2, no. 42 (October 21 1991): 783.

33. Martin Walker, "The More Things Change: Europe Slips Into Old Roles," *The Los Angeles Times*, May 30 1993, M2.

34. Owen Harries, "The Collapse of the West," *Foreign Affairs* 72, no. 4 (September-October 1993): 49; and Doder, "Yugoslavia," 4.

35. George Soros, "Bosnia and Beyond," *The New York Review of Books*, October 7 1993, 15.

36. James O. Jackson, "A Lesson in Shame," *Time*, August 2 1993, 38.

37. Jonathan S. Landay, "Bosnian Serbs Make a Business Out of Ethnic Cleansing," *The Christian Science Monitor*, June 10 1994, 1.

38. Kenneth Blackwell, "Status of Detention Centers in Bosnia-Hercegovina," *U.S. Department of State Dispatch* 3, no. 38 (September 21 1992): 717.

39. Gutman, *A Witness*, 80; Roger Cohen, "In Town Cleansed of Muslims, Serb Church Will Crown the Deed," *The New York Times*, March 7 1994, A1.

40. Andrew Bell-Fialkoff, "A Brief History of Ethnic Cleansing," *Foreign Affairs* 72, no. 3 (Summer 1993): 116.

41. Dan Morgan, "Serbia May in Fact Have Lost the War," *The Washington Post Weekly Edition*, June 27–July 3 1994, 24.

42. Morgan, "Serbia," 24.

43. George Bush, "News Conference, August 7 1992," *Weekly Compilation of Presidential Documents* 28, no. 32 (August 10 1992): 1396.

44. Kenny, "Does Bosnia Matter?" 644.

45. Richard Cohen, "In No Man's Land," *The Washington Post National Weekly Edition*, June 6–12 1994, 29.

46. "Statement on the United States Recognition of the Former Yugoslav Republics, April 7 1992," *Weekly Compilation of Presidential Documents* 28, no. 15 (April 13 1992): 601.

47. Johnson, "U.S. Efforts," 782.

48. "UN Security Council Resolutions 761 and 762 on Bosnia-Hercegovina," *U.S. Department of State Dispatch* 3, no. 27 (July 6 1992): 544.

49. Kirkpatrick, "Statement," 8.

50. "Deputy Secretary Eagleburger Meets With Serbian Official," *U.S. Department of State Dispatch* 3, no. 5 (February 3 1992): 84.

51. Roger P. Winter, "Statement," in *Implementation of the Helsinki Accords*, Hearing Before the Commission on Security and Cooperation in Europe, 103rd Cong., 1st Sess. February 4 1993 (Washington, D.C.: U.S. Government Printing Office, 1993), 101.

52. Eagleburger, "Intervention at the London Conference," 674.

53. Chuck Sudetic, "Serbs Bar Aid Convoy to Besieged Bosnian Town," *The New York Times*, March 16 1994, A4; and "Bosnian Serbs List Demands on Talks," *The New York Times*, March 25 1994, A6.

54. "Implementation of the Helsinki Final Act," *U.S. Department of State Dispatch* 3, no. 6 (September 1992): 29.

55. Chuck Sudetic, "Gorazde Pounded By Serb Gunners," *The New York Times*, April 19 1994, A1.

56. George Bush, "Remarks on Hurricane Andrew and the Situation in Iraq, and an Exchange With Reporters, August 26 1992," *Weekly Compilation of Presidential Documents* 28, no. 35 (September 13 1992): 1513.

57. Michael Mandelbaum, "The Reluctance to Intervene," *Foreign Policy*, no. 95 (Summer 1994): 12.

58. Zimmerman, "Why America," 23.

59. George Bush, "Question and Answer Session, October 22 1992," *Weekly Compilation of Presidential Documents* 28, no. 43 (October 26 1992): 2058.

60. Carroll J. Doherty, "Vets Add Weight to Hill Debate On Use of Military Power," *Congressional Quarterly Weekly Report*, April 30 1994, 1078–1079.

61. See Steven Kull and Clay Ramsay, "Public Attitudes on Bosnia," *The Christian Science Monitor*, June 9 1993, 19; George Gallup, Jr., *The Gallup Poll: Public Opinion 1993* (Wilmington, Delaware: Scholarly Resources, 1994), 42.

62. *The Gallup Poll*, 96.

63. Leslie McAneny, "Huge Majority Backs Shift from International to Domestic Agenda," *The Gallup Poll Monthly*, no. 316 (January 1992): 12.

64. George Bush, "News Conference With Foreign Journalists, July 2 1992," *Weekly Compilation of Presidential Documents* 28, no. 27 (July 6 1992): 1195.

65. Christopher Madison, "Not on Our Beat," *National Journal* 23 (August 10 1991): 2032.

66. "The Halyard Mission Rescue Operation," *American Srbobran*, May 18 1994, 1.

67. James Baker, "Address Before the UN Security Council, September 25 1991," *U.S. Department of State Dispatch* 2, no. 39 (September 30 1991): 723.

68. "Serbia: A Bully, But Our Bully," *The Economist*, June 20 1992, 49.

69. George Bush, "News Conference in Kennebunkport, Maine, August 8, 1992," *Weekly Compilation of Presidential Documents* 28, no. 33 (August 17 1992): 1408; and Douglas Jehl, "Clinton Bids Navy Graduates Heed World War II Lessons," *The New York Times*, May 26 1994, A3.

70. Joseph R. Biden, *To Stand Against Aggression: Milosevic, the Bosnian Republic, and the Conscience of the West*. A Report to the Committee on Foreign Relations, U.S. Senate (Washington, D.C.: U.S. Government Printing Office, 1993), 2.

71. David Gompert, "How to Defeat Serbia," *Foreign Affairs* 73, no. 4 (July-August 1994): 35.

72. Warren Christopher, "Statement," in *Foreign Assistance Legislation for Fiscal Year 1994, Parts 1 and 8*. Hearing and Markup before the Committee on Foreign Affairs, House of Representative, 103rd Cong., 1st Sess. March 3 (Washington, D.C.: U.S. Government Printing Office, 1993), 93.

73. "Presidential Debate in St. Louis, October 11 1992," *Weekly Compilation of Presidential Documents* 28, no. 41 (October 12 1992): 1916.

74. David Owen, "The Future of the Balkans," *Foreign Affairs* 72, no. 2 (Spring 1993): 2.

75. *The Gallup Poll 1993*, 244.

76. William J. Clinton, "Letter to Congressional Leaders on the Conflict in the Former Yugoslavia, February 17 1994," *Weekly Compilation of Presidential Documents* 30, no. 7 (February 21 1994): 324.

77. Michael R. Gordon, "NATO Craft Down 4 Serb Warplanes Attacking Bosnia," *The New York Times* April 5 1994, A6.

78. Michael R. Gordon, "No Green Light for Serb Attacks, Clinton Says," *The New York Times*, April 5 1994, A6.

79. Douglass Jehl, "U.S. Seeks to Persuade Serbs NATO and UN Are Neutral," *The New York Times*, April 15 1994, A4.

80. "UN Security Council Resolution 713, September 25 1991," Reprinted in *U.S. Department of State Dispatch* 2, no. 39 (September 30 1991): 725

81. "UN Security Council Resolution 757, May 30 1992," Reprinted in *U.S. Department of State Dispatch* 3, no. 23 (June 1992): 449–450; George Bush, "Executive Order 12808—Blocking Yugoslav Government Property and the Property of the Governments of Serbia and Montenegro, May 30 1992" *Weekly Compilation of Presidential Documents* 28, no. 23 (June 8, 1992): 975–977; George Bush, "Executive Order 12810—Blocking Property of and Prohibiting Transactions With the Federal Republic of Yugoslavia (Serbia and Montenegro), June 5 1992," *Weekly Compilation of Presidential Documents* 28, no. 23 (June 8 1992): 1009-1011.

82. George Bush, "Statement on United States Recognition of the Former Yugoslav Republics, April 7 1992," *Weekly Compilation of Presidential Documents* 28, no.15 (April 13 1992): 601.

83. Albert Wohlstetter, "Genocide by Mediation," *The New York Times*, March 3 1994, A15.

84. Curtis, *Yugoslavia*, 270.

85. Michael R. Gordon, "Iran Said to Send Arms to Bosnians," *The New York Times*, September 10 1992, A10.

86. "Presidential Debate in St. Louis," 1916.

87. Doherty, "Vets Add Weight," 1077.

88. William J. Clinton, "Remarks on Bosnia and an Exchange With Reporters Prior to Departure for Milwaukee, Wisconsin, April 18 1994," *Weekly Compilation of Presidential Documents* 30, no. 16 (April 25 1994): 826.

89. Katherine Q. Seelye, "Senate Wants Clinton to Lift Bosnia Embargo," *The New York Times*, May 13 1994, A4.

90. Seelye, "Senate Wants Clinton to Lift," A4; Claiborne Pell and Lee H. Hamilton, "Don't Arm Bosnia," *The New York Times*, May 15 1994, A19.

91. Huntington, "The Clash of Civilizations," 37.

92. "OIC Foreign Ministers Meet in Karachi," *The Monthly Newsletter of the Royal Embassy of Saudi Arabia*, June 1993, 2.

93. Gordon, "Iran Said to Send Arms to Bosnians," A10.

94. George Bush, "Statement on Humanitarian Assistance to Bosnia, October 2 1992," *Weekly Compilation of Presidential Documents* 28, no. 40 (October 5 1992): 1845.

95. Ralph Johnson, "U.S. Efforts to Promote A Peaceful Settlement in Yugoslavia," *U.S. Department of State Dispatch* 2, no. 42 (October 21 1991): 782.

96. William J. Clinton, "Letter to Senate Leaders on the Conflict in Bosnia, October 20 1993," *Weekly Compilation of Presidential Documents* 29, no. 42 (October 25 1993): 2123.

97. George Bush, "Remarks on the London Economic Summit and an Exchange With Foreign Journalists," *Weekly Compilation of Presidential Documents* 27, no.27 (July 8 1991): 867.

98. Robert McCloskey, "Statement," in *Implementation of the Helsinki Accords*. Hearing before the Commission on Security and Cooperation in Europe, 103rd Cong., 1st Sess. War Crimes and the Humanitarian Crisis in the Former Yugoslavia, January 25 1993 (Washington D.C.: U.S. Government Printing Office, 1993): 5.

99. R.W. Apple, "Allow Miscalculation, Open the Way to War," *The New York Times*, April 24 1994, Section 4, 1.

100. William E. Schmidt, "Peace Talks Suspended Pending Efforts by U.S.," *The New York Times*, March 1 1994, A4.

101. Jonathan S. Landay, "Bosnian Serbs Demand Own State in Exchange for Peace," *The Christian Science Monitor*, March 28 1994, 7.

102. William J. Clinton, "News Conference, November 10 1993," *Weekly Compilation of Presidential Documents* 29, no. 45 (November 15 1993): 2320.

103. Alfonse D'Amato, "Statement," *Implementation of the Helsinki Accords*, February 4 1993, 12.

104. George Bush, "News Conference, August 7 1992," *Weekly Compilation of Presidential Documents* 28, no. 32 (August 10 1992): 1397.

105. Owen, "The Future of the Balkans," 2.

106. Roger Cohen, "Bosnia Map: Bitter Pill," *The New York Times*, July 7 1994, A1.

107. Alan Riding, "Bosnian Serbs Said to Reject Mediators' Partition Plan," *The New York Times*, July 21 1994, A3.

Chapter 7

1. Roger Cohen, "West's Fears in Bosnia: Chaos and Islam," *The New York Times*, March 13 1994, E3.

2. Lucia Mouat, "U.S. to Propose Phased Sanctions on North Korea," *The Christian Science Monitor*, June 13 1994, 1.

3. Roger Fisher and Willaim Ury, *Getting to Yes: Negotiating Agreement Without Giving In* (New York: Penguin, 1983), 27.

4. Alan Riding, "U.S. and North Korea in Accord to Seek Diplomatic Links," *The New York Times*, August 13 1994, A1.

5. I. William Zartman, "Conflict and Resolution," *Annals of the American Academy of Political and Social Science* 518 (November 1991): 19.

6. Richard J. Payne, "Black Americans and the Demise of Constructive Engagement," *Africa Today* 33, no. 1 (1986): 71–90.

7. Richard J. Payne, *Opportunities and Dangers of Soviet-Cuban Expansion* (Albany: State University of New York Press, 1988), 145.

8. Ibid., 145.

9. Ibid., 146.

10. Richard L. Millett, "The Aftermath of Intervention: Panama 1990," *Journal of Interamerican Studies and World Affairs* 32, no. 1 (Spring 1990): 5.

11. George Bush, "Address to the Nation Announcing U.S. Military Action in Panama, December 20 1989," *Weekly Compilations of Presidential Documents* 25, no. 51 (December 1989): 1974.

12. Zartman, 15.

13. David Skidmore, "Foreign Policy Interest Groups," in *Jimmy Carter*, eds. Herbert D. Rosenbaum and Alexej Ugrinsky (Westport, CT.: Greenwood Press, 1994); 299.

14. William G. Hyland, "Setting Global Priorities," *Foreign Policy*, no. 73 (Winter 1988–89): 23.

15. J. William Fulbright, *The Arrogance of Power* (New York: Random House, 1966),22.

16. Joseph Biden, "Statement," *Congressional Record: Senate. Proceedings and Debates of the 102d Congress, First Session, January 12 1991* (Washington, D.C.: U.S. Government Printing Office, 1991), S339.

17. Charles Krauthammer, "The Unipolar Moment," *Foreign Affairs* 70, no. 1 (1990/91): 33.

18. Adam Watson, *Diplomacy: The Dialogue Between States* (New York: McGraw-Hill, 1983), 34.

19. Zbigniew Brzezinski, *Power and Principle* (New York: Farrar, Straus, Giroux, 1983), 547.

20. Jimmy Carter, "Remarks at the Closing Banquet of the Biennial Convention of B'nai B'rith International, September 4 1980," *Public Papers of the Presidents of the United States: Jimmy Carter* (Washington, D.C.: U.S. Government Printing Office, 1982): 1660.

21. Richard Nixon, *Memoirs* (London: Sidgwick and Jackson, 1978), 884.

BIBLIOGRAPHY

Adas, Michael. *Machines as the Measure of Men: Science, Technology, and Ideologies of Western Dominance*. Ithaca, New York: Cornell University Press, 1989.

Anthony, Dick and Thomas Robbins. "Spiritual Innovation and the Crisis of American Civil Religion." *Daedalus* III, no.1 (Winter 1992): 215–234.

Armacost, Michael H. "Military Power and Diplomacy: The Reagan Legacy." *Department of State Bulletin* 88, no. 2140 (November 1988): 40–44.

Aspin, Les. *The Aspin Papers: Sanctions, Diplomacy, and the War in the Persian Gulf*. Washington, D.C.: The Center for Strategic and International Studies, 1991.

Atiyeh, George N. *Arab and American Cultures*. Washington, D.C.: American Enterprise Institute, 1977.

Axtell, James. *The Invasion Within: The Contest of Cultures in Colonial North America*. New York: Oxford University Press, 1985.

Baker, James. "America's Strategy in the Persian Gulf Crisis." *U.S. Department of State Dispatch* 1, no. 15 (December 1990): 307–09.

Bandura, Albert. "Selective Activation and Disengagement of Moral Control." *Journal of Social Issues* 46, no. 1 (1990): 27–46.

Baritz, Loren. *Backfire: A History of How American Culture Led Us Into Vietnam and Made Us Fight the Way We Did.* New York: William Morrow and Company, Inc., 1985.

———. *City On A Hill: A History of Ideas and Myths in America.* New York: John Wiley and Sons, 1964.

Beck, Robert J. "Munich's Lessons Reconsidered." *International Security* 14, no. 2 (Fall 1989): 161–91.

Bellah, Robert N. "Civil Religion in America." *Daedalus* 96, no.1 (Winter 1967): 1–21.

———. *Habits of the Heart: Individualism and Commitment in American Life.* Berkeley: University of California Press, 1985.

Bellah, Robert N., et al. *The Good Society.* New York: Alfred A. Knopf, 1991.

Bennett, Lance W. and David L. Paletz, eds. *Taken By Storm: The Media, Public Opinion and U.S. Foreign Policy in the Gulf War.* Chicago Press, 1994.

Bercovitch, Sacvan. *The American Jeremiad.* Madison: University of Wisconsin Press, 1978.

Booth, Ken. *Strategy and Ethnocentrism.* New York: Holmes and Meier Publishers, 1979.

Brady, Linda P. *The Politics of Negotiation: America's Dealings with Allies, Adversaries, and Friends.* Chapel Hill: The University of North Carolina Press, 1991.

Bulloch, John and Harvey Morris. *Saddam's War: The Origins of the Kuwait Conflict and the International Response.* London: Faber and Faber, 1991.

Buruma, Ian. *Behind the Mask.* New York: Penguin Books, 1984.

Bush, George. "Address to the Nation Announcing Allied Military Action in the Persian Gulf." *Weekly Compilation of Presidential Documents* 27, no. 3 (January 21 1991): 50–52.

———. "Address to the Nation Announcing Allied Military Ground Action in the Persian Gulf Conflict, February 3 1991." *Weekly Compilation of Presidential Documents* 27, no. 9 (March 1991): 207–08.

———. "Address to the Nation Announcing the Deployment of United States Armed Forces to Saudi Arabia." *Weekly Compilation of Presidential Documents* 26, no. 32 (August 1990): 1216–18.

———. "Address to the Nation Announcing U.S. Military Action in Panama, December 20 1989." *Weekly Compilation of Presidential Documents* 25, no. 51 (December 1989): 1974–75.

———. "Letter to the Speaker of the House and the President Pro Tempore of the Senate on the Deployment of Additional United States Armed Forces to the Persian Gulf." *Weekly Compilation of Presidential Documents* 26, no.46 (November 1990): 1834–35.

———. "The Persian Gulf Crisis: Going the Extra Mile for Peace." *U.S. Department of State Dispatch* 2, no. 1 (January 1991): 1.

———. "Press Conference at Huntsville, Alabama, June 20 1990: Suspension of Talks with the PLO." *Foreign Policy Bulletin: The Documentary Record of United States Foreign Policy* 1, no. 1 (July/August 1990): 68–70.

———. "Proclamation 6272—Jewish Heritage Week, April 17 1991." *Weekly Compilation of Presidential Documents* 27, no. 16 (April 1991): 454–55.

———. "Radio Address to the Nation on the Persian Gulf Crisis, January 5 1991." *Weekly Compilation of Presidential Documents* 27, no.2 (January 1991): 15–16.

———. "Remarks at the All-Star Salute to the Troops at Andrews Air Force Base, Maryland, April 3, 1991." *Weekly Compilation of Presidential Documents* 27, no. 14 (April 1991): 385.

———. "Remarks at the Annual Southern Baptist Convention in Atlanta, Georgia, June 6 1991." *Weekly Compilation of Presidential Documents* 27, no. 23 (June 1991): 726–28.

———. "Remarks on Fast Track Legislation and Question-Answer Session with Reporters, May 23 1991." *Weekly Compilation of Presidential Documents* 27, no. 21 (May 1991): 658–61.

———. "Remarks at the National Prayer Breakfast, January 31, 1991." *Weekly Compilation of Presidential Documents* 27, no. 5 (February 1991): 100–01.

———. "Remarks to Participants in the Rally for Life, April 28 1990." *Weekly Compilation of Presidential Documents* 26, no. 18 (May 1990): 673.

———. "Remarks at a White House News Conference on the Crisis in the Gulf, January 12 1991." *U.S. Department of State Dispatch* 2, no.2 (January 1991): 14–16.

———. "The United Nations in a New Era." *U.S. Department of State Dispatch* 2, no. 39 (September 1991): 718–20.

Carter, Jimmy. *Keeping Faith: Memoirs of a President.* New York: Bantam Books, 1982.

Chace, James and Caleb Carr. America Invulnerable: *The Quest for Absolute Security from 1812 to Star Wars.* New York: Summit Books, 1988.

Chagnon, Napoleon A. *Yanomamo*. Fort Worth, Texas: Harcourt Brace Johvanovich, 1992.

Chay, Jongsuk, ed. *Culture and International Relations*. New York: Praeger, 1990.

Cheesebrough, David B. *God Ordained This War*. Columbia, S.C.: University of South Carolina Press, 1991.

Clinton, William J. "Letter to Senate Leaders on the Conflict in Bosnia, October 20 1993." *Weekly Compilation of Presidential Documents* 29, no. 42 (October 25 1993): 2123.

———. "News Conference, November 10, 1993." *Weekly Compilation of Presidential Documents* 29, no. 45 (November 15 1993): 2320.

———. "Remarks on Bosnia and an Exchange With Reporters, April 18 1994." *Weekly Compilation of Presidential Documents* 30, no. 16 (April 25 1994): 826.

Cohen, Raymond. *Negotiating Across Cultures: Communication Obstacles in International Diplomacy*. Washington, D.C.: United States Institute of Peace Press, 1991.

Coker, Christopher. *Reflections on American Foreign Policy Since 1945*. New York: St. Martin's Press, 1989.

Colley, Linda. *Britons: Forging the Nation 1707–1837*. New Haven: Yale University Press, 1992.

Congressional Record: Proceedings and Debates of the 102nd Congressional First Session, January 10 1991. Washington, D.C.: U.S. Government Printing Office, 1991.

Congressional Record: Proceedings and Debates of the 102nd Congressional First Session, January 11 1991. Washington, D.C.: U.S. Government Printing Office, 1991.

Congressional Record: Proceedings and Debates of the 102nd Congressional First Session, January 12 1991. Washington, D.C.: U.S. Government Printing Office, 1991.

Dallek, Robert. *The American Style of Foreign Policy: Cultural Politics and Foreign Affairs*. New York: Alfred A. Knopf, 1983.

DeBenedetti, Charles. *The Peace Reform in American History*. Bloomington, Indiana: Indiana University Press, 1980.

Degler, Carl N. *Out of Our Past: The Forces That Shaped Modern America*. New York: Harper and Row Publishers, 1984.

DeMesquita, Bruce Bueno and David Lalman. *War and Reason: Domestic and International Imperatives*. New Haven: Yale University Press, 1992.

Dixon, William J. "Democracy and the Management of International Conflict." *Journal of Conflict Resolution* 37, no. 1 (March 1993): 42–68.

Dower, John W. *War Without Mercy: Race and Power in the Pacific War*. New York: Pantheon Books, 1986.

Drinnon, Richard. *Facing West: The Metaphysics of Indian-Hating and Empire-Building*. Minneapolis: University of Minnesota Press, 1980.

Dunn, Charles W., ed. *Religion in American Politics*. Washington, D.C.: Congressional Quarterly Press, 1989.

Dunn, Richard S. and Mary Maples Dunn, eds. *The World of William Penn*. Philadelphia: University of Pennsylvania Press, 1986.

Dutter, Lee E. "The Seventy-Five Years' War, 1914–1989: Some Observations on Psychology of American Foreign Policy Making." *Political Psychology* 12, no. 3 (Sept. 1991): 523–554.

Eccles, W.J. *France in America*. East Lansing, Michigan: Michigan State University Press, 1990.

Elshtain, Jean Bethke and Sheila Tobias, eds. *Women, Militarism, and War*. Savage, Maryland: Rowman and Littlefield, 1990.

Elwarfally, Mahmoud G. *Imagery and Ideology in U.S. Policy Towards Libya*. Pittsburgh: University of Pittsburgh Press, 1988.

Esposito, John L. *The Islamic Threat: Myth or Reality*. New York: Oxford University Press, 1992.

Falk, Richard. "Reflections On Democracy and the Gulf War." *Alternatives* 16, no. 2 (Spring 1991): 263–274.

Farer, Tom. "Israel's Unlawful Occupation." *Foreign Policy*, no. 82 (Spring 1991): 37–58.

Federal Bureau of Investigation. *Uniform Crime Reports for the United States*. Washington, D.C.: U.S. Government Printing Office, 1987.

Findley, Paul. *They Dare to Speak Out: People and Institutions Confront Israel's Lobby*. Westport, CT.: Lawrence Hill and Company, 1985.

Fischer, Fritz. *Germany's Aims in the First World War*. New York: W.W. Norton, 1967.

Fisher, Glen. *International Negotiation: A Cross-Cultural Perspective*. Chicago: International Press, 1980.

Fisher, Roger and William Ury. *Getting to Yes*. New York: Penguin, 1983.

Fredrickson, George M. *White Supremacy: A Comparative Study in American and South African History*. New York: Oxford University Press, 1981.

Freilich, Morris, ed. *The Relevance of Culture*. New York: Bergin and Garvey, 1989.

Fulbright, J. William. *The Arrogance of Power*. New York: Random House, 1966.

Gaenslen, Fritz. "Culture and Decision Making in China, Japan, Russia, and the United States." *World Politics* 39, no. 1 (October 1986): 78–103.

Gallup, George Jr. and Jim Castelli. *The People's Religion: American Faith in the 90's*. New York: Macmillan Publishing Company, 1989.

Gallup, George Jr. and Frank Newport. "First Anniversary of Iraqi Invasion of Kuwait: Most Americans Strongly Positive About U.S. Role," *The Gallup Poll Monthly*, no. 310 (July 1991): 34–38.

———. "Majority Says No to Intervening on Behalf of Iraqi Rebels," *The Gallup Poll Monthly*, no. 307 (April 1991): 2-3.

———. "Most Americans Favor Attacks on Iraq If Nuclear Materials Not Destroyed," *The Gallup Poll Monthly*, no. 310 (July 1991): 32.

———. "Death Penalty Support Remains Strong," *The Gallup Poll Monthly*, no. 309 (June 1991): 40–45.

Geertz, Clifford. *The Interpretation of Cultures*. New York: Basic Books, 1973.

Gibson, Charles, ed. *The Spanish Tradition in America*. New York: Harper and Row, 1968.

Gil, David G. *Violence Against Children: Physical Child Abuse in the United States*. Cambridge, Mass.: Harvard University Press, 1970.

Glad, Betty. "Black-and-White Thinking: Ronald Reagan's Approach to Foreign Policy," *Political Psychology* 4, no.1 (March 1983): 33–76.

Glenny, Misha. *The Fall of Yugoslavia: The Third Balkan War*. New York: Penguin Books, 1992.

Graham, Hugh Davis and Ted Robert Gurr, eds. *Violence in America: Historical and Comparative Perspectives*. Beverly Hills: Sage, 1979.

Greven, Philip. *Spare the Child: The Religious Roots of Punishment and the Psychological Impact of Physical Abuse.* New York: Alfred A. Knopf, 1991.

Grose, Peter. *Israel in the Mind of America.* New York: Alfred A. Knopf, 1983.

Gutman, Roy. *A Witness to Genocide.* New York: Macmillan, 1993.

Hamilton, Michael P. ed. *American Character and Foreign Policy.* Grand Rapids, Michigan: William B. Ferdman's Publishing Co., 1986.

Hartz, Louis. *The Liberal Tradition in America.* New York: Harcourt, Brace, and Company, 1955.

Harris, William V. *War and Imperialism in Republican Rome.* Oxford: Clarendon Press, 1979.

Hatch, Nathan O. *The Democratization of American Christianity.* New Haven: Yale University Press, 1989.

Hoffmann, Stanley. "The Political Psychology of Peace and War: Critique and an Agenda," *Political Psychology* 7, no. 1 (March 1986): 1–21.

———. *Gulliver's Troubles, Or The Setting of American Foreign Policy.* New York: McGraw-Hill Book Company, 1968.

Hofstadtler, Richard. *The Paranoid Style in American Politics.* New York: Alfred A. Knopf, 1965.

———. *Social Darwinism in American Thought.* Boston: Beacon Press, 1955.

Horowitz, Mardi J. "Self-righteous Rage and the Attribution of Blame," *Archives of General Psychiatry* 38, no. 11 (November 1981): 1233–1238.

Horsman, Reginald. *Race and Manifest Destiny.* Cambridge, Mass.: Harvard University Press, 1981.

Hunt, Michael H. *Ideology and U.S. Foreign Policy.* New Haven: Yale University Press, 1987.

Hunter, James Davison. *Culture Wars: The Struggle to Define America.* New York: Basic Books, 1991.

Huntington, Samuel P. "The Clash of Civilizations?" *Foreign Affairs* 72, no. 3 (Summer 1993): 22–49.

Ikle, Fred Charles. *How Nations Negotiate.* New York: Praeger, 1967.

James, Patrick and John R. Oneal. "The Influence of Domestic and International Politics on the President's Use of Force." *Journal of Conflict Resolution* 35, no. 2 (June 1991): 307–332.

Jensen, Kenneth M. and David Wurmser, eds. *The Meaning of Munich Fifty Years Later*. Washington, D.C.: United States Institute of Peace, 1990.

Jervis, Robert. *Perception and Misperception in International Politics*. Princeton: Princeton University Press, 1976.

Jonsson, Christen. *Communication in International Bargaining*. New York: St. Martin's Press, 1990.

Kaplan, Robert D. *Balkan Ghosts*. New York: St. Martin's Press, 1993.

Kaplowitz, Noel. "National Self-Images, Perceptions of Enemies, and Conflict Strategies: Psychopolitical Dimensions of International Relations." *Political Psychology* 2, no. no. 1 (March 1990): 39–82.

Karsh, Efraim and Inari Rautsi. *Saddam Hussein: A Political Biography*. New York: The Free Press, 1991.

Kegley, Charles W. et al. "Conflict at Home and Abroad: An Empirical Extension." *The Journal of Politics* 40, no. 3 (August 1978): 742-752.

Kennan, George F. "Morality and Foreign Policy." *Foreign Affairs* 64, no. 2 (Winter 1985/86): 205–218.

———. *The Other Balkan Wars*. Washington, D.C.: Carnegie Endowment for International Peace, 1993.

Kerry, Richard J. *The Star Spangled Mirror: America's Image of Itself and the World*. Savage, Maryland: Rowman and Littlefield Publishers, 1990.

Kremenyuk, Victor A.. ed. *International Negotiation: Analysis, Approaches, Issues*. San Francisco: Jossey-Bass Publishers, 1991.

Larson, Erik. *Lethal Passage: How the Travels of a Single Handgun Expose the Roots of America's Gun Crisis*. New York: Crown Publishers, 1994.

Lerner, Max. *America As A Civilization: Life and Thought in the United States Today*. New York: Henry Holt and Company, 1987.

Levy, Daniel S. "Why Johnny Might Grow Up Violent and Sexist: Interview with Myriam Miedzan." *Time*, Sept. 16 1991: 16–19.

Levy, Jack S. "Misperceptions and the Causes of War," *World Politics* 36, no. 1 (October 1983): 76–99.

Lipset, Seymour Martin. *The First New Nation: The United States in Historical Perspective*. New York: W.W. Norton, 1979.

——. *Continental Divide: The Values and Institutions of the United States and Canada*. New York: Routledge, 1990.

Maoz, Zeev and Bruce Russett. "Alliance, Continuity, Wealth and Political Stability: Is the Lack of Conflict Among Democracies a Statistical Artifact." *International Interactions* 17, no. 3 (1992): 245–267.

Marius, Richard. "Musings on the Mysteries of the American South." *Daedalus* 113, no. 3 (Summer 1984): 143–176.

Mautner-Markof, Frances, ed. *Processes of International Negotiations*. Boulder, Colo.: Westview Press, 1989.

——. "A Necessary War?" *Foreign Policy*, no. 82 (Spring 1991): 159–177.

McNaught, Kenneth. *The Pelican History of Canada*. Middlesex, England: Penguin, 1969.

Mearsheimer, John J. "Back to the Future: Instability in Europe After the Cold War." *International Security* 15, no. 1 (Summer 1990): 5–56

Miedzian, Myriam. *Boys Will Be Boys: Breaking the Link Between Masculinity and Violence*. New York: Doubleday, 1991.

Morgan, Clifton and Sally Howard Campbell. "Domestic Structure, Decisional Constraints, and War." *Journal of Conflict Resolution* 35, no. 2 (June 1991): 187–211.

Moses, Rafael. "Empathy and Dis-Empathy in Political Conflict." *Political Psychology* 6, no.1 (March 1985): 135–39.

Myrdal, Gunnar. An American Dilemma: The Negro Problem in Modern Democracy, vol. II. New York: Harper Torchbooks, 1962.

——. *Policy and Opinion in the Gulf War*. Chicago: University of Chicago Press, 1994.

Nash, Roderick. *Wilderness and the American Mind*. New Haven: Yale University Press, 1973.

Neustadt, Richard E. and Ernest R. May. *Thinking in Time: The Uses of History for Decision-Makers*. New York: The Free Press, 1986.

Newsom, David D. *Diplomacy and the American Democracy*. Bloomington, Indiana: Indiana University Press, 1988.

Niebuhr, Reinhold. *The Irony of American History*. New York: Charles Scribner's Sons, 1952.

Novik, Nimrod. *The United States and Israel: Domestic Determinants of a Changing U.S. Commitment*. Boulder, Colo.: Westview Press, 1986.

Opotow, Susan. "Moral Exclusion and Injustice: An Introduction." *Journal of Social Issues* 46, no. 1 (1990): 1-20.

Ostrom, Charles W. and Brian L. Job. "The President and the Political Use of Force." *American Political Science Review* 80, no. 2 (June 1986): 541–566.

Paine, Thomas. *Common Sense and Other Political Writings*, edited by Nelson F. Adkins. Indianapolis: The Bobbs-Merrill Co., 1953.

Patchen, Martin. *Resolving Disputes Between Nations: Coercion or Conciliation?* Durham: Duke University Press, 1988.

Payne, Richard J. *The West European Allies, The Third World, and U.S. Foreign Policy*. New York: Praeger, 1991.

Pfaff, William. "Invitation to War." *Foreign Affairs* 72, no. 3 (Summer 1993): 97–109.

Polenberg, Richard. *One Nation Divisible: Class, Race, and Ethnicity in the United States Since 1938*. New York: The Viking Press, 1980.

Post, Jerrold M. "Saddam Hussein of Iraq: A Political Psychological Profile." *Political Psychology* 12, no. 2 (June 1991): 279–290.

Prothrow-Sith, Deborah and Michele Weissman. *Deadly Consequences*. New York: HarperCollins, 1991.

Pruitt, Dean G. *Negotiation Behavior*. New York: Academic Press, 1981.

Pye, Lucian W. *Asian Power and Politics: The Cultural Dimensions of Authority*. Cambridge, Mass.: Harvard University Press, 1985.

Redman, Charles. "Iraq's Use of Chemical Weapons." *Department of State Bulletin* 88, no. 2141 (December 1988): 44.

Risse-Kappan, Thomas. "Public Opinion, Domestic Structure, and Foreign Policy in Liberal Democracies." *World Politics* 43, no. 4 (July 1991): 479–512.

Ross, Marc Howard. "International and External Conflict: Cross-Cultural Evidence and a New Analysis." *Journal of Conflict Resolution* 29, no. 4 (December 1985): 547–579.

Russett, Bruce M. *Controlling the Sword: Democratic Governance of National Security*. Cambridge, Mass.: Harvard University Press, 1990.

Russett, Bruce M. and Alfred Stephan, eds. *Military Force and American Society*. New York: Harper and Row Publishers, 1973.

Said, Edward W. *Covering Islam: How the Media and the Experts Determine How We See the Rest of the World.* New York: Pantheon Books, 1981.

Shadid, Mohammed K. *The United States and the Palestinians.* New York: St. Martin's Press, 1981.

Shafer, Byron E., ed. *Is America Different? A New Look at American Exceptionalism.* Oxford: Clarendon Press, 1991.

Shaheen, Jack G. *The T.V. Arab.* Bowling Green, Ohio: Bowling Green State University Popular Press, 1984.

Sheffer, Gabriel, ed. *Dynamics of Dependence: U.S.-Israeli Relations.* Boulder, Colo.: Westview Press, 1987.

Shehadeh, Raja. *Occupier's Law: Israel and the West Bank.* Washington, D.C.: Institute for Palestine Studies, 1988.

Slade, Shelley. "The Image of the Arab in America: Analysis of a Poll on American Attitudes." *The Middle East Journal* 35, no. 2 (Spring 1981): 143–162.

Slotkin, Richard. *Regeneration Through Violence: The Mythology of the American Frontier.* Middletown, CT.: Wesleyan University Press, 1973.

———. *Gunfighter Nation: The Myth of the Frontier in Twentieth Century America.* New York: Atheneum, 1992.

Smith, Gaddis. *Morality, Reason, and Power: American Diplomacy in the Carter Years.* New York: Hill and Wang, 1986.

Snyder, Glenn H. and Paul Diesing. *Conflict Among Nations: Bargaining, Decision Making, and System Structure in International Crises.* Princeton: Princeton University Press, 1977.

Soderlund, Jean R. *Quakers and Slavery: A Divided Spirit.* Princeton: Princeton University Press, 1985.

Stoll, Richard J. "The Guns of November: Presidential Reelection and the Use of Force, 1947–1982." *The Journal of Conflict Resolution* 28, no. 2 (June 1984): 231–246.

Suleiman, Michael W. *The Arabs in the Mind of America.* Brattleboro, Vermont: Amana Books, 1988.

Terry, Janice J. *Mistaken Identity: Arab Stereotypes in Popular Writing.* Washington, D.C.: American-Arab Affairs Council, 1986.

Timmerman, Kenneth R. *The Death Lobby: How the West Armed Iraq.* Boston: Houghton Mifflin Co. 1991.

Thompson, W. Scott, et al. eds. *Approaches to Peace: An Intellectual Map*. Washington, D.C.: United States Institute of Peace, 1991.

Tocqueville, Alexis de. *Democracy in America* vol.1. New York: Doubleday and Company, 1969.

Toolin, Cynthia. "American Civil Religion From 1789 to 1981: A Content Analysis of Presidential Inaugural Addresses." *Review of Religious Research* 25, no. 1 (Sept. 1983): 39–49.

Tutwiler, Margaret. "Loan Guarantees to Israel." *U.S. Department of State Dispatch* 2, no. 40 (Oct. 1991): 754.

United Nations. *UN Security Council Resolution 660, Aug. 2 1990*. Washington, D.C.: United Nations Information Center, 1990.

UN Security Council. "Resolution 562, May 10 1985." *Resolutions and Decisions of the Security Council 1985*. New York: United Nations, 1985.

U.S. Congress. House. *Foreign Assistance Legislation for the Fiscal Years 1988–89* (Part 1). Hearings Before the Committee on Foreign Affairs. 100th Congress, 1st sess., February 18, 19, and 24 1987. Washington, D.C.: U.S. Government Printing Office, 1987.

———. ———. *United States-Iraqi Relations*. Hearings Before the Subcommittee on Europe and the Middle East of the Committee on Foreign Affairs. 101st. Congress, 2nd sess., April 26 1990. Washington, D.C.: U.S. Government Printing Office, 1990.

———. ———. *Human Rights Abuses in Kuwait and Iraq*. Hearings Before the Committee on Foreign Affairs. 102nd Congress, 1st sess., January 8 1991. Washington, D.C.: U.S. Government Printing Office, 1991.

U.S. Congress. Senate. *Chemical Weapons Use in Kurdistan: Iraq's Final Offensive*. A Staff Report to the Committee on Foreign Relations. Oct. 1988. Washington, D.C.: U.S. Government Printing Office, 1988.

———. ———. *U.S. Policy in the Persian Gulf*. Hearings Before the Committee on Foreign Relations. 101st. Congress, 2nd sess., Sept. 5, 20, and October 17 1990. Washington, D.C.: U.S. Government Printing Office, 1990.

———. ———. *U.S. Policy in the Persian Gulf*. Hearings Before the Committee on Foreign Relations. 101st Congress, 2nd sess., December 4 and 5 1990. Washington, D.C.: U.S. Government Printing Office, 1991.

——. ——. *U.S. Policy in the Persian Gulf.* Hearings Before the Committee on Foreign Relations. 102nd Congress, 1st sess., January 8 1991. Washington, D.C.: U.S. Government Printing Office, 1991.

——. ——. *Persian Gulf: The Question of War Crimes.* Hearing Before the Committee on Foreign Relations. 102nd Congress, 1st sess., April 9 1991. Washington, D.C.: U.S. Government Printing Office, 1991.

U.S. Department of State. *Realism, Strength, Negotiation: Key Foreign Policy Statements of the Reagan Administration.* Washington, D.C.: U.S. Department of State, 1984.

——. *PLO Commitments Compliance Act.* Report Prepared for the Committee on Foreign Affairs, U.S. House of Representatives, March 1990. Washington, D.C.: U.S. Government Printing Office, 1990.

U.S. Institute of Peace. *The Gulf Crisis: Finding a Peaceful Solution.* Washington, D.C.: U.S. Institute of Peace, 1990.

Varley, H. Paul, Ivan Morris, and Nobuko Morris. *Samurai.* New York: Dell, 1970.

Vlahos, Michael. "The End of America's Postwar Ethos." *Foreign Affairs* 66, no. 5 (Summer 1988): 1091–1107.

——. "Culture and Foreign Policy." *Foreign Policy*, no. 82 (Spring 1991): 59–78.

Waltz, Kenneth N. *Man, the State, and War.* New York: Columbia University Press, 1959.

Watson, Adam. *Diplomacy: The Dialogue Between States.* New York: McGraw-Hill Book Company, 1983.

Whitfield, Stephen J. *The Culture of the Cold War.* Baltimore: Johns Hopkins University Press, 1991.

Wiarda, Howard J. *Ethnocentrism in Foreign Policy: Can We Understand the Third World?* Washington, D.C.: American Enterprise Institute, 1985.

Wilkenfeld, Jonathan, ed. *Conflict Behavior and Linkage Politics.* New York: David McKay, 1973.

Wilkinson, Rupert. *American Tough: The Tough-Guy Tradition and American Character.* Westport, CT.: Greenwood Press 1984.

——. *The Pursuit of American Character.* New York: Harper and Row, Publishers, 1988.

Wittkopf, Eugene R. *Faces of Internationalism: Public Opinion and American Foreign Policy*. Durham: Duke University Press, 1990.

Woodward, Bob. *The Commanders*. New York: Simon and Schuster, 1991.

Wright, Quincy. *A Study of War*. Chicago: The University of Chicago Press, 1964.

Wuthnow, Robert. *The Restructuring of American Religion: Society and Faith Since World War II*. Princeton: Princeton University Press, 1988.

Zartman, William I., and Maureen R. Berman. *The Practical Negotiator*. New Haven: Yale University Press, 1982.

INDEX

Abdallah, Munzer, 151
Adams, John, 37
Afghanistan, 65, 66
African-Americans, 63, 142
    role in U.S. foreign policy, 204–
        205, 212
    United States negative atti-
        tude toward, 31, 40
    vigilantism toward, 54–55
Africans
    U.S. policy toward, 33
    enslaved in United States, 74
Americans sensitivity to Nazi-like
        actions, 103
    of Iraq in Gulf, 93, 98, 128
    of Serbia in Bosnia, 193–197
Aidad, Mohamed, 35
Akawi, Mustafa, 149–150
Al Aqsa Mosque, 145–146
Al-Assad, Hafez, 163
Al-Sabah, Sheikh Jabir, 110
Al-Sadat, Anwar. See Sadat,
        Anwar
Aladdin (Disney movie), 97

Algeria, 201
America. See United States
American Academy of Pediatrics,
        59
American Civil War
    religion and, 29
    vigilantism following, 51
American Creed, 10, 14, 90
American cultural values, 123,
        172, 196
    and right to bear arms,
        191–192
    Cold War's effect on, 64
    complexity of, 131, 148
    distant cultures and, xiii–xiv,
        93, 182
    humanitarian aspect of, 140,
        141, 144, 151
    role in U.S. foreign policy,
        36, 128, 166, 181,
        204–205
    violence in, 57
American exceptionalism, 89–90
    and diplomacy, 82–87

and U.S. foreign policy, 22–25,
        85–86
American historical experiences
    and rule of law, 54–56
    in Cold War, 64–65
    in Vietnam, 106
    in World War II, 104–106, 136
    U.S. foreign policy and, 2,
        47–54, 74
    with Native Americans, 49–50
American Indian Wars, 55
American Israel Public Affairs
        Committee (AIPAC),
        137–138, 154
American Medical Association, 58
American national myths, xiv, 20,
        21. See also specific
        myths
    Americanism, 14
    and nationalism, 2
    Reagan's use of, 16
American patriotism
    religion's role in, 21
American political thought, 48
American Revolution, 7, 24–25,
        28, 200–201
    violence in, 48
American Way, 2, 14
Americans. See also United
        States
    and violence, 48, 57, 64
    competitive nature of, 89–90
    impatience of, 90–92
    perceptions of and cultural
        links to Israel, 134–138
    perceptions of Arabs, 96–98
    perceptions of Palestinians,
        139–141
    perceptions of race, 31–32
    role in U.S. foreign policy, 66,
        67, 191
    self perceptions, 26, 49
Americans for Peace Now, 146
Americanism, 14
Amnesty International, 101, 149
Analogy. See also U.S. foreign pol-
        icy; Munich analogy

    in foreign policy, 68
    U.S. inaction in Bosnian con-
        flict and Vietnam,
        182–189
    U.S. Gulf War policy and
        Vietnam and World War
        II, 104–106
    Pearl Harbor, 69
Ancient Greece, 41
Angola, 65
Anthropology, 2
Anti-communism, 69, 87
Anti-Semitism, 45
Aoun, Michael, 102–103
Apartheid, 204–205
Appeasement
    in Munich analogy, 69–70,
        104–106, 176
Apple, R. W., 194
Arab leaders
    role in Gulf Crisis, 106
    support for negotiation, 157,
        160
Arab culture
    Disney's Aladdin negative por-
        tayal of, 97
    perceived as distant by
        Americans, 97
    U.S. sensitivity to, 146
Arab League, 98, 110
Arab solution, 106, 110
Arab states, 115, 132, 154, 156
    diplomatic initiatives in Gulf
        War, 109–110
Arab-Americans
    Americans' hostility toward, 96
    and Palestinian-Israeli
        Conflict, 140
Arab-Israeli Conflict. See also
        Palestinian-Israeli
        Conflict
    links between Gulf Crisis and,
        145, 154, 163
Arab-Israeli War
    Hussein's linking his with-
        drawal from Kuwait to,
        141

Israeli annexation of West
    Bank and Gaza Strip
    during, 143
Arabs
    American perceptions of, 96–98
    communication style, 78
    European support of, 143
Arafat, Yasir, 76, 162
Ares (Greek war god), 41
Armegeddon, 158
Arms sales
    Iraq and, 102–103
    United States and, 65–66
Asians, 32, 78
Aspin, Les, 41, 138
ATF (Bureau of Alcohol, Tobacco,
    and Firearms)
    conflict with Branch
    Davidians, 58, 65
Attitudes (cultural)
    and international conflicts, 36
    and television, 61
    definition of, 9
    internal and external link of,
    72
    U.S. racial, 31
Austin, Hudson, 206
Austria-Hungary, archduke of,
    167
Axtell, James, 52, 53, 54
Aziz, Tariq, 106, 108, 111

Baker, James
    and Bosnian conflict, 174, 186
    and Gulf War, 106–107, 108,
    111, 114–115
    and Palestinian-Israeli conflict,
    154, 164
Balkan wars. See Bosnian conflict
Balkans, 171, 175, 178. See also
    Bosnian conflict
    Americans' views of, 166–167
    United States cultural distance
    from, 170
Banca Nazionale del Lavoro, 128
Baritz, Loren, 24, 32–33
Barre, Siad, 66

Battle of Blackbird Fields, 178
BBC (British Broadcasting
    Corporation), 154
Begin, Menachem, 143, 144, 159
Bedouins, 97
Beliefs (cultural), 10
    American, 4, 11, 117, 131
    belief systems, 10–11, 24
    role in international conflicts,
    36, 72
Bentley, Helen Delick, 185
Berger, Peter L., 8
Bickerman, Elias J., 42
Biden, Joseph, 210
Bihac, 182
Bishop, Maurice, 206
Bismark, Otto von, 44
Blackwell, Kenneth, 177
Blake, William, 23
Blum, Douglas W., 10
Boschwitz, Rudy, 138
Bosnia. See also Bosnian conflict
    ethnic complexity of, 171
    people perceived as violent, 167
    U.S. inaction in Bosnian con-
    flict and terrain of, 183
Bosnian conflict. See also Vance-
    Owen plan
    as an international threat,
    171–176
    complexity of, 171–172, 194
    European and Russian involve-
    ment in, 196
    role of cultural differences
    within, 6, 166–170, 199
    UN arms embargo during,
    189–193
    UN role in, 179–180
    U.S. reluctance to use
    force in, 69, 104,
    166–170, 182–189,
    201–202
Bosnia-Hercegovina. See Bosnia
Bosnian Croats
    U.S. support of, 196
Bosnian Muslims, 166–171, 177,
    185

cultural distance to West, 166,
        201
ethnic cleansing, 178
Islamic world linked to,
        169–170, 193
reluctance to negotiate with
        Bosnian Serbs, 195
UN arms embargo effect on,
        189–193
Bosnian Serbs, 175, 196. *See also*
        Serbs; Serbia; Ethnic
        cleansing
cultural distance from West,
        168
perception of as violent, 167
reluctance to negotiate with
        Bosnian Muslims, 195
ultimatum to close detention
        camps, 196
U.S. cultural links to,
        168–169
Boucher, Richard, 127
Boutros-Ghali, Boutros 179–180,
        188–189
Bowers, Stephen R., 174
Bradley, Bill , 138
Brady, Nicholas F.
        and shuttle diplomacy, 115
Branch Davidians, 58, 65
Brezhnev, Leonid, 213
Britain, 204
        and Arab-Israeli conflict,
                142–143
        and Munich Agreement, 104
        Anglo-American link, 110,
                200–201
        in Gulf War, 123, 128
        war and national identity in,
                40, 43
Brown, Richard Maxwell
        on violence in American val-
                ues, 48, 57
        on vigilantism in United
                States, 54
Browning, Bp. Edmond, 30
Brzezinski, Zbigniew, 107, 211
Buruma, Ian, 46

Bush, George, xvi–xvii, 16, 29–30,
        38, 135, 141, 143, 164
        and new world order, 129, 173
        and religion, 29–30
        and rule of law, 56
        and use of analogy, 10, 38,
                68–69, 104–105
        in Bosnian conflict, 85, 130,
                165, 172, 176, 178–183,
                186,
        in Operation Desert Storm, 35,
                93–95, 98–101, 113–118,
                120, 125–126, 145
        relating to Saddam
                Hussein, 62–63, 78–79,
                103–110, 126
        in Operation Restore Hope, 35
        in Palestinian-Israeli conflict,
                154–155, 162–163
        sanctions against Iraq,
                102–103

Calvinist doctrine, 86
Camp David Accords, 75, 87
        Carter's role in, 131, 159, 211
Canada
        reliance on negotiation, 55
        rule of law in, 54–55
Capital punishment, 64
Carr, Caleb, 68
Carter, Jimmy, xvi, 4, 25, 38, 86,
        87
        ability to empathize, 37, 131,
                148, 153
        and Middle East peace process,
                87, 131, 158–161
        and North Korea dispute,
                203–204
        and Panama Canal treaties,
                208
        negotiations with distant cul-
                tures, 34, 74
Castelli, Jim, 27
Catholics (Roman), 50, 54, 205
        Croatian, 167
        French, and Native
                Americans, 51–54

Spanish, and Native
    Americans, 50–51
Chace, James, 68
Chagnon, Napoleon A., 47
Chamberlain, Neville, 69, 104
Chechnya, 174
China, People's Republic of, 86
Christianity
    and Native Americans, 50, 51
    comparisons between
        American and European,
        28
    fundamentalists in, 29–30, 136
Christopher, Warren, 187–188
CIA (Central Intelligence
    Agency), 128, 130
"City on the Hill" myth, 20
Civil religion, 28–29
    American, 29–31, 120, 122
Civil rights movement (U.S.), 11
Clinton, Bill, xvii, 10, 38
    ambivalence toward diplomacy
        in Bosnian conflict,
        193–197
    and dispute in North Korea,
        202
    and rule of law, 56
    and Saddam Hussein, 63
    as symbolic of a new genera-
        tion, 212
    focus on domestic policy, 41,
        69, 166
    role in Bosnian conflict, 85,
        188–189, 191, 193
    role in Gulf crisis, 81, 125
Codewords, 69, 80, 98, 110, 117
Cohen, Roger, 201
Cold War
    effect on American cultural
        values, 64
    American political conformity
        based on threats of, 209
    Yugoslavia in, 168
Collectivist societies
    in negotiations, 78–79
    Iraq as, 74
Colley, Linda, 23, 43

Communism, 64, 69, 132, 157
    Christian fundamentalists
        view of, 29
Comprehensive Antiapartheid
    Act, 205
Conflict, 71, 74, 81
    Americans and foreign, 80
    cultural modes of dealing with,
        36
    dualism in, 79
Conflict, external, 40
Conflict resolution
    nonviolent, 74
    political systems role in, 76
Contact Group, 194, 197
Convention for the Limitation of
    the Spread of Missile
    Technology, 143
Coser, Lewis, 40
Costa Rica, 205
Croatia
    as similar culture to West,
        167–168
    ethnic cleansing by, 178
    Serbia's Greater Serbia policy
        in, 171
    use of religion to gain support,
        169
Cuba, 60, 71–72
Cultural barriers
    to negotiations, 71–75
Cultural conflicts
    factors influencing prevalence
        of, xiii
    differing responses to, 6–7
Cultural differences
    affect on international rela-
        tions, xiii, 6, 72,
    between Bosnia and Croatia,
        167
Cultural influences, 1–4, 34
    on foreign policy, 4–14
Cultural proximity
    between Croatia and West,
        167–168
Cultural relativism, 53–54
Cultural reservoir, 5

Israeli and United States
    shared, 135
Culture, 2, 7, 8, 9, 15, 16–18, 37
    American, 74–75, 89
        U.S. subculture, 4, 8, 86
        U.S. dominant, 5, 10, 12,
            31–33, 56, 86, 90–91,
            100–101, 125, 186, 194
        U.S. popular, 60
    and foreign policy, 4–14
    clashing of, 174
    enculturation, 11
    external stimuli effect on,
        12–13
    role in policymaking, 17
Cyprus, 145
Czechoslovakia, 69, 176

D'Amato, Alfonse, 103, 188
Daponte, Beth Osborne, 126
Darwinism, 33
de Tocqueville, Alexis, 15, 28, 50,
    90–91
Declaration of Independence
    (U.S.), 27
Dehumanization
    in international conflict, 36–37
    link to moral exclusion, 37
    of non-Europeans, 32, 60, 207
Dellums, Ronald, 117–118
Democracies
    as similar cultures, 7
    use of force, 38–39
Democracy
    American, 39, 55, 83–84, 148
    Kantian view of, 38–39
    views of Croatia as, 168
    views of Israel as, 148
Democratic individualism, 53
Détente, 86
Diplomacy, 91, 88, 104. See also
    negotiations
    American exceptionalism and,
        82–87
    and American society, 78,
        82–83

U.S. presidents' popularity
    and, 208
    shuttle, 115, 158–159
Distant cultures, 7, 87–90
    in international relations, 200
    in European conflicts with
        non-Europeans, 49
    and United States, 6
        approach to negotiations
            with, 74–75, 79–80, 92,
            123
        double standards with, 146,
            173–174
        response to Gulf crisis, 94,
            97, 110
        response to Bosnian con-
            flict, 166, 170
        support for humanitarian
            aid to, 114
        television and, 60–61
        use force with, xvi, 39, 49,
            71, 123, 200–201
Diversity, 88–89
Dixon, William J., 39
Djerejian, Edward P., 170
Doctors Syndicate, 170
Dole, Robert, 185
Domestic violence, 47, 57–58
Dualism, 13, 62, 84–85, 211
    consistent with U.S. world-
        view, 209
    role in conflict, 79, 95, 185
Dugan, Michael J., 18
Durkheim, Emile, 8

Eagleburger, Lawrence, 181
    shuttle diplomacy, 115
    relationship with Serbia,
        168–169
East Jerusalem, 148
Eastern Orthodox, 169
East-West Conflict, 85–86, 132,
    208–213
EC (European Community)
    in Gulf War, 109, 186–187
    in Bosnian conflict, 172, 187

Egypt
    aid to Bosnian muslims, 170
    diplomatic role of, 98, 132
    in Camp David Accords, 81, 87,
        157
Eirene (Greek peace goddess), 41
Eisenhower, Dwight, 132,
        142–143
El Salvador, 65, 205
Elliot, J. H., 53
Elshtain, Jean Bethke, 41
Empathy, 11, 37
Enculturation, 11, 116
England. See Britain
Equality for women movement
        (U.S.), 11
Ethnic cleansing, 210. See also
        genocide
    Bosnian Muslims' policy
        of, 178
    by Croatian Utashi, 178
    in Nazi Germany compared to
        in Bosnia, 176–179, 194
    Milosevic's role in, 168, 176
    Serbian policy of, 129–130
    West's indirect role in, 165,
        167, 176–179
Ethnic conflict, xiii, 199
    in Bosnia, 171, 172, 186
Ethnocentrism, 17, 54
    and international relations, 73
Ethnonationalism, 3, 171
Europe, 4, 78, 80, 115
    concept of racial hierarchy, 32
European-Americans, 40, 54
Europeans, 67–68
    and Bosnian conflict, 166, 173,
        186, 188, 196
    cultural links with Americans,
        31–32
Exceptionalism, 23
    American, 25, 89–90
    as barrier to negotiations, 85
    British, 23
External violence
    link to internal violence, 38–47

Falklands War, 201
Farer, Tom, 148
FBI, 59, 96
Fedayeen, 142
Ferdinand, King (of Spain), 50
Findley, Paul, 138
Firearms. See guns
Fischer, Fritz, 44
Fisher, Glen, 73
Fisher, Roger, 79, 203
Force, 36–37, 72, 76, 149
    impatience as factor in use of,
        91
Ford, Gerald, 156
Foreign Affairs, 209
Foreign policy, 2–3, 6, 12
    analogy in, 68–70
    and culture, 4–14, 201
    and public opinion, 14–18
Fourth Geneva Convention, 142,
        149, 150–152
France, 142–143
    in Gulf crisis, 110–111
    relations with Native
        Americans, 51–54
    Catholic, 44
French Revolution, 18
Frontier myth, 20
    in Vietnam, 106
Fulbright, J. William, 37, 209

Galluci, Robert L., 203–204
Gallup, George, 27
Gaza Strip. See also Occupied
        Territories
    Israeli occupation of, 132, 143,
        154
    American-Jews' views of,
        138
GATT (General Agreement on
        Tariffs and Trade), 92
Geertz, Clifford
    on culture, 7–8, 9
    on ideology, 18, 19
Genocide
    in World War II, 176–179

Gephart, Richard, 138
Germany. *See also* Nazi Germany
and Gulf War, 110–111, 115
Kultur concept in, 7
links between internal and ex-
ternal violence in, 44–45
reunification of, 199
Global interdependence. *See*
Interdependence
Golan Heights, 144
Goldstone, Richard J., 195
Gorazde, 182, 189
Gorbachev, Mikhail, 81, 87, 120
Gordon, Michael, 191
Gore, Al, 125, 128, 172–173
Graham, Rev. Billy, 30
Graham, Hugh Davis, 57
Great Britain. *See* Britain
Greece, 174. *See also* Ancient
Greece
Greeks, Eastern Orthodox, 169
Grenada
U.S. invasion of, 206–207
Grose, Peter, 134
Grossman, Steve, 138
Guernica, 103
Gulf Crisis
barriers to negotiated settle-
ment in, 106–112
as an international threat,
98–101
links between Arab-Israeli
Conflict and, 163
Gulf Crisis Financial
Coordination Group
(GCFCG), 115
Gulf War (Persian), 115
civilian deaths in, 66, 122–123
compared to Bosnian conflict,
180, 186–187
compared to Palestinian-
Israeli conflict, 145
diplomacy in, 109–110
cultural distance as a factor in,
94–95
new world order's birth from,
128–130, 209–210

North African states call for
pause in air strikes, 123
religion's role in, 27, 118–121
United States' participation in,
105, 119–125, 183
analogy's role in, 10, 62,
66, 104
American cultural values
in, 112
Bush's role in, 36, 93–94,
106
opposition to, 94, 119
support for, 94, 119
U.S. avoidance of
responsibility in,
126–128
U.S. self-perception and,
112–115
Gulf region (Persian), 82
Guns
in United States, 58–59, 61
and culture of violence, 54–55
Gurr, Ted Robert, 43

Hague, the
Balkan war crimes tribunal
in, 195
Regulations of 1907, 148
Haiti, 212
Halajaba, 102
Hall, Edward T., 9
Hall, Mildred Reed, 9
Halperin, Morton H., 13
Hamas, 152
Handzar, 178
Hanke, Lewis, 51
Hardliners, 81
Harkin, Tom, 138
Harris, William V., 42
Hartz, Louis, 14, 49
Harvard University School of
Public Health, 59
Hassan, King (of Morocco), 163
Hatch, Orin, 117
Henry Kissinger Associates, 168
Hiroshima, 122
Historical experiences, 36

Hitler, Adolf
and Munich analogy, 69, 104,
105
Saddam Hussein compared to,
96, 101–104, 178
Slobodan Milosevic compared
to, 177
Hobbes, Thomas, 38
Hoffmann, Stanley, 49, 89
Hofstadter, Richard, 33
Holbrooke, Richard, 169
Holocaust. See Jewish Holocaust
homicide
in U.S. culture of violence,
56–59
rates compared, 57
hostages, 100
in Grenada, 206–207
in Iran, 33
Hufbauer, Gary Clyde, 113
human rights abuses
CIVAD, 149
IDF, 149–151
Iraqi, 101–103
Serbian, 177
Humphrey, Hubert, 160–161
Hunt, Michael, 21, 32
Huntington, Samuel P., xiii, 6, 27,
169
Hurd, Douglas, 163
Hussein, Saddam, 38, 63, 78–79,
93. See also Gulf War
alliance with United States,
101–103, 128
compared to Adolf Hitler, 96,
101–104, 178
dualistic view, 121
in Gulf War, 95–96, 100–101,
113–115, 120, 122–123
invasion of Kuwait, 68, 128
personalization of Gulf crisis,
109
suppressing Kurdish and
Shiite rebellions,
209–210
use of religion, 120–121
violating international law, 180

violations of human rights,
102–103
Hussein, King (of Jordan), 110
Hyland, William G., 209
Hyman, Irwin A., 58

Ideology, 2, 18–22
Images, 18
Impatience
as a barrier to negotiation,
90–92
in American culture, 90–91,
112–115
Imperialism, 24
Individualist societies
in negotiations, 78
U.S. as, 112–113
Interdependence, 87–90, 200
Internal conflicts, 72
Internal violence
in Ancient Greece, 41
in Britain, 43
in Catholic France, 44
in Germany, 44–45
in Japan, 45–46
in Roman Republic, 41–42
in Yanomami, 46–47
link to external violence,
38–47
International Atomic Energy
Agency, 202
International conflicts. See also
specific conflicts
culture as a factor in, xiv, 1–2,
36, 72
International environment, 3
Bosnian conflict as threat to,
171–176
Gulf crisis as threat to, 98–101
International law
U.S. Supreme Court circumventing, 56
violations of, 141, 153, 180
International relations. See also
Negotiation; Diplomacy
analogy and, 176
culture and, 5–6, 72, 199

ethnocentrism and, 73
perceptions and, 9
realism as approach to, 2
Intifada, 140
IDF response to, 150
Iran, 78, 103, 110
American hostage crisis in, 33
assistance to Bosnian
Muslims, 170, 193
Iraqi human rights abuses
against, 102
Iran-Iraq War, 102
Iraq, 17, 41, 75, 98, 102. *See also*
Gulf War
as distant culture to United
States, 103, 107
cultural values of, 11, 73
hostages taken during Gulf
War, 100
human rights abuse by,
101–102
invasion of Kuwait, 28, 82,
163, 174
petroleum and, 99, 109, 113
sanctions against, 112
U.S. use of force against, 56,
81, 95, 108, 121–125,
209–210
Iraqis
Americans' lack of empathy
for, 95
Iraq's Republican National
Guard, 122
Isabella, Queen (of Spain), 50
Islam
Americans' fear of, 97, 170
fundamentalism in, xiii, 170,
193, 201
Islamic Jihad, 153
Islamic world
support for Bosnian Muslims,
169–170, 193
United States' double standard
in Bosnia and Gulf, 170
Isolationism
and interdependence, and negotiations, 87–90

United States' embrace of, 69,
88, 89
in Bosnian conflict, 166, 176,
187
Israel, 142–143, 157, 161. *See also*
Palestinian-Israeli con-
flict
American cultural links to,
132–138, 141, 146–148
and UN resolutions, 141–142,
144, 151
government's policies toward
Palestinians, 147, 150
invasion of Lebanon, 144–145
occupation of Arab territories,
153–154, 163
U.S. foreign aid to, 154–155
violations of human rights in
Occupied Territories,
145–153
Israeli Civil Administration
(CIVAD), 149
Israeli Defense Forces (IDF)
alleged use of torture, 149–150
demolition of Palestinian
homes, 150–151
Israeli-Palestinian Conflict. *See*
Palestinian-Israeli
Conflict
Izetbegovic, Alija, 171

Jacobs, Michael T., 91
Jackson, Andrew, 32
Jacksonian democracy, 11
Janus (Roman god), 42
Japan, 202. *See also* Samurai
link between internal and ex-
ternal violence, 45–46
nonviolence in culture of,
45–46
policy during Gulf War, 112,
115
Japanese, 78
Jefferson, Thomas, 27
Jenks, Chris, 8
Jerusalem, 147, 157. *See also*
East Jerusalem

violence at Al Aqsa Mosque,
145–147
Jervis, Robert, 17, 68
Jesuits, 51–53, 205
Jewish-Americans
and Palestinian-Israeli conflict,
133, 146, 162
cultural links with Israel, 134
views of Israeli government,
138, 155
Jewish Holocaust, 45
effect on Americans' perception
of Israel, 136
ethnic cleansing in Bosnia
compared to, 176–179
perceptions of different role in,
176
Jews, 177
Israeli, 153–154
victimized in Westward expansion, 50
Job, Brian L., xv, 36
John Paul II, 119
Johnson, Haynes, 12
Johnson, Lyndon B.
use of war metaphors, 38
and Palestinian-Israeli conflict,
136, 157, 161
Johnson, Ralph, 193
Joffe, Josef, 172
Jordan, 132, 153
Just war, 118
in Gulf, 118–119
in Bosnia, 181

Kaplan, Robert D., 167
Karadzic, Radovan, 171, 195
Kegley, Charles, 39–40
Keen, Sam, 5
Kelly, John H., 102
Kennan, George, 3, 166
Kennedy, Edward, 117
Kennedy, John F., 38
Kennedy, Paul, 104
Kenny, George, 173
Kerry, John F., 116–117, 184
Khe Sanh, 105

Kim, Il Sung, 202–203
Kim, Jong Il, 203
Kirchner, Robert, 150
Kirkpatrick, Jeane, 173, 180
Kissinger, Henry, 86, 91
and Palestinian-Israeli conflict,
158–160
Korean War, 202
Kristallnacht, 176
Krauthammer, Charles, 210
Ku Klux Klan, 51
Kultur, 7
Kurds
Bosnian Muslims compared to
Northern Iraqi, 181
Iraqi government's human
rights abuses against,
101–102
rebellion following Gulf War,
126–127, 209–210
Kuwait. See also Gulf War
Iraq's invasion of, 68, 81, 93,
128, 141, 173
Bush's response to, 95,
103–107
Iraq's human rights abuse in,
82
petroleum and, 109
uranium as health threat to
civilians of, 124–125

Language
as barrier to negotiations,
77–78, 108
Lantos, Thomas, 185
Las Casas, de Bartholome (bishop
of Chiapas in
Guatemala), 50
Latin Americans, 78
Law and order. See rule of law
League of Communists of
Yugoslavia (LCY), 171
Lebanon, 152
Iraq and, 102, 103
Israel's invasion of, 144–145
Levin, Carl, 138
Levine, Mel, 138

Levy, Jack S., 9
Libya, 98
Lieberman, Joseph, 114
Likud, 154, 155
Lind, Michael 5, 172
Lipset, Seymour Martin, 55
Locke, John, 21
Lockean liberalism, 21
London Economic Summit, 194
Louis XIV, King (of France), 53
Luckman, Thomas, 8
Lugar, Richard, 188

Maastricht Treaty, 175
Mandelbaum, Michael, 183
Manifest Destiny, 34
Massachussetts Peace Society, 86
Material culture, 7
Maynes, Charles William, 33–34
McCain, John, 184
McCarthyism, 14
McCloskey, Robert, 194
McNamara, Robert, 113
McNaught, Kenneth, 54–55
Media. See also television
    and cultural values, 12
    and national identity, 18
Meernik, James, xvi, 39, 56
Mexicans, 31, 33
Mein Kampf, 166, 167
Middle East, 153
    U.S. role in, 78, 102, 158
    violence in, 147
Mihailovich, Draza, 185
Militarization, 40, 45
Milosevic, Slobodan
    and ethnic cleansing in Bosnia,
        168, 185–186
    and Greater Serbia policy, 173,
        177
    compared to Adolf Hitler, 177
    violations of international law,
        180
Missiles, 95, 103, 122
Mission creep, 187
Mitterand, Francois, 111, 163
Morgenthau, Hans J., 3

Morocco, 98
Moody, Jim, 185
Moral exclusion, 37
Moral Majority, 119
Mubarak, Hosni, 163
Munich analogy. See also U.S.
        foreign policy
    Britain's role in, 69, 104
    in U.S. foreign policy, 69–70,
        104, 179
    in Bosnian conflict, 176
Murtha, John P., 184
Muslim countries, 193
Myrdal, Gunnar, 55
Myth, 19, 20. See also national
        myths; American nation-
        al myths
    ideology, and U.S. foreign
        policy, 18–22

Napoleonic Wars, 7
Nasser, Gamal Abdul, 142
Nation
    as a cultural entity, 4
National Association of
        Evangelicals, 119
National Council of Churches, 119
National identity, 18
    external conflict and, 40–47
    ideology and, 19
    war and, 40
National interests, 3
    U.S., 4
National Institute for Mental
        Health Initiatives, 59
National leaders, 17, 68
National myths, 19–21
National Religious Broadcasters,
        30–31
National security, U.S., 14,
        65, 70
    quest for absolute security,
        67–68
National Security Education
        Act, 78
National Security Council, U.S.
    and U.S. culture of violence, 64

Nationalism, 4, 21, 36
    American, 32, 40–41
    ethnicity's role in, 174
    link with sports, 61–63
    religion's role in, 11–12
Native Americans, 49–54
    Canadian relations with,
        54–55
    France's relations with, 51–54
    Quakers and, 86
    Spanish relations with, 51
    U.S. relations with, 31–33, 54
NATO (North Atlantic Treaty
        Organization), 175, 187,
        189
Nazi Germany, 44, 103
    Iraq compared to, 105
    Munich agreement compared
        to Iraqi aggression,
        103–105
    Serbian ethnic cleansing com-
        pared to genocide in,
        176–179
Negotiations. See also diplomacy
    between similar cultures, 71
    cultural barriers to, 71–76,
        79–80, 85–86, 90–92
    communication's role in, 73,
        212–213
    and isolationism, and interde-
        pendence, 87–90
    in Bosnian conflict, 178–182
    in Gulf crisis, 73, 95, 106–112
    in North Korea, 202–204
    in Palestinian-Israeli conflict,
        156, 164
    process of, 73, 75–82
    ripeness, 76
New Deal, 11
New Jerusalem, 51, 52, 134
New world order, 22, 65, 179
    Bosnian conflict and, 173
    Gulf War and, 128–130
    Palestinian-Israeli conflict and,
        162
New York Peace Society, 86
New York Times, 56, 97, 101, 125

New Zionists, 154
Newsom, David D., 62, 82–83
Nicaragua, 38, 55, 65, 205
Nixon, Richard, 86–87
    and Palestinian-Israeli
        conflict, 131, 137, 140,
        157, 161
Non-Europeans, 30–32, 49, 166
Nonmaterial culture, 7
Nonviolence
    tradition in United States,
        86–87
Nonwesterners, 79
Noriega, Manuel, 56, 207
North Korea
    U.S. dispute with Kim Il Sung,
        202–204
Normandy, 105
Norway, 164
Novello, Antonia C., 57
NOW (National Organization for
        Women), 58
NRA (National Rifle Association),
        58
Nuclear Non-Proliferation Treaty,
        203
Nuclear weapons, 85–86
    North Korean threat,
        202–204

Obey, David, 138
Occupied Territories. See also
        West Bank, and Gaza
        Strip
    links between Gulf Crisis and
        Arab-Israeli Conflict, 163
    Israeli settlements in, 153–154
    Israel's violations of human
        rights in, 147–153
    UN role in, 146, 147, 151
Oklahoma City bombing, 58
OPEC (Organization of Petroleum
        Exporting Countries), 99
Operation Desert Shield. See also
        Gulf War
    barriers to negotiation in, 82
    Bush's role in, 36, 83

Operation Desert Storm. *See* Gulf War

Operation Just Cause, 207–208. *See also* Panama

Operation Restore Hope. *See also* Somalia

U.S. use of force during, 35–36

Ostrom, Charles W., xv, 36

Owen, David, 188, 194, 196

Pacifism, 86, 119

Paine, Thomas, 24–25, 27, 129

Palestine Liberation Front, 162

Palestinian uprising. *See* Intifada

Palestinian-Israeli Conflict

Arabs support for negotiated settlement in, 132, 157

cultural distance as a factor in, 148

Israeli government's defiance of UN resolutions on, 163

United States role in, 6, 17, 75, 131–134, 145, 155–162, 164, 210–211

Gulf War's role in negotiated settlement of, 162–164

Palestinians, 132, 143. *See also* PLO

American perceptions of, 139–141, 156, 162

Israeli treatment of, 154

United States failure to address concerns of, 160

Panama, 56, 75

Carter's negotiations with, 208

Machos del Monte, 207

U.S. invasion of, 207–208

Panama Canal Treaty, 75, 87, 208

Panic, Milan, 169, 196

Paul, III, 50

Pell, Clairborne, 103, 138

Pentagon, U.S., 38

Perceptions, 9

effect on international relations, 9, 79–80

Perry, William J., 189

Persian Gulf. *See* Gulf region

Persian Gulf War. *See* Gulf War

Petroleum

Iraq's dependence on trade of, 113

U.S. dependence on, 99, 119, 166

Western Europe and Japan's dependence on, 100

Pfaff, William, 167

Phalange, 144

Pickering, Thomas R., 146

PLO (Palestine Liberation Organization)

belief in negotiations, 132, 157, 164

United States' communications with, 160–162

renouncing terrorism, 140, 162

Pluralism, 8

Polish Jews, 191

Political leaders, 18, 36, 72

Political science, 2

Pork Chop Hill, 105

Post, Jerrod M., 109

Post-Cold War era, 174, 183

effect on Palestinian-Israeli conflict, 153, 164

and Gulf Crisis, 98, 113

United States in, 38, 170, 197, 208–213

Powell, Colin, 116

Protestant Ethic and Spirit of Capitalism, 10

Protestants

American, 26

Early American (English), 49–54

Prothow-Smith, Deborah, 61

Public opinion, U.S., xv–xvi, 4

and foreign policy, 14–18, 74

on Bosnia, 185

subcultures' growing influence on, 15

Quakers (Society of Friends), 81, 86, 205

Qaddafi, Muammar, 98

Rabin, Yitzhak, 76, 152
Race
    as a factor in treatment of
        Native Americans, 48–49
    hierarchy of, 32,
    Hitler's ideology of, 103
    in Bosnian conflict, 186
    in United States, 31–34, 59,
        74, 86
    in Zimbabwe settlement, 204
Ramadan, 112
Ramaila Field, 109
Reagan, Ronald, 4, 16, 25, 36, 162
    and religion, 29–30
    and rule of law, 55–56
    domestic policy of, 29–30
    in Palestinian-Israeli conflict,
        158
    policies in Central America, 73,
        205–206
    relations with Saddam
        Hussein, 102–103
    view of East-West struggle,
        85–86, 204
Realism, xiv, 2–4, 5, 38, 199–200
Redman, Charles E., 196
Religion, 11–12. See also Civil re-
        ligion; specific religions
    and war, 118–121
    in Bosnian conflict, 169, 171,
        177–178
    in Gulf War, 30–31, 118
    in Palestinian-Israeli conflict,
        154, 157, 160
    in United States, 12, 25,
        26–31, 86, 97
Religious right, 158
Republicans, 29
Richardson, Neil R., 39–40
Richter, Gunther, 39–40
Robb, Charles S., 184
Roelofs, H. Mark, 19–20
Roman Catholics. See Catholics
Roman Republic, 41–42
Roosevelt, Franklin D., 38, 69
Rose, Sir Michael, 182
Rosenthal, A. M., 60

Rostow, Eugene W., 2, 7
Rule of law
    in post-Cold war, 210
    Iraqi violations of, 95
    selective application of, 142
    Serbian violations of, 179–182,
        189
    UN resolutions and, 141–147
    United States and, 54–56, 142
Rubinstein, Alvin, 33
Russett, Bruce M., 39
Russia, 7, 193
Russian, Eastern Orthodox, 169
Rwanda, 6, 173–174

Sabra and Shatilla massacre, 144
Sadat, Anwar, 81, 157, 159
SALT (Strategic Arms
        Limitations Talks
        Treaties), 92
Samurai, 45
Sanctions
    and Americans' cultural impa-
        tience, 112–115
    in Gulf, 125
Sandinistas, 73
Sarajevo,188–189
Saudi Arabia
    and Gulf War, 110, 115, 145
    support for Bosnian Muslims,
        193
Savimbi, Jonas, 38
Schlesinger, James, 86
Schools, 11, 18
    in United States, 58, 59
Schultz, George, 137
Scowcroft, Brent, 168–169
SDI (Strategic Defense Intiative),
        85–86
Sentencing Project, 63
Serbia, Republic of. See also
        Bosnian conflict
    ethnic cleansing policy of,
        129–130, 176–177, 194
    Greater Serbia plan, 171
    weapons advantage over
        Bosnia, 172, 190–191, 195

Serbs. *See also* Bosnian Serbs
  appeal to Western cultural
    fears of Muslims,
    169–170
  cultural links to United States,
    185
  human rights abuse, 177–178,
    188
  ignoring rule of law in Bosnian
    conflict, 179–182,
    188–189
  United States patience with,
    195–196
Shiites, 130
  rebellion in Iraq following Gulf
    War, 126–127, 209–210
Silajdzic, Haris, 195
Similar cultures, 6–7
  U.S. and Israel as, 134–138,
    156
  U.S. tendency to use diplomacy
    with, xvi, 71, 200–201
Simon, Paul, 138
Six Day War. *See* Arab-Israeli
  War
Skidmore, David, 208
Slavery, 74, 86
Slotkin, Richard, 20, 48, 50
Slovenia, 172, 175
Smith, Donald, 33
Smith, Ian, 204
Society of Friends. *See* Quakers
Somalia. *See also* Operation
  Restore Hope
  U.S. policy toward, 4, 35,
    65–66
South Africa, 4, 49, 143
  Boers' similarity to American
    settlers, 22
  cultural factors in U.S. policy
    toward, 204–205
South Korea, 202
Southern Baptist Convention, 119
Soviet Union, 3, 4, 157
  Americans negative views of,
    81, 85–86
  disintegration of, 154, 199

Spain, Catholic
  treatment of Native
    Americans, 49–54
Spanier, John, 14, 58, 85
Spanish Inquisition, 51
Sports
  and violence, and U.S. foreign
    policy, 61–63, 95, 183
Steiner, David, 138
Stereotypes, 80–81
Suez Canal, 142
Suleiman, Michael W., 97
Sweden, 74
Sweigart, Frank, 124
Symbols, 9, 12
  guns as, 47, 54
  in history, 16
Syria, 157

Technology, 167–168
Television
  and culture of violence, 42,
    59–61
  impact on U.S. foreign policy,
    12, 96, 140, 186
Thatcher, Margaret, 100, 174, 188
Third World, 33, 34, 81
  U.S. involvement in, 69
Thomas Jefferson High School, 59
Timmerman, Kenneth R., 128
Tito, Marshal Josip, 168, 171
Torrey, Barbara Doyle, 126
Tradition, 8
Tunisia, 98
Turkey, 145, 156, 174–175
Tutwiler, Margaret, 126, 152, 172

Unilateralism
  as deterrent to negotiation, 76
  United States tendency to use,
    112–113
United Arab Emirates, 115
United Nations
  investigations and reports,
    102, 124–125
  Israel's defiance of, 142–143
  role in international environ-
    ment, 141, 179–180

U.S. role in, 186–187
UN arms embargoes
   during Bosnian Conflict, 170,
      172, 189–193
   during Gulf Crisis, 113,
UN coalition against Hussein, 56
UN Interim Force in Lebanon
      (UNIFIL)
   Israeli bypass of, 144
UN Protection Forces (UNPRO-
      FOR)
   in Bosnian conflict, 180
   Serbians aggression toward,
      181–182, 189
UN resolutions
   and rule of law, 141–147
   United States interpretations
      of, 181
   on Bosnian Conflict, 179,
      189–190
   on Gulf Crisis, 75, 112–113,
      117,
   on Palestinian-Israeli Conflict,
      140–147, 151–152, 159
UN Security Council, 113, 121,
      142
United States, 2, 4–7. *See also*
      other U.S. headings
   and Bosnian conflict, 165–168,
      170, 172, 175, 178, 181
   and diplomacy, 71–75, 77–79,
      81–87, 102–103, 109, 115
   and Gulf War, 73, 93, 97–101,
      106–107, 121–125
   and Israel, 132–138, 144–148,
   and national security, 67–68
   and Palestinian-Israeli conflict,
      131, 150–162, 164
   and religion, 12, 26–31,
      128–130
   and rule of law, 54, 56,
      141–142, 179–182
   and Serbia, 168–169
   Anglo-American link, 200–201
   avoidance of responsibility,
      66–67, 126–127, 207
   characteristics of

impatient, 90–93
individualistic, 78
isolationist, 88, 89
sensitive to agression, 103
dependence on petroleum, 99,
   116, 166
perceptions of Palestinians,
   139–141
self-perception, 20, 22
   and Gulf War, 115–118
treatment of Native
   Americans, 49–54
unilateral actions and, 68
use of sanctions, 98, 113–114
views on military force and
   diplomacy, xvi, 64,
   193–197
violence and, 39, 47, 49, 50,
   54–56
   culture, 56–66
Ury, William, 79, 203
U.S. Congress, 3
   cultural factors effect on South
      Africa policy of, 204–205
   differing views on Bosnian con-
      flict, 185, 188, 192
   inquiry concerning health
      threats from Gulf War,
      125
   pressured by Bush about Gulf
      War, 112
   pro-Israel groups funding of
      members, 138
U.S. Constitution, 74
U.S. culture of violence, 56–59
   Branch Davidians as example
      of, 58
   democratic individualism in,
      53–55
   domestic violence in, 57–58
   government's role in, 63–66
   public's role in, 56–57
   NRA's role in, 58
   Oklahoma City bombing as ex-
      ample of, 58
   Selective Service reinforcing,
      64–65

television and, 59–61
U.S. domestic policy, 3–4, 69
U.S. foreign policy, 13–14, 16–17,
    68–69, 176
  ambivalence toward relying on
    diplomacy, 194
  American exceptionalism and,
    22–25, 89
  analogy in, 68–70, 101, 176
  avoidance of responsibility in,
    127
  avoidance of appeasement in,
    70
  confrontational language in,
    133–134
  culture and, 2, 5–6, 15, 20, 160
  democratic individualism and,
    100
  domestic politics role in, 3–4
  double standards in, 6, 141,
    145–146, 170
  ideology, myth and, 18–22
  in Bosnian conflict, 166–170,
    182–183, 186–187,
    193–197
  in Central America, 205–206
  in Grenada, 206–207
  in Gulf crisis, 121–125, 146
  in Israel, 148, 154–156
  in North Korean dispute,
    202–204
  in Panama, 207–208
  in South Africa, 204–205
  in Zimbabwe, 204
  isolationism in, 88–89
  link with American cultural
    values, 98–99, 117–118
  national security and, 67–68
  negotiation and, 86–87, 164
  race, culture, and, 31–34
  religion and, 26, 84–85
  sports, and violence, 61–63
  subcultures impact on, 86
  television violence link to, 60
U.S. government, 78, 91, 149
  role in U.S. culture of violence,
    63–66

U.S. political culture, 15
  American policymakers and,
    xvii, 4, 68, 96, 133, 166,
    171, 176
  political leaders, 14–15, 86–87
  presidents, 14, 16, 48,
    133–134, 136
U.S. State Department
  concern for diplomacy, 64
  documentation of human
    rights abuse, 101,
    148–152
U.S. Supreme Court
  and rule of law, 56
U.S use of force, xiv–xv, 40,
    47–54, 55, 66–67, 70, 91
  and presidents' popularity, 208
  analogy and, 69
  in Grenada, 206
  in Gulf, 81, 98–101, 114–115,
    122
  in Panama, 206
  in Somalia, 35–36
  lack of in Bosnia, 182–189
  military might in, 104
  national security and, 67, 81
  popular support necessary for,
    36, 56
Ustashi, 178

values (cultural), 4, 7, 9–10, 16
  in foreign policy, 36, 39, 201
  as factor in Gulf War, 94–95
  influence on negotiations, 72,
    73
  television and, 61
  violence and, 41–48
Vance, Cyrus, 196
Vance–Owen Plan, 84, 196
Varley, H. Paul, 43
Vietnam War, 62
  Agent Orange in, 66
  effect on Americans' beliefs,
    10, 40
  U.S. foreign policy and analogy
    of, 106, 182–189, 202,
    206

vigilantism
    in American South following
        Civil War, 55
    role of cultural differences in,
        54–55
violence. *See also* U.S. culture of
        violence; Domestic
        Violence
    international comparisons of
        external, 40–44
    in United States, 47
    link between internal and ex-
        ternal, 38–47
    and sports, and U.S. foreign
        policy, 61–63
Vlahos, Michael, 1–2, 10

Waco Conflict. *See* Branch
        Davidians
war
    Americans and, 84, 91, 95
    concept of "just," 118–119
    metaphors used by U.S. presi-
        dents, 38
    role of religion in, 118–121
War of 1812, 7, 201
Washington, George, 27
Weber, Max, 11
Weissman, Michele, 61
West, The
    Arabs cultural clash with,
        97–98
    "just war" concept in, 117
    and Bosnian conflict, 165,
        169–170, 190, 193
West Bank, 132. *See also*
        Occupied Territories
    Israeli annexation of, 138, 143
    Jewish settlers in, 154
West European allies, 156
West Europeans, 112
Westward expansion, 24
    vigilantism in, 54

Whitfield, Stephen J., 13
Wiarda, Howard, 34
Wills, Garry, 25
Wilson, Charles, 145
Wilson, Woodrow, 29
Winter, Roger P., 181
Wohlstetter, Albert, 190
Wolpe, Howard, 138
Woods, Jeanne M., 13
Woodward, Bob, 116
World Trade Center bombing, 66,
        170
World War I, 7, 29, 167
    American exceptionalism and,
        25
World War II, 2, 31
    Anglo-American cultural links
        in, 201
    U.S. policy in Gulf War based
        on analogies of, 104–106,
        191
    Bosnian conflict compared to,
        171, 176–179
Worldview
    connection to ideology, 19
Wright, Quincy, 36

Yanomami, 46–47
Yates, Sidney, 138
Young, Andrew, 162
Yugoslav People's Army, 190–191
Yugoslavia, 4, 168, 190–191. *See
        also* Bosnia; Croatia;
        Serbia; Slovenia;
        Bosnian conflict
    Americans' perceptions of, 167
    disintegration of, 171–172

Zimbabwe, 81
Zimbabwe Settlement, 75
    as example of U.S. negotiation
        with distant culture, 204
Zimmerman, Warren, 174, 183